28 YEARS
HAUNTED

The Life and Adventures of
World-Renowned Psychic Medium
BRANDY MARIE MILLER

To Deb,
Happy Trails and...
Happy Haunting!

B.D. Prince

B. D. Prince

Ghastly Press

Cover Designed by B.D. Prince
Book Layout ©2017 BookDesignTemplates.com, modified by B.D. Prince

28 Years Haunted/ B.D. Prince. -- 1st Edition.
ISBN 978-1-0880-7913-3

I wish to dedicate this book to my sweet, loving mother, Renee, who was taken from us far too soon.

And to my children Austin, Autumn, Anthony, Lucas, and Carter.
Always remain true to yourself no matter what you go through in life's journey. Remember your late Nana's words that helped me through my journey.... ALWAYS BE YOU!

And to all my family and friends who stood by my side through thick and thin and helped guide me to where I am today.
I owe it all to you.

Brandy Marie Miller

Contents

INTRODUCTION

Ever wonder what it's like to be a Psychic Medium? To see ghosts and shadow figures since you were a child? Hear disembodied voices? To communicate with the dead? Then join world-renowned Psychic Medium Brandy Marie Miller on the front lines in the spiritual battle between light and dark. Experience her most terrifying adventures growing up in a haunted house and investigating some of the most haunted locations in America—the famous and the obscure. From abandoned asylums to haunted hospitals, possessed mirrors and portals to the underworld, Brandy has seen it all!

Then, follow Brandy as she embarks on the opportunity of a lifetime—starring in the hit Netflix series *28 Days Haunted*. But it doesn't come without cost. Locked down without contact with the outside world for 28 days to test Ed and Lorraine Warren's 28-Day Cycle theory, Brandy must deal with the spirit of a mass murderer and other forces even more dangerous. Relive Brandy's journey from audition to post-production during the most harrowing paranormal investigation of her life, including exclusive behind-the-scenes content you won't find anywhere else.

I first met Brandy in 2019 while in an asylum. Now, before you jump to conclusions, we were on a paranormal investigation at the haunted Eloise Psychiatric Hospital in Westland, Michigan. Brandy led the investigation with her fellow Detroit Paranormal Expeditions (DPX) partners Todd Bonner and Jeff Adkins for Ghost Magnet podcast host and former Playboy playmate Bridget Marquardt. I also invited my friend and fellow author Josh Malerman and his fiancé Allison.

I didn't know what to make of Brandy at first. I'd never met a psychic medium before, and I admit I was skeptical. As a man of faith, I do believe in the supernatural. My first paranormal experience came at the infamous Stanley Hotel, the inspiration for Stephen King's book, The Shining. I attended a horror writer's retreat there with featured guests Jack Ketchum and Josh Malerman, which is how Josh and I met.

One night, around 11:00 p.m., as I stood near the master staircase chatting with fellow writer Cathleen Marshall, I was suddenly shoved from behind, knocking me off balance. I spun around to discover who pushed me, and to my horror, there wasn't a living soul behind me!

I turned back to Cathleen to find out if someone had somehow managed to sneak up behind me, shove me, and escape without a trace. Since she was facing me, she would know. All she could do was shake her head in amazement and chalk it up to the ghosts of The Stanley Hotel.

While at the writer's retreat, I also met Rob Cohen, producer of the Ghost Magnet with Bridget Marquardt podcast. Rob later introduced me to Bridget, who invited me to join her when she investigated Eloise with DPX. Like my stay at The Stanley Hotel, I wasn't expecting a paranormal encounter at Eloise. But once again, I was wrong.

While walking down the second-floor hallway of the abandoned asylum, I ran into what felt like a wall of invisible energy, and my breath was sucked out of my lungs! I'd never experienced anything like it in my life. So, as any good husband would do, I yelled down the hall to my wife, Deanne, "Hey honey, come here!"

My wife strolled down the hallway, unsuspecting, as I watched to see if she experienced the same phenomenon. Sure enough, when she reached the same spot in the hallway, she stopped and exhaled sharply. When I asked her about it, she described the same uncanny sensation I had.

After recovering from our initial shock, my wife and I explored the rooms at the end of the second-floor hallway. After a few minutes, I wandered back toward the other end of the hallway where the others had gathered. Instead of following me, my wife ventured into room 217, ironically, the same room number as the most haunted suite at The Stanley Hotel.

While in the empty room, she attempted to take a picture with her phone, but the screen went black. She struggled with it for a moment, turned it off and on again, but still had difficulty taking a picture. As she grappled with her phone, she felt me walk up behind her and breathe on her neck. Turning to ask for help with her phone, she screamed, seeing she was alone.

I heard Deanne yelling my name from the other end of the hallway. I bolted down the hall to make sure she was okay. Rushing into the room, I found her wide-eyed and shaking. She begged me to assure her that I had been in the room with her and just stepped out. Like my encounter at The Stanley Hotel, I could only shake my head and chalk it up to restless spirits.

That evening, Brandy and I ended up in jail. Before you get the wrong idea, the group of us from Eloise drove to the former 6th Precinct in downtown Detroit to explore another one of Brandy's favorite haunted locations in Southern Michigan. Although I didn't experience any paranormal phenomena there, Brandy and her partners at DPX have encountered plenty, which we'll discuss in more detail later in this book.

In 2020, Brandy and I went to prison together. The Ohio State Reformatory in Mansfield, Ohio, to be exact. If it sounds familiar, it's likely because it was the location where the film *The Shawshank Redemption* was filmed. It's also notoriously haunted. While touring the East Cell Block area, my wife yelled out in pain and grabbed her lower back. I was a few steps behind her, powerless to help.

"What's the matter?" I asked, rushing to her side.

Brandy turned back and answered my question. "You're being shanked!"

Fortunately, as suddenly as the attack began, it ceased. Did a former inmate have an issue with blondes? Or did my wife relive the prison shanking of another prisoner? I guess we'll never know. But I guarantee she'll never forget her visit to Ohio State Reformatory.

In the fall of 2022, after filming her hit Netflix series 28 Days Haunted, Brandy contacted me to see if I'd be willing to help write her biography. I have to admit I was hesitant at first. As a fiction author and screenwriter, biographies are not really my area of expertise. And to be honest, most people are not that interesting. But after listening to Brandy recount her life story and her incredible experiences during the filming of 28 Days Haunted, I was sold.

I trust you will find Brandy's life and adventures as a psychic medium as intriguing and inspirational as I did. I encourage you to find a comfortable place to sit and a blanket just in case you notice a cold spot develop near you. The blanket will also come in handy if you need to pull it over your eyes when you wish to hide from the watcher in the shadows. But whatever you do, don't turn out the lights. How are you supposed to read in the dark?

- **B.D. Prince**

Brandy and Bryan at Father John's Microbrewery

Brandy and Bryan at Ohio State Reformatory

FOREWORD

I've never read a book like this before.

I've never heard a story like Brandy Marie Miller's before. Certainly not to this degree. Those of us who are interested, even partially, in the paranormal lifestyle, have read of investigations and hauntings: rarely novel-length accounts and more often brief histories of unsettling events at specific (likely well-known) locales. But here we have the life story of a complex medium, complete with childhood and young adulthood traumas, yes, but just as profoundly: the joys and bravery of self-discovery along the way.

I think this is what strikes me most about the book you are about to read:

Brandy Marie Miller's epic journey with the paranormal does not come off as "dark" as much as it does "responsible." Here, a woman has refused to turn her back on what she's seen, choosing not to "ignore" the entities of her life, but to actively investigate, research, to *face* the sort of things that would send many of us (likely me included) to the nearest bar instead. From childhood to the present, Brandy has had to juggle her abilities with a desire to live a "normal" life. And while it must sometimes be appealing to leave the hauntings behind... at what cost?

Once you've seen behind the curtain, how can you possibly pretend there's nothing there?

Especially a curtain on stage as big as this one.

That stage being: *life.*

Because the life Brandy leads is multifold. And while us horror fanatics are thrilled by scary stories, is there anything more optimistic than the discovery of... the other side? Life (and its ilk) beyond death (and its ilk) suggests there is *more.* And what's more optimistic than *more?*

Still, as Bryan Prince so deftly dramatizes, Brandy's journey has been intense. From the possibility of two distinct entities warring for her soul in childhood, to juggling the growing "magnet" she and her own five children later make, the abilities Brandy possesses do not come easy. There are headaches, there is exhaustion, there is a constant sense of double-checking what her children (and later her investigative teammates) have seen for themselves.

And there is, of course, *seeing.*

A life of seeing, documented here in the form of an occultist's life story, and the incredible pressures that come with it.

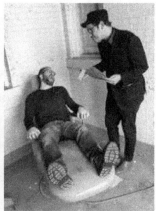

Left: Josh Malerman smokes and Brandy sizzles.
Right: Josh psychoanalyzes B.D. Prince at Eloise.

I met Brandy on an investigation myself. At the Eloise Psychiatric Hospital here in Westland, Michigan. Bryan was there. So was the brilliant Bridget Marquardt, she of *Ghost Magnet*, a paranormal investigator all her own. After a perfunctory meeting of the minds in the parking lot, we all entered the legendary place, where I told Todd (you'll read about him in these pages) that I was, indeed, scared. He told me something Brandy confirms in this very book:

The ghost hunter is just as scared as you are.

And therein lies the bravery.

Brandy Marie Miller isn't naïve to the scares of her profession. Yet, she endures.

And it was in that psychiatric hospital that I received one of the most unexpected compliments of my life:

Walking the length of the second-floor hall with my fiancée Allison Laakko (gripping her arm for the duration), we chanced upon Brandy seated upon a bench. Brandy looked to be thinking (I wonder now, after reading these pages, if she wasn't experiencing a bit of a headache from the overwhelming energy of that place). Then Brandy heard us, looked up, and said to me:

Oh, you are definitely sensitive. You are dripping with it.

Now, these words might have passed quietly by the ears of someone with less reverence for the very thing we were doing there. But not me. And rather than feeling horror at the fact that the investigation's medium just told me I was likely to *feel* and *sense* things within Eloise, I was immediately and genuinely *warmed* by her comment. It was a compliment of the highest order. One I cherish. Brandy had, in a sense, given me agency with her words. She'd told me to trust my experience. And, more: I've spent many hours in many homes, apartments, buildings, campsites, writing nooks, and offices, wondering if perhaps I'm not able to sense a little more than most.

Brandy Marie Miller had given me a cosmic wink. She'd said, *You can feel things, too.*

And, perhaps, you *deserve* to.

Now, the unbelievable experience Brandy had while shooting *28 Days Haunted* is no doubt a centerpiece of this book, and it's possibly even the reason you're reading. I don't blame you. Just wait till you get to that part. But these pages could've led up to Brandy sitting alone on a front porch, sipping lemonade, and the story would be just as riveting. Because what you are about to experience is *a life*. A fascinating, brilliant one at that.

And if you're anything like me, you'll discover an abundance of ardor, passion, hard work, and stamina. For, while Brandy Marie Miller may spend her time investigating the highest mysteries of this thing we call life, she has displayed here, for the world, the details of her own.

And for that, and more, I thank her.

Josh Malerman
Michigan
Autumn, 2023

I SEE DEAD PEOPLE

The first time the spirits came to me, I was five. It's hard enough for a kindergartner to make sense of the natural world around them, let alone the supernatural realm. Yet children seem more open to the paranormal world: those shapes, shadows, and faces you see out of the corner of your eye but adults are quick to dismiss. Parents, grandparents, aunts, uncles, and teachers all convince you that what you saw was just your own shadow or perhaps a reflection. Or, more likely, the product of a child's overactive imagination.

I believe we're all born with some measure of sixth sense, though some to a greater extent than others. As for me, I came from a long line of psychic mediums. This gift, which sometimes seemed more like a curse, was present in my mother, aunt, grandmother, and great-grandmother. And, for all I know, many generations before that.

A few of us chose to embrace our gifts more than others, while most failed to develop their abilities to their full potential due to the stigma from those who would shame them for dabbling in things that ought not to be dabbled in. Others tried to ignore it altogether, convincing themselves they were just imagining things because they were afraid to ponder the alternative.

Although we may all be born with some degree of sixth sense, most tend to lose touch with it as they age. Many suppress it out of fear or have it "taught" out of them by others who deny the spiritual world altogether. As for myself, I didn't fully

11

embrace my abilities until I was in my twenties. But I always knew they were there. How could I not, having seen the things I've seen? Although I tried to suppress it for many years, I wasn't always successful in keeping the spirits at bay.

I remember my first paranormal experience like it was yesterday. Like most harrowing experiences, this one is ingrained in my memory, even down to the most intricate details. If you've ever had a terrifying or traumatic experience, I'm sure you know what I'm talking about. Since this first entity visited me every day for two years, I can still visualize his ghostly appearance, even today. Although he never told me his name, I will always think of him as *The Man in White*.

Left: Brandy and her mom
Right: Four generations of psychic mediums

The Man in White

I first saw The Man in White when I was five. Up until then, I slept in the nursery downstairs. When my brother was born, he moved into the nursery, so my dad turned the upstairs into my new bedroom. The second story of our house was just one open space, kind of like a loft. At first, I was excited to have a room to myself again. But that was before I discovered something else had already made its home there.

As a child, my bedtime ritual was always the same. Mom would give me a bath and then help me into my pajamas. Next, I would brush my teeth and smile so she could see how clean my teeth were. Then, we would go into the nursery, where I'd say my prayers, and Mom would tuck me in, kiss me on my forehead, and say goodnight. Lastly, she'd turn off the lights on her way out of the room and wish me "sweet dreams."

But everything changed the first night I slept upstairs in my new bedroom. My sweet dreams turned into dark nightmares.

As we climbed the staircase and peered into my new bedroom, I was excited to see how big it was. So much room to play! Not only did I have a new bedroom, but I also got a new big-girl bed. And the best part was that my daddy made it himself, just for me. Running into my new room, I jumped on my special bed and bounced on the springy mattress, giggling.

Mom came around to the side of my bed like always and reminded me that we needed to say our prayers. In all the excitement, I'd forgotten. I climbed back out of bed, got on my knees next to her, and said our nightly prayers together. Once we finished, my mom tucked me in, kissed me on the forehead, and wished me "sweet dreams" before turning out the light.

Listening to my mom's footsteps fading down the stairs, I realized I wasn't alone.

As my eyes adjusted to the darkness, I sensed someone else in the room watching me. The feeling grew stronger with every step my mom took down the stairs. Out of the corner of my eye, I suddenly noticed someone standing in the shadowy corner next to my bed. I slowly turned to look, afraid of what I might see. That's when I first saw *him*.

Lurking in the shadows stood a tall, slender man wearing a clean, white suit with tails, pointed white dress shoes, and a white top hat. In his right hand, he held a white cane with a gold stripe at the top and bottom. Beneath his top hat hung long, wavy white hair down to his shoulders and an equally impressive beard. But the most striking feature was his icy blue eyes, eyes that now stared back at me.

"Mommy!" I bawled, terrified to move for fear of drawing the stranger's attention. What if he came toward me? I screamed for my mom again. Suddenly, a horrific thought crossed my mind. What if my mom couldn't hear me all the way downstairs? The stranger in the shadows was so close that, even if she heard my cries, there was no way she could rescue me in time if he started thrashing me with his cane!

I continued crying out for my mom. What else could a five-year-old do? I glanced over at the Man in White again to see if he had gotten any closer. But he just stood there in the same spot, gazing ahead stoically, like a sentry guarding something.

Finally, I heard my mother's footsteps pounding up the stairs. She flipped on the light and rushed to my side.

"What's the matter?" she asked.

I tried to describe the white-clad man I saw standing in the corner, but when I looked again, he was gone.

Or so I thought.

Once my mom calmed me down and tucked me back in, she turned off the light and made her way back downstairs. I glanced back at the corner, and to my dismay, he was back. But it appeared like he never left since he stood in the exact same spot, still looking straight ahead. Did the light make him disappear? Was it possible he was only visible in the dark?

I burst into tears and yelled for my mother again. After a few moments, I could hear her stomping back up the stairs. She turned on the light and strolled back over to my bed. I told her the strange man was back. Most parents usually tell their terrified children that the monster they think is under the bed or in the closet isn't real, that it's just the product of their overactive imagination. But my mom was different. She glanced at the corner where the Man in White lurked and told me to "just ignore him."

After I was a little older, I realized how odd it was that she never told me the ghostly figure I saw wasn't real. She didn't blame it on my imagination or deny that the apparitions existed. She only told me to ignore them. Once I became an adult, she finally confided in me that she saw things too. And so did my grandma. And great grandma. And my aunt. She revealed that this second sight or "third eye" ran in the family, and the way she learned to deal with seeing ghosts and shadow figures was just to ignore them. Eventually, she said, if she ignored them long enough, they would just go away.

I eventually discovered that if you have "the gift," you can't turn it off. The switch was always on. The best you could hope for was the ability to ignore or block the energies when you detected their presence.

Once she calmed me down again, I convinced her to leave the light on. As she disappeared down the stairs, I hid under the covers. In my five-year-old mind, I thought that if I couldn't see The Man in White, he couldn't see me either. And if he couldn't see me, he might forget about me and leave me alone.

I still sleep with the lights on to this day with a blanket covering half my face. I also leave the TV on or use some kind of white noise to help block out anything that might be trying to communicate with me. Otherwise, I would never get any sleep!

Despite my best efforts to ignore him, The Man in White didn't forget about me that night and leave. He was still there every night when the lights went out. Even when I couldn't see him, I could feel his presence. Over the next two years, I never got comfortable knowing he was there, watching me sleep.

Looking back on it now, I've come to believe that The Man in White wasn't a malevolent force after all, but quite the opposite; he was my protector, my guardian angel. As my psychic abilities developed over the years, I wondered if he wasn't still there, watching over and guiding me.

Once my little brother outgrew his crib downstairs, my dad decided to remodel the second floor and convert it into two bedrooms, one for each of us, with a hallway running down the middle. After the remodel, I didn't see The Man in White again. But I still felt his presence.

It's common for renovations to stir up the spirits that haunt a location. Our house was no different. After my dad completed the upstairs remodel, the atmosphere up there gradually grew darker and heavier. Around this time, I also encountered my first dark entity, an evil spirit I called, *The Dingy Man*.

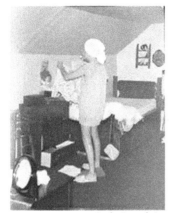

Left: Brandy's upstairs bedroom
Right: Bedtime Prayers

The Dingy Man

The raspy voice startled me as I sat on the floor downstairs. My little brother and I were playing in the nursery-turned-playroom when I first heard it. As I glanced up, my heart nearly leaped out of my chest, seeing this strange, dingy old man leaning over me, scowling. His eyes reminded me of the droopy, bloodshot eyes of an old basset hound, except instead of brown, his eyes were black as night.

His dark, greasy hair was finger-combed back over his scalp. A rough, stubbly, five-o-clock shadow covered his weathered, dirt-smeared face. The vile stranger wore a stained, long-sleeve flannel shirt, torn, filthy jeans, and scuffed-up work boots. He looked like a hobo. The kind that offered little kids candy to follow him into a back alley.

"Bite him," The Dingy Man commanded, nodding toward my little brother. A sinister grin stretched across his face, chilling me to the bone. This dark stranger was the exact opposite of The Man in White. The Yang to his Yin. If The Man in White was my guardian angel, The Dingy Man was a fallen angel who'd crawled up from the pits of hell.

My ears started ringing. My heart raced. I wanted to run to my mom, but I was afraid to leave my brother alone with this stranger, fearing he might do the things to my brother he was encouraging me to do. Or worse.

The Dingy Man leaned closer, threatening me with his menacing glare. I never felt so powerless. I sensed him taking control. He told me my brother was a dirty little boy who deserved to be punished.

A noise came from the kitchen. I don't recall if it was the clang of a pan or the clinking of ice dropped into a glass, but the sound temporarily broke the spell The Dingy Man held over me, long enough for a cry to escape.

"Mommy!"

The Dingy Man's brow furrowed with rage. The ringing in my ears grew louder. Although his lips didn't move, I could hear his deep, raspy voice egging me on.

"Bite him! Bite him really hard!"

I became confused and lost, his thoughts mingling with mine. Before I lost complete control to the dark stranger, I cried out again, "Mommy!"

My mother poked her head out of the kitchen to see what was wrong. Seeing her released the flood of tears bottled up inside me, which made my brother cry, too. My mom's curiosity turned into concern, and she rushed over. As she passed through The Dingy Man to pick me up, he vanished.

Feeling how bad I was shaking, my mom tried to calm me, rocking me and stroking my hair. My brother clung to her leg as she gently shushed our cries. Once I'd calmed down enough to explain what I'd seen, my mom did what she always did.

"Just ignore him, honey."

The next day, my brother and I were downstairs piecing together a puzzle when my ears started ringing again. A heaviness descended as I felt a dark sense of dread overtaking me.

He's coming.

Nervously, I looked up, and there was The Dingy Man looming over me again, grinning that menacing grin, his black eyes boring inside me, willing me to do things to my brother. Awful things.

I never heard The Dingy Man speak with my ears, only in my mind. It's like we could communicate telepathically. And once he got inside my head, he was able to coerce me into doing things I wouldn't normally do. Hurtful things. He had a way of confusing my thoughts, making wrong seem right. I loved my little brother. I didn't want to harm him, but The Dingy Man convinced me that he deserved those nasty things he wanted me to do to him.

Inside my mind, I told the evil man to go away and leave me alone. I just wanted that horrible feeling of dread to disappear. But he convinced me that if I did what he asked, he would be satisfied and leave me alone. His Faustian bargain turned out to be a lie.

Every day, The Dingy Man did his best to convince me to hurt "the dirty boy." I didn't want to do the awful things the bad man told me to do, but he wouldn't leave me alone. He was relentless. I finally concluded that if I did what he wanted, he would eventually disappear. So, I did.

It began with me performing small requests like slapping my little brother, pinching him, or pulling his hair. But instead of satisfying The Dingy Man and making him leave, it seemed to encourage him instead. Empower him, even. It also got me in trouble with my mom whenever my brother cried and told her what I did to him.

Whenever my mother scolded me for hurting my little brother and lectured me to be nice to him, The Dingy Man would come right behind her and tell me not to listen to her. Tired of constantly getting in trouble for doing what The Dingy Man said, I finally tried to take my mom's advice and ignore the evil entity. The longer I resisted his manipulation, the weaker he seemed to get and the stronger I became.

I didn't know it then, but along with the ability to see and interact with supernatural entities, I also had the ability to block them. Although, it wasn't as easy as just flipping a switch. Depending on the type of spirit, some take longer than others to dispel. But the less energy I gave them, the less power they had over me until, eventually, I could close that connection for good.

My struggles with The Dingy Man persisted for over a year. He continued tormenting me in the playroom until my dad finally remodeled the downstairs, combining the playroom with the living room to open things up more. Even though I didn't see The Dingy Man downstairs after that, I still felt his negative presence in the house and could still hear his deep, raspy voice whispering my name in the night.

Looking back on my experiences with The Man in White and The Dingy Man, I believe a battle was being waged for my soul. Light vs. dark. Good vs. evil. Angel vs. devil. Who would win the tug of war, the spirit drawing me toward the light or the one pulling me down into darkness and despair? As a mother of five, it's frightening to consider that there's a battle being fought for my children's souls. Have I done enough to help them in that fight?

There always seemed to be a black cloud hanging over my childhood home, casting a dark shadow of anger, fear, and negativity. I noticed it most whenever I left the house and went to school or one of my friends' houses. It felt like having a weight lifted off my chest. Like storm clouds driven away by a warm summer breeze, the sun finally poking through. But once I entered the door to my house, the storm clouds reappeared, and the heaviness returned as if The Dingy Man was sitting on my chest.

The darkness and negativity reached its peak by the time I turned ten. That's when I began hearing strange noises upstairs during the night—the floor creaking, my name whispered, and the introduction of a shadow haunting the hallway outside my bedroom door.

Brandy staring at The Dingy Man

The Shadow

One of the most terrifying events of my childhood happened when I was ten. I was lying in bed, the lights on as usual, when I heard the floorboards creak in the hallway outside my bedroom. It sounded like someone was pacing outside my room.

I peeked out from under the covers to see light spilling from my brother's bedroom into the hallway. I figured that my brother must be up and walking around. But why? Did he get up to use the bathroom?

The footfalls came closer. I watched the doorway, expecting to see my brother peek into my room. Instead, a tall, dark shadow filled the door. I nearly screamed! After a breathless moment, the shadow continued down the hallway.

I tried to make sense of what I'd just seen. Was it my brother's shadow cast by the light from his bedroom? Shaking, I mustered up the courage to get out of bed and check. If I could prove it was my brother walking around, I could put my fears to rest and go back to sleep.

Slipping out of bed, I crept to the doorway and peeked out. Like the Night Before Christmas tale, not a creature was stirring, not even a mouse. But it had to be my brother. Who else could it be? Could he have already made it downstairs, heading for the bathroom? Most nights, I tried to hold it until morning so I wouldn't have to walk all the way downstairs in the dark.

I knew I'd heard footsteps. If it wasn't my brother's shadow, whose was it? I had to know for sure. I tip-toed into my brother's bedroom, and there he was, eyes closed, mouth open, fast asleep. Had I just dreamed it? Was I dreaming now? I pinched myself. Nope. I was definitely awake.

Then it hit me. Maybe Mom came upstairs to check on us. Yes, that must be it. What else could it have been? But wouldn't I have heard her thumping down the stairs?

Tired and confused, I finally started back toward my bedroom when a loud CRASH came from inside! Was the person who cast the shadow in my room?

I tiptoed back to the doorway and peeked inside. To my shock, there on the floor lay the porcelain cross my mom had hung on the wall, shattered to pieces. But how?

My mind raced. What could've made the crucifix fly off the wall and shatter on the floor? I thought about the shadow, and it made my blood run cold. Could the shadow have been The Dingy Man coming upstairs to get me? Was he the one who smashed the crucifix? Or was it just collateral damage in the battle between The Dingy Man and The Man in White? The battle of dark vs. light? Good vs. evil? And the most important question, who won?

I waited for the shadow to return. But it didn't. I often wondered if The Man in White saved me that night. Or had the Jesus from the crucifix sacrificed Himself to save me? Still shaking, I stepped around the broken crucifix, climbed back into bed, and pulled the covers over my head, praying that Jesus and The Man in White would continue to protect me in my sleep.

Until then, I thought the scary things I saw were all because of the house. There was no doubt that our house was haunted. I'd seen and felt too many supernatural things not to believe. Once I became an adult, I learned that my grandfather on my father's side previously owned the house and that our home possessed a long history of paranormal activity. My aunt and uncle, who lived there as kids, admitted that they too were haunted by dark entities there.

My uncle told me that growing up, he also slept upstairs. At night, he'd awaken to a black mass hovering above his bed. He felt totally powerless to fight it. The shadow figure would hold him down, pinning him to the mattress, completely immobilizing him. He was so frozen with fear that he couldn't even scream. So, it hadn't just been my imagination!

The ceramic crucifix on the wall

To Grandmother's House We Go

Imagine my surprise and horror to discover that even my grandmother's house wasn't safe from the dark entities haunting me. If I could see shadow figures at Grandma's, then nowhere was safe!

The closest person to me growing up, next to my mother, was my grandma Theresa. She was the most loving, caring, and generous person I've ever had the pleasure to know. She would give the shirt off her back to a total stranger. I miss the way we used to talk all the time. Whenever she came over, or I visited her house, she'd always hug me and say how much she loved me. Her grandchildren were her life. One of my favorite memories of staying at my grandma's was lying in bed with her at night while she read romance novels and shared York Peppermint Patties with me.

Grandma Theresa always made me feel safe when I was with her. When I did get afraid, she would comfort me and make me feel as if nothing could hurt me as long as she was there. She was like my earthly guardian angel. Which was good because there were terrifying things in her house that were not of this earth.

My grandma lived with my aunt Serena in the upper half of a two-story house built in Detroit in the early 1900s. It was basically a duplex, separated by level. Before I turned one, my parents and I lived on the first floor. But even though we moved across town, we remained close to Grandma and regularly visited each other's houses.

As a kid, the one thing I hated about the upper level where my grandma lived was this pair of porcelain clown faces hanging on the living room wall. Whenever I came to visit, my eyes were immediately drawn to those painted faces staring down at me with their grotesque makeup. It gave me the creeps the way their eyes seemed to follow me everywhere I went!

My aunt's bedroom was off the second-floor living room in the front, while Grandma's bedroom was in the back of the house next to the dining room and kitchen. Whenever I spent the night, my grandma would fashion a makeshift bed out of spare blankets and pillows on the living room floor for me.

After the lights were out and everyone had gone to bed, I would lie there and try not to think about the clowns glaring down at me. It wasn't long before I discovered they were the least of my worries.

Grandma always left the kitchen light on at night so I could find my way to the bathroom and to ease my fear of sleeping alone in the living room. As I closed my eyes and tried to fall asleep, I sensed something watching me. This time, it wasn't the clowns or The Man in White. It felt like a male energy, which was strange since my grandma and aunt were the only people living here. I didn't want to open my eyes for fear of what I might see. But eventually, curiosity got the best of me.

When I opened my eyes, I noticed movement on the other side of the house, near my grandma's bedroom. Expecting to see Grandma shuffling to the bathroom, I was stunned to discover a dark, shadowy figure instead. I watched in horror as a dark apparition floated from the bathroom, across the dining room, and into the kitchen. I was so shocked at first that I couldn't make a sound. But once the shadow figure disappeared into the kitchen, I finally managed to release the scream building in my chest.

Grandma rushed into the living room to comfort me. I thought these kinds of things only happened at my house! Seeing this dark entity here made me realize that if Grandma's house wasn't safe from these things, then I wasn't safe anywhere.

Once my grandma calmed me down, she let me sleep in her room. So, we gathered the blankets and pillows, carried them into her bedroom, and made a new bed for me on the floor. From where I lay, I could see straight into the kitchen. The same kitchen that the shadow man had disappeared into. I asked Grandma if she could close her door halfway to block some of the light. But mostly, it was to block my view in case the apparition returned. Unfortunately, Grandma's bedroom didn't have a door for some strange reason.

Despite my fear, I found myself staring into the kitchen, waiting for something to move. I thought about the missing door. What if the shadow man decided to float from the kitchen into Grandma's room? There'd be nothing to stand in its way!

Terrified at the thought, I pulled the blanket over my eyes. Like most children, I believed this thin layer of material possessed some magical powers, like a cloak of invisibility or a supernatural force field capable of warding off evil. Besides, if the monsters couldn't see me, they might forget I was there and move on to some other kid's bedroom who wasn't as diligent not to expose any fingers or toes for them to nibble on.

Once again, that nagging feeling of being watched returned. I tried not to peek, but once again, curiosity got the better of me, and I slowly lowered my covers. To my horror, silhouetted by the kitchen light, stood a tall, dark shadow figure watching me. I cried out for Grandma.

Even though she didn't acknowledge the apparition, she humored me and moved my bedding between her bed and the wall. From there, I couldn't see the open doorway, plus Grandma could provide an additional barrier of protection from the dark figure lurking outside.

I stayed at Grandma Theresa's house numerous times and must've witnessed the same repetitive loop of the phantom floating from bathroom to kitchen at least a dozen times. The pattern never changed. Was it some kind of residual energy from a former resident?

Whenever I spent the night at my grandma's house, I tried to fall asleep early before the shadow man revealed himself. People may wonder why I kept sleeping at her house, knowing I'd likely see a ghost. Well, for one thing, the shadow man was predictable. He never deviated from his routine of floating between the bathroom and the kitchen. He also never threatened me like the Dingy Man. So, by comparison, the shadow man wasn't nearly as frightening.

But mostly, it was because of the special relationship I had with my grandma. She was such a wonderful, loving person. And I'm so glad I spent so much time with her when I was little because, when I was ten, she unexpectedly passed away. Although I didn't have long with her, I cherish every minute. I wouldn't trade those memories for anything. To this day, I regularly visit Grandma's gravesite when seeking guidance or just a place where I can feel safe in her loving presence.

When recounting the memories at Grandma's house for this book, I reached out to my Aunt Serena to see if she remembered anything strange happening when she lived there with Grandma. And I wasn't disappointed.

Aunt Serena was only nine years older than me. She felt more like a big sister than an aunt. Although she didn't see the shadow man herself, Serena often felt like something was watching her. She also sensed a similar "male energy" whenever she visited my house, particularly in the downstairs playroom and upstairs, where my bedroom was.

The most frightening thing Serena remembers from living at my grandmother's house wasn't what she felt or saw there but what she often heard. She remembers hearing strange noises coming from the attic, an experience made all the more disturbing when she found out that a previous tenant hanged herself in that very same attic!

Serena described the unnerving sound as a repeating *Click-Clack* noise. But what could make a sound like that? Was it the spirit of the hanged lady pacing around the attic, her heels echoing on the hardwood floor? *Click-Clack! Click-Clack!* Or could it have been the sound of the former tenant hanging from the rafters, her stretched-out neck cracking as her body swung from side to side? *Crick... Crack! CRICK... CRACK!*

My aunt finally gathered the courage to convince Grandma to go up into the attic with her to investigate. They discovered a wind-up baby swing someone had stored in the attic long ago. The swing was rocking on its own, making that same telltale sound, *Click-Clack, Click-Clack*, even though no one had wound the mechanism in many years. Could the hanged lady be using the baby swing to communicate with the living?

The baby swing that moved on its own wasn't the only strange thing uncovered in that attic. When I asked my dad if he remembered any unusual occurrences at Grandma's house, he confessed that he once went up in the attic by himself and stumbled across a tooth! We have no idea who the tooth belonged to, how it got knocked out of their mouth, or even if someone just yanked it out themselves. But it isn't uncommon for human artifacts to have their owner's spirit energy attached. Could it have belonged to the hanged lady?

When Grandma Theresa was diagnosed with breast cancer, everything turned upside down for me. My grandma and I were practically inseparable. I couldn't imagine a world without her. My mom cared for her mom until she finally had to be admitted to the hospital. I stood by her bed every chance I could, holding her hand.

I brought her a glass rabbit candle holder, which she proudly displayed on the nightstand beside her bed, along with all the flowers people brought to her.

I'll never forget the day I came home from school and found grandma's things at the house. Seeing the candle holder I'd given her, I knew she had died. It felt like my whole world came crashing down around me. I was inconsolable and cried myself to sleep.

Grandma Theresa's funeral was the first I can remember attending. I was scared to approach the casket at first. I'd never seen a dead body before. My mom reminded me it was just Grandma, and I didn't need to be afraid. She offered her hand and slowly led me to the front, where the casket was displayed. Grandma looked like she was sleeping. Oh, how I wished that were true. But deep down, I knew she would never wake up.

I remember thinking that Grandma wore more makeup than I'd ever seen on her before. Tears streaming down my mom's face, she made the sign of the cross, kissed her fingers, and patted Grandma's folded hands. Not knowing how to process all of this, I did the only thing I could. I sobbed.

A handful of relatives filed in. Some I knew, many I didn't. The adults stood around and talked like adults do. They shared stories about how wonderful Grandma was and how much everyone loved her. They each had a story about her generosity and how she helped, encouraged, and prayed for them. She always had a way of making others feel better.

After the viewing, the last stragglers wandered into the hallway, but I hung back alone, still crying. I finally mustered up the courage to approach the coffin one last time. Once I saw her face, I broke down again, sobbing and hugging her. I didn't want to let her go.

Then I heard a soft, comforting voice say, "I'm okay, honey."

I glanced up and saw a translucent glow at the head of the casket. I couldn't believe my eyes as I witnessed my grandma's spirit floating in mid-air! She was visible only from the shoulders up; below that, the rest of her faded away. But all that mattered to me was seeing her smile and hearing her soothing voice, assuring me that everything was okay.

Grandma's funeral wasn't the last time I saw her. A few years later, during one of the most traumatic experiences of my childhood, Grandma Theresa was there again to comfort me.

I was fourteen and had become seriously ill. My throat felt like it was on fire, and I could barely swallow. My mom took me to the doctor's office, where he diagnosed me with tonsillitis. I overheard people say that the older you are, the more dangerous a tonsillectomy can be. Since I had never had any surgery before, I was afraid that I was going to die!

My anxiety shot through the roof as they wheeled me into the operating room. The thought of the doctor taking a scalpel, reaching into the back of my throat, and cutting out my tonsils horrified me.

I couldn't stop crying, even when the anesthesiologist placed the mask over my nose and mouth. It felt as if he were trying to suffocate me! My whole body tensed as I listened to the hiss of the gas pumping into the mask.

I squeezed my eyes shut as the anesthetist told me to count backward slowly from ten to one.

As the anesthesia took hold and I drifted into that zone between consciousness and sleep, I heard a familiar voice call my name. My eyes fluttered open, recognizing Grandma's voice. I was confused. The only faces around me were the doctor and attending nurses.

I closed my eyes again. Once again, I heard Grandma's reassuring voice.

"Brandy, my dear. You're going to be okay."

The bright glow of the operating room intensified. Grandma's voice seemed to be coming from the light. I wanted to go into that light to be safe with her and escape the doctor with the razor-sharp scalpel.

"You're not coming here, darlin'. Not now. It's not your time."

As the anesthesia swept me away, I gradually let go of the fight.

"Don't be afraid, Brandy, you're going to be fine. You'll be just fine..."

That was the last thing I remember until I awoke in my hospital bed. Grandma was right. It wasn't my time.

Grandma's House in Detroit

The Divorce

My tenth year was one of the darkest and most tumultuous times of my life. After saying goodbye to my grandma, I no longer had anyone to go to when things at my house got stressful. My house was thick with negative energy. Mom and Dad fought more and more, and the yelling got louder and louder. It's like the dark energy fed off of the conflict. Encouraged it, even. Like how the Dingy Man fed off the bad things he made me do.

Did the arrival of The Dingy Man cause all the fighting and negativity, or was this dark entity drawn by the conflict already here? Did one feed the other, or did they both feed off each other equally? And what was my part in all of this?

The darkness and negativity finally reached its peak when my parents decided to get a divorce. My dad packed up his things and moved out. Now, I'd lost not only my grandma but my father as well. Then, to top it off, my other grandma died a year later. So much loss in such a short time took its toll on me.

I continued to live in the house with my mom and brother until I was 15 when we moved into a new place. My childhood home is still just down the street from where I live today. Even now, it gives me chills when I drive past it, dredging up so many dark and frightening memories. But it also brings up many fond memories of a time when my family was whole.

Teen Years – The Life of an Empath

My teen years were quiet when it came to the paranormal, likely due to all the high school distractions, typical teen drama, and running around with friends. It was easier to block out the spirits that wanted to communicate with me when I was active and had so many other things competing for my attention. But one aspect of my abilities did seem to blossom during these years: my empathic skills.

I've always been independent, wanting to do my own thing, be my own person, and forge my own path. I've also felt things deeper than most, experiencing higher highs and lower lows. Despite my independence, I could never completely distance myself from others.

As an empath, my energy reacts to what others are feeling, which often makes my emotions mirror those around me, but to a greater extent. The biggest downside is that others' negativity gets magnified in me tenfold. Whether at a party, walking through the store, or even eating at a restaurant, being around others can dramatically affect me. Sometimes, the negative emotions become so overwhelming that I have to distance myself physically.

Sometimes, when I'm out in public, I feel like I can hear a million thoughts simultaneously. It can be so overwhelming! It's challenging to block them all out or to focus on a single voice. It's enough to make me crazy at times.

Like when I was thirteen, one of my best friends, who was like a sister to me, moved up to Traverse City. I was devastated.

I remember talking and crying with her before she moved. She didn't want to go but didn't have a choice. I remember feeling her emotions so deeply; it was like I was experiencing both our emotions combined. I didn't know how to handle these elevated feelings at first.

As a developing empath, I struggled with how deeply I felt the emotions of those around me, whether it be the turmoil of what my single mom was going through with her divorce, the teenage angst of all my friends with their family drama, breakups, or dealing with the mean girls at school. It finally got too much to handle, so I looked for an escape.

Runaway Emotions

After my parents' divorce, I still saw my dad. He often came over to visit me and my brother, but it always seemed to end with my parents fighting again. So, at 13, I got fed up with all the negative energy and drama in the house and decided to run away from home. During the next two years, I ran away multiple times. I'd be gone for days, sometimes weeks, staying at various friends' houses.

The first time I ran away from home, I was gone for two weeks. I didn't leave a note or anything. When I didn't come home, my mom called the police to report that I had run away, but she didn't know where. All she knew was the name of the guy I was dating, and she figured that I must have run away with him. So, she gave the police my boyfriend's name, and they used that to locate the house where he lived with his parents.

I'll never forget the day the police tracked me down. I was living at my boyfriend's house when I heard this loud banging on the front door. It sounded like someone was trying to break into the house. My boyfriend's mom answered the door. A moment later, she called up to me.

"Brandy, the police are here, and they want to talk to you."

I almost had a heart attack!

I slunk downstairs, and there at the front door were two uniformed officers. They told me that they were there to take me home. I was petrified. I had never had any run-ins with the police before. What was I going to do? There was nothing I could do except gather all my stuff and leave with them.

The officers put me in the back of their cruiser and sped off. The drive back to my house seemed to last forever. I shook the whole time. The officers interrogated and lectured me the entire way. First, they asked me why I ran away and why I was staying at my boyfriend's house. I told them it was because I hated living at my house. It was depressing being in the middle of all my parents' issues and living in a place that always felt dark and threatening.

They warned me that if I kept running away, I would end up in an all-girls home. And they assured me that it was even worse than it sounded. They also made sure I knew that no matter how tough I thought I was, the girls there would be much tougher. Juvie wasn't summer camp. The picture the officer painted scared the crap out of me.

The police cruiser rolled up in front of my house, and the officers walked me to the door. My mom answered, and her expression said it all. She was mortified to have the police bring me home and was livid that I'd run away in the first place. She stood in the doorway with her arms crossed, giving me that mom look that told me I was in big trouble.

I didn't want to get into it with my mom, so I just stomped upstairs and slammed my bedroom door. The next day, I stayed in my room, trying to avoid any more conflict with my mom. When I finally came downstairs, she wouldn't even talk to me. Her silent treatment was almost worse than if she'd yelled at me.

Unfortunately, things didn't get any better at home. I ran away again about a month later. It wouldn't be the only time, either. I must've run away over a dozen times in total. Sometimes, it was only for a few days; others, it was for weeks at a time. One thing I will never forget was the last time I ran away. It's a miracle I survived.

One night, when I was fourteen, I was hanging out with one of my friends down the street when we decided to score some weed. Maybe a little cannabis would help me deal with my heightened emotions and stormy home life. She gave me the number of a guy that a mutual friend vouched for as a reliable source. I called him, and he said he'd happily hook me up.

When the guy showed up, we asked him for the weed. He said he didn't have it on him but knew where to get it and could take me there. I got in the car with him and told my friend I'd be right back. We drove awhile before I noticed that the neighborhoods were getting sketchier and sketchier. We finally stopped at a building in downtown Detroit.

The place looked okay from the outside compared to some others nearby. We got out of the car, and he led me up to one of the doors and let me in. Once I stepped inside, I was shocked to find the place was empty. On closer inspection, I realized that it was abandoned. A dark, negative energy enveloped me, and my heart began to race. What had I gotten myself into?

I tried to convince myself that I was overreacting. Maybe this is just where the guy kept his stash hidden. Or perhaps someone else who had the weed would meet us here to make the deal. Growing increasingly uncomfortable, I turned to the guy and asked him where the weed was. That's when I saw the gun pointed at my head.

He told me to get down on the floor. I was so terrified I almost puked. What had I been thinking? How could I have been so naive? I started shaking uncontrollably, feeling a hot tear run down my cheek. I quickly swiped it away because I didn't want to let him see me cry; didn't want to seem weak.

He shoved the gun in my face and repeated his demands. What was a fourteen-year-old girl to do? I did the only thing I could think of if I hoped to survive this ordeal. I got down on the dirty floor, closed my eyes, and prayed it would be over quickly.

When it was finally over, he took me back to my friend's house. She asked me where the weed was. He made an excuse for why he couldn't get his hands on the weed and told her he would be back later to pick me up, and we could score it then. After he left, I got extremely nervous. He knew I was a runaway and probably figured he could talk me into doing whatever he wanted and that no one would care.

Dark thoughts clouded my mind. What if the creep came back later and brought some of his friends? What if they not only came back to kidnap me but my friend, too? I'd heard horrifying stories of young runaways being forcibly hooked on heroin and driven into prostitution.

My legs were still shaking from what he did to me. I fought back the tears, not wanting my friend to see how terrified I was. I finally broke down and called my mom to tell her what had happened. She immediately called the police.

My friend and I sat tight until the police could arrive. The whole time we waited, I feared my attacker would return before the officers showed up. My heart sank every time a car came down the street. Then, I saw a dark automobile slowly cruising down the block. As it drew closer, I recognized the vehicle. I was never so happy to see the police!

The officers drove me to the hospital, where a nurse performed a rape kit on me. It was so humiliating, but I didn't want my attacker to get away with what he'd done to me. What if I didn't report him or provide the physical evidence needed to convict him, and he did this to someone else? I'd have a hard time living with myself.

The next day, my mom and dad took me to the local police station to issue a formal statement. It was bad enough having to explain what happened to the first pair of officers and then the nurse at the hospital, but to have to recount the experience for a third time in front of my parents was the hardest.

After the warrant was issued, I was terrified to leave the house. What if the guy who assaulted me came back? Did he know where I lived? And what if he and his friends decided to break into our house? I didn't think he knew where to find me since he picked me up at my friend's house. But what if he came after her?

My fears finally eased when we got the call from the police that they had arrested my attacker. He later got sentenced to 12 years in prison.

After returning home, I was made to feel as if the sexual assault was all my fault. It would never have happened if I hadn't run away. Why did I get in a car with a guy I didn't know? I wouldn't have even met my assailant if I hadn't been looking to buy drugs in the first place. And so on. That was when I first began blocking my emotions and retreated into myself.

It felt like I didn't have anyone else to turn to. My mom was struggling with being a single mother and dealing with her divorce. And with Grandma gone, too, I felt I had to deal with everything myself. And by the grace of God, I did.

But it didn't mean that there weren't still struggles. You can't block out everything, especially as an empath. Even when I buried my own feelings, I couldn't block the emotions of those around me. It was like I needed to make sure that others felt okay, even at the expense of my own well-being. The happier those around me were, the happier an empath like me felt. That might be why I believe it's my mission to help others.

But I wasn't immune to the consequences of my actions. I was put on probation for being a repeat runaway. I skipped a lot of school during that rebellious time, especially when I wasn't living at home. The principal contacted law enforcement concerning how much time I had missed, and they charged me with truancy. The court ordered my parents and I to appear in court. When the court date arrived, my dad showed up, but my mom didn't, so the court assigned custody of my brother and me to my dad.

I was fifteen when my brother and I moved in with our dad. Moving is always stressful, especially when it meant leaving the only home I'd ever really known. But maybe the change of scenery would be good for me, with so many dark memories at the old house, like The Dingy Man, the shadow in the hall, all the negativity and dark energy seemingly permeating every room, not to mention all the yelling and arguing leading up to my parent's divorce. Maybe a fresh start would be best for all of us.

It Runs in the Family

I became pregnant with my first child when I was twenty. After suppressing my emotions for most of my teen years, I was surprised at how having children brought those feelings back stronger than ever. It also opened up new feelings. Between the love I developed for my children and the heightened emotions of the children themselves, my empathic abilities once again blossomed.

It had been years since I had seen or been contacted by any spirits. Or if any of them had tried to connect with me, I was so closed off that they couldn't make contact. I actually hadn't even thought much about the supernatural in ages.

Despite coming from a long line of psychic mediums, The thought never really crossed my mind that I might pass this trait down to my children. That is until my firstborn began seeing "The Boy."

"The Boy"

When my oldest son Austin turned two, I became pregnant again. I was thrilled when the doctor told me it would be a girl. My mom was ecstatic. Not long after, I became pregnant with my third child, another boy. Even though I saw spirits as a child, I never considered whether my children might see them as well. All of that changed when Austin and his younger brother, Anthony, began seeing *The Boy*.

It started one day when Austin was around seven. While playing in his bedroom, he suddenly pointed and said, "The boy!" It seemed like such a strange thing to say. The Boy? What boy? Anthony wasn't in the room, and even if he had been, why would Austin refer to his brother as *The Boy*?

I followed his gaze and looked in the direction Austin was pointing, thinking maybe he saw his reflection or something. But there weren't any mirrors or reflective surfaces where Austin would see his reflection. And why would he refer to himself as The Boy, anyway?

But Austin was insistent and kept pointing.

"The Boy!"

Was it possible he saw a spirit that I couldn't? Then I remembered when I was a child, my mom didn't see The Man in White or The Dingy Man, even though she seemed to sense their presence at times. Or maybe I was reading too much into the imaginary play of a seven-year-old. I finally dismissed it, choosing to believe he was just playing a game or had developed an imaginary friend.

A little while later, my younger son Anthony, who was three, walked into the living room and said, "Mommy, there's a boy under my bed."

It stopped me in my tracks. I flashed back to when Austin had pointed at *The Boy*. Could this be the same boy Anthony's brother had been talking about?

My son's demeanor was what struck me most. It wasn't like he was making something up to avoid going to bed or that he was afraid a monster might be under his bed. He didn't seem scared of The Boy at all. He was just matter-of-factly letting me know that there was a boy under his bed.

Was he parroting his older brother? Or did he actually see someone under his bed? I decided to test him.

"What does the boy look like?"

"He's a dark boy," Anthony explained. "His skin is brown, and he has short curly hair." As he described what sounded like an African-American boy, I was struck by how specific his description was.

"His name is J.J."

He was starting to blow my mind! And if that wasn't enough, Anthony added one more disturbing detail.

"The boy says he got in a car accident, and he died."

A chill raced up my spine. Could it be that my son was talking to a dead boy living under his bed? Surprisingly, my sons didn't seem to be disturbed or threatened by The Boy at all. My biggest concern was that sometimes evil spirits took on the form of children to trick people into lowering their guard so they could manipulate or even jump (possess) them. But in this case, it didn't feel like a dark entity or demon. Just the spirit of a lost little boy.

I decided to start tuning in to my psychic abilities again. It concerned me that spirits might be trying to communicate with my children, and I wasn't aware of it. I remembered how scared

I'd been when I first started seeing spirits and the dead tried to contact me. Were my children also caught in a spiritual battle between dark and light? This sobering thought made me focus my energies to tune in to what my children were experiencing. It was time to open my 3rd eye again.

My mom came over later to see the kids and stay the night. I got her some blankets and a pillow and arranged a spot for her on the couch. It reminded me of when my grandmother used to fashion a makeshift bed for me in her living room when I spent the night at her house. This time, it was my mom's turn to see shadow figures.

The following day, while I was making breakfast for the boys, my mom strolled into the kitchen. At first, she didn't say anything. She just watched me fix breakfast. Then, she reluctantly said, "You'll never guess what I saw last night."

The way she said it stopped me in my tracks. She nervously recounted how she had been asleep on the couch when something had awakened her. She wasn't sure what it was at first. Then she confessed that she had experienced this nagging sensation of being watched. Unable to shake the feeling, she sat up and looked down the hallway connecting the living room to the boys' bedroom. That's when she saw the dark figure.

At first, she thought one of her grandchildren had gotten up to use the restroom in the middle of the night. Only something wasn't right. The figure didn't resemble any of her grandkids. The dark mass was too solid to be a shadow. It almost looked like a young African-American boy stood in the hallway, watching her.

She tried to convince herself that she was dreaming, but it seemed so real.

I told her about the spirit of the boy who lived under Anthony's bed. She stared at me in disbelief. The boys wandered into the kitchen, hearing us talking. I asked them to tell their grandma about The Boy. She stared in disbelief as they described the dead boy under the bed.

My mom was now the third person to confirm seeing The Boy. And she wouldn't be the last.

It Follows

A couple of years after our encounter with The Boy, we packed up and moved into a new home. My youngest son Anthony had just turned five. Another house, another chance for a fresh start. I hoped that the troubles of the past wouldn't follow us. Sadly, I was wrong.

Shortly after we moved in, my son Austin came running up the stairs yelling, "I saw the boy! I saw the boy!" It didn't register at first what he was saying. He must've seen the confusion on my face as he tried to explain.

"The boy that died. He's here! I saw him under my bed again!"

Was that even possible? I'd never had a spirit follow me from one place to another before. I always associated spirits with the house I was in at the time. It was the house that was haunted, right? Then, an ominous thought hit me. What if it wasn't the *houses* that were haunted? What if it was *me*? Or, in this case, my children!

This new revelation renewed my drive to understand what my kids were experiencing and what followed them here. I needed to know how to protect my children from any malevolent spirits that might try to attach themselves to them or negatively influence them as The Dingy Man had done to me. Or worse.

Honing My Gifts

My journey toward realizing the true potential of my spiritual gifts began when I joined a private Spiritualist group on Facebook. The group was created to encourage those who had just discovered their gifts and to help those with psychic abilities practice their craft with others. At first, I was just a silent observer, seeing what I could learn from others in the group and what I could apply to myself. I soon began to develop the confidence to interact with other group members.

After watching others perform psychic readings, I decided to try it myself. I asked if anyone had any family members I could practice reading. Several members responded. Surprisingly, I discovered I was getting things right from the very start.

However, my ability to read others and connect with their deceased family members really took off once I began experimenting with automatic writing. Psychography, more commonly known as "Automatic Writing," is the process of taking a writing instrument and allowing the unconscious part of one's psyche to write spontaneously, letting their hand be guided, not by conscious thought, but by spirits or psychic forces.

The more I practiced performing psychic readings and mediumship, the more I realized how good I was at it. For anyone unfamiliar with these terms, *Psychic Reading* is when somebody taps into their psychic abilities to intuit information for someone else. These can include *clairvoyance* (vision), *clairaudience* (hearing), *clairsentience* (feeling), and *Claircognition* (knowing). *Mediumship* is the practice of acting as a mediator to communicate between familiar spirits (the spirits of the dead and the living).

The admin of the Spiritualist Facebook group was a wonderful mentor to me. She was careful not to over-influence me but encouraged me to explore my gifts and find my own way. Since not everyone is the same, my path wouldn't necessarily be the same as hers.

The more I practiced and explored my abilities, the more I realized my capabilities as a psychic medium. That explained my earliest encounters with various spirits/entities like The Man in White and The Dingy Man, not to mention the visits from my grandmother. I realized I could see, hear, and talk with the dead!

Time after time, members of the group confirmed my findings. It wasn't long before the group leader encouraged me to start my own psychic group. She thought I was ready to step out on my own and expand my abilities on a broader scale. And so, I did.

So, I created a new, private Facebook group for psychics to discuss their abilities and answer each other's questions. I wanted to encourage others struggling to understand their abilities and let them know they weren't alone. It was important to me to create a safe place for others to explore and strengthen their gifts and learn how to use them better. And who knows, with some help, more of us might discover latent abilities that we didn't even know we had!

My journey started by working with mentors who were more experienced than me. Now, I had developed to the point where I was ready to pass on what I had learned to others. The student was now becoming the teacher.

Strengthening my psychic mediumship abilities became a blessing and a curse. I loved being able to help others connect with lost loved ones and help them find peace and hope. But as I opened up my 3rd Eye, it seemed to act like a beacon of light for spirits to find me and attempt to connect with my energy. It wasn't long before the shadow figures returned.

Dark Shadows

After being blessed with twins, I was now the mother of five. And with my older children having exhibited their own psychic medium abilities, it was like we were a 6x super-magnet, drawing spirit energies from near and far. Unfortunately, the spirits in our new house were some of the darkest I'd experienced yet, and they appeared to be coming from the basement.

My first encounter with these mysterious shadow figures came one night while watching TV in the living room. The kids were in bed, and I was relaxing on the couch. From where I sat, I could see the dining room and the stairwell leading down to the basement. While engrossed in my program, I glimpsed movement out of the corner of my eye. The kids should all be asleep by now, so to see a shadow bolt from the basement stairs into the dining room startled me.

Austin's bedroom was in the basement, and for a moment, I thought maybe he had come up the stairs to get something from the kitchen. But as I turned, I caught what looked like a disembodied shadow float through the dining room and disappear into the kitchen.

A chill ran up my spine as I felt the temperature drop. I tried to dismiss what I'd seen as just a shadow cast by the TV. But then I flashed back to the shadow I'd seen as a child at my grandma's house, floating from the bathroom into the kitchen. Had the shadow man followed me here from my grandma's house? Or was this a different entity altogether?

I tried to focus on the TV program, but I sensed the shadow figure was more than just an optical illusion. I quickly discovered that I was right.

I found myself glancing toward the basement stairwell every few minutes. Something felt... *off*. It didn't take long before I glimpsed another dark figure out of the corner of my eye. To my horror, I witnessed a tall, dark mass travel from the basement, through the kitchen, and then disappear into the wall leading to the kids' bedrooms!

I was so terrified that I jumped off the couch and turned on all the lights in the living room, dining room, and kitchen, hoping the light would dispel the darkness creeping up from below.

My heart still racing, I sat back down on the couch and tried to leverage my developing psychic abilities to determine what these shadow figures might be. I hoped they were nothing more than another residual loop like the one at my grandma's house. But to my dismay, these entities turned out to be something much darker and potentially much more dangerous.

I opened up my 3rd eye to tune into these spirits, but all I could see was utter darkness. It was like gazing into the empty eye sockets of the Grim Reaper. A feeling of deep dread gripped me, but I had to know what I was dealing with and what my children might be facing.

I extended my psychic tendrils further, attempting to connect with the spirits, but the harder I pushed and the deeper I explored, the heavier and darker everything became. This feeling of impending doom threatened to drag me deeper into the abyss. I grew more and more afraid for myself and my children. A sense of hopelessness overwhelmed me, and I began to cry.

Something deep inside me told me not to let go but to fight for myself and my children. An inner voice warned me not to be absorbed by the darkness but to return to the light. I knew I was sinking, the shadowy forces pulling me deeper and deeper into their lair, and if I didn't stop it soon, this torrent of despair could become a permanent reality.

Leveraging all the strength I had left, I tried to close my 3rd eye to sever the connection I'd made with the dark entities. I desperately needed a lifeline to pull me back toward the light. I thought of my children and what it would do to them to lose their mother. Focusing on my need to protect my little ones, I concentrated on a distant pinprick of light. It began to grow brighter and brighter the harder I focused on it. I longed to escape the darkness and draw closer to that light full of love and warmth.

As I squeezed my eyes shut, it was as if I cut the rope tethering me to the bottom. I gradually felt myself ascending toward the light. The shadows began to fade into the distance beneath me, and the light grew brighter and brighter until I finally broke the surface of that black lake and gasped for air. I opened my eyes and was suddenly back in my living room, the television still droning in the background.

As the cobwebs cleared, I thought of Austin, who had chosen the bedroom in the basement where the shadow figures originated. With my room upstairs on the other side of the house, I worried about being too far away if one of these things set its sights on him. To my dismay, it wasn't long before my fears came true.

Not long after our move, Austin began seeing tall shadow figures creeping around the basement outside his bedroom door. They mostly appeared to travel from one side of the basement to the other as if traversing some invisible passageway. At first, he thought he was just seeing things, or maybe it had all been a dream. When he finally mustered the courage to tell me, I asked him what he thought they were. He said that they were nothing like the boy from under the bed. These things seemed evil.

One night, while Austin was down in the basement, he felt something dark building outside his bedroom door. He pulled the covers up to his chin, eyes glued to the doorway, afraid one of the shadows might creep into his room.

A shadow passed in front of his doorway, giving him a start. Then came another. And another. How many of these things were there? He waited nervously, hoping they would keep moving past his room and disappear up the stairs like before. But this time, the shadow-things assembled as if gathering their collective strength, then turned and headed for his room! Had they heard him gasp?

Austin held his breath as they neared his doorway. He readied to scream. The thought of these phantoms creeping into his room and surrounding his bed terrified him. Cornered, he had nowhere to run. Austin's heart pounded, his whole body shaking. Could shadows harm flesh and bone?

Then, as the horde of shadow figures reached the threshold, they suddenly came to an abrupt halt. Austin held his breath. What were they waiting for? Why weren't they coming into his room? Were they like vampires who needed an invitation to enter? Or could something more powerful be keeping them at bay?

What if they were only trying to get his attention? Wanted to show him something? Something unspeakable. Austin closed his eyes, terrified of what they might see that could never be unseen. What if he kept his eyes shut? Would they lose interest and retreat? After all, isn't that what his mom would do? But what if they were creeping into his room even now, surrounding him, preparing to attack? Would it be better to see it coming?

Austin opened his eyes and found the shadowy apparitions still congregated outside his doorway. Even though they hadn't left, at least they hadn't advanced. He shut his eyes again, struggling to block them out. He was too frightened to open his eyes again, fearing they might interpret his attention as an invitation to enter his room, or worse, enter *him*!

Still terrified, Austin forced himself to keep his eyes shut to block out the curious creatures. He focused on his breathing to reduce his heart rate. Before Austin realized it, he drifted off to sleep.

When he opened his eyes the following morning, the shadows were gone.

* * *

Unfortunately, that wasn't the last time we witnessed shadow figures in this house. For the most part, they primarily seemed to haunt the basement area outside Austin's bedroom. It was almost as if an open portal existed in the basement.

I often witnessed the shadows rise from the basement and travel through the wall in the kitchen, which troubled me the most since that wall separated the kitchen from the youngest kids' bedrooms.

One of the most disturbing aspects of the shadow figures was that they didn't seem to have any fear of us. It was as if this was *their* house and *we* were the trespassers.

After telling my brother about the shadowy intruders, he and his wife decided to come over with their video camera to see if they could document the phenomenon and validate our stories. It would also prove we weren't crazy.

I greeted my brother and sister-in-law at the door. After some small talk, I led them down into the basement. Austin didn't want to have any part of the investigation, so he stayed upstairs. I can't say that I blame him since he was the one who had to sleep down there.

We didn't have infrared cameras back then, so we had to turn the lights on for the camcorder to pick up anything. My sister-in-law stood at the foot of the stairs and started recording. I'm not sure if it was because she thought it was the best angle or because she wanted the ability to escape up the stairs quickly if something did show up!

As my brother's wife recorded, I gradually opened myself up to the energies in the room. Immediately, I sensed a dark energy down there. I got the impression we were intruding on whatever inhabited the basement. The more I opened up to the dark passengers, the more I sensed that our basement possessed some type of portal that dark energies used to travel from the spirit world into ours.

I didn't want to say anything that might influence my brother or his wife, so I didn't tell them what I sensed. I figured I'd wait to see if they detected anything first. And then it happened. The first shadow figure materialized from the basement wall and moved toward me.

I stepped aside to let the shadow pass and watched it travel from one corner of the basement to the other. My sister-in-law gasped and told me that we had to stop what we were doing so she could show us what she witnessed through the lens finder.

We gathered around the camcorder's small video screen as my sister-in-law rewound to the beginning and pushed play. As the tape played back, we were amazed to see this towering, dark, shadow figure with what looked like a long black robe trailing behind it, rush from the corner of the basement and past Austin's bedroom before disappearing into the wall.

After witnessing the apparition fly across the room, my brother and sister-in-law never questioned me again.

Shadow figures continued to roam through the house the entire time we lived there. They seemed to originate from the basement, possibly wayward passengers from an ancient portal between dimensions we inadvertently disturbed. They seemed drawn to us once they realized we could see them and acknowledged their existence. No longer were they content to pass through the basement portal but instead began wandering upstairs and throughout the house. Were they trying to bring us messages from the other side? Or were they attempting to lure us down into the abyss from where they came? I wasn't sure if I really wanted to know the answer.

PARANORMAL INVESTIGATING

B y 2013, I regularly performed psychic readings for people in my private Facebook group. I also joined several paranormal groups to connect with others interested in the supernatural to increase my knowledge.

While performing an online reading for one of the group members, I detected multiple supernatural phenomena occurring in their house. The client was shocked by how many details from my reading directly coincided with her family history. She confirmed everything I had picked up during our session.

The founder of a local paranormal team came across the thread of my psychic reading and was impressed with my accuracy and the ability to read my client's location remotely. He shot me a private message asking if I would be interested in joining their paranormal investigation team.

I was hesitant to commit to anything exclusive or long-term, but I was curious to test my abilities at an actively haunted location. He offered to let me come with them on their next investigation and said I could decide if I wanted to join them from there.

I wasn't familiar with very many haunted locations at this early stage. But, I figured, how bad could this place be? I asked them where they were going, and he told me they were heading to Kentucky to investigate a place called Waverly Hills Sanatorium. Little did I know at the time that Waverly Hills was considered by many to be the most haunted location in America!

First Investigation — Waverly Hills

I f I had known then what I know now, I would not have chosen one of the most active haunted locations in the nation as my first foray into paranormal investigating. Talk about trial by fire!

Waverly Hills Sanatorium started in 1910 as a two-story facility meant to accommodate roughly 40-50 tuberculosis patients. Back then, Tuberculosis was a highly contagious and deadly disease. Most of those who contracted TB had to isolate themselves from the rest of the population and were quarantined at locations where they could get plenty of fresh air and rest.

As the tuberculosis epidemic grew, the headcount at Waverly Hills multiplied to nearly 150 patients. Bursting at the seams, they eventually expanded the overcrowded clinic into a massive, gothic-style Sanatorium in 1926, which is what you see today. The new sanatorium could accommodate over 400 patients and was considered one of the most modern, well-equipped facilities of its time.

The facility continued serving as a tuberculosis hospital until 1961, when an antibiotic was discovered to successfully treat and even cure the disease, ultimately rendering the sanatorium obsolete. After that, it served as a nursing home for two decades before the state shuttered it for good in 1981. After years of weather damage and vandalism, Waverly Hills nearly became condemned before the Waverly Hills Historical Society rescued it.

But I didn't know any of this going in. Even from the start of my paranormal investigation pursuits, I wanted to go into every investigation knowing as little as possible to avoid any outside influences. I prefer to read a location cold to ensure I can interpret what I see, hear, and feel accurately, without bias. So, when I went into Waverly Hills Sanatorium, I went in blind.

We pulled off the highway onto a narrow, blacktop road that cut deep into the remote Kentucky hillside. The asphalt beneath us was faded and crumbling. Trees towered over us on either side, casting ominous shadows as we wound our way up the hill to the abandoned sanatorium. It was late in the day, and the sun was completing its retreat behind the forest of trees.

The long, gloomy drive up the hill only added to the suspense and my feeling of dread. The twisting road finally dumped us out into a courtyard of cracked concrete, where I got my first glimpse of the imposing, gothic structure.

My initial reaction when stepping out of the car was awe at the sheer size of the building. Next, I was struck by how dark the sky had already gotten. After we extinguished our headlights, the only light out here in the boondocks was the pale moonlight illuminating our path. But once we step inside, we only have a handful of flashlights to light our way. That's the problem with investigating abandoned structures – no electricity. What did I get myself into?

Waverly Hills Sanatorium loomed over us as we hiked toward the entrance. The closer I got, the more overwhelming the negative energy became. My heart picked up its pace as I experienced a sudden crisis of confidence. Until now, performing mediumship for clients, I'd only connected to light energies. Nothing negative like this. I'd had run-ins with a few dark entities in my lifetime, like the Dingy Man and various mysterious shadow figures, but this was on a totally different level. It was like encountering a thousand voices chattering all at once, some whispering, others wailing. I was scared to death to venture inside.

Historians have determined from surviving hospital records that at least 8,000 patients died at Waverly Hills' during its operation. Others have theorized that the number could be as many as 60,000. What worried me most was how many of those thousands of spirits were still wandering the halls of this place, waiting for us.

I turned to the others and said, "I don't think I can do this!"

"We'll just go slow," they said, attempting to put me at ease. "Why don't we just see how it goes since we're already here?"

They had a point. It would be a shame to come all this way just to chicken out at the last minute. But I couldn't help but be nervous exploring a haunted sanatorium at night. The others had investigated here before, so they knew their way around. But they swore to stay with me the whole time, so I didn't need to worry.

"You'll be okay," they promised.

I took a deep breath to calm my nerves and tried to ignore all the negative energies assaulting me. Call it peer pressure or pride, but I didn't want to be the only person too afraid even to step foot in the place. But if they could sense what I did, I wonder how many of them would be brave enough to go into this haunted of a location.

I stood there a moment, taking it all in, my whole body tense.

The sprawling red brick building's entrance offered an ornate, white-stone archway accompanied by hideous gargoyles perched on top, glaring at us. A wrought iron embellishment crowned the center arch with a message welcoming us to Waverly Hills Sanatorium.

I gawked at the ominous structure, speechless. Somebody finally broke the silence.

"Everybody ready to go in?"

I wanted to yell, "Hell no!" But I ignored my psychic instincts warning me against it and agreed to enter with everyone else. Besides, what choices did I have? Ruin everyone else's night by making them take me to the hotel? Or sit in the car by myself while everyone else had fun investigating? I was already here, and the sanatorium did look amazing. I decided to go ahead and give it a try. What's the worst that could happen? I quickly realized it was better not to ponder that.

The moment we first stepped into Waverly Hills, it felt like something was slowly squeezing my head in a vice. The atmosphere was so heavy in there!

We began our investigation with an initial walkthrough to just get the lay of the place.

The outer walls of the building were exposed to the outside with large open windows designed to allow the fresh air in to aid the tuberculosis patients' recovery. During the day, hospital beds were wheeled into the outer hallways so the patients could get as much sun and fresh air as possible.

When we ventured into the inner hallways, the thick, stale air made it feel like someone had tossed a bag over my head. Dust motes cascaded down from above, whirling around in our flashlight beams. Rusty pipes ran the length of the hallway's ceilings. The eerie silence struck me as we wandered deeper into the sanatorium, the only sound coming from our echoing footsteps.

The peeling walls bore the markings of teenage vandals, with chunks of plaster knocked out and graffiti tags spray-painted throughout. Many left their mark, though most of their scrawlings were indecipherable. A few left their names behind to prove they'd been brave enough to make it this far.

Several rooms still contained medical equipment, beds, and furniture covered in a decades-old blanket of dust. I half expected to see a patient in one of the beds suddenly sit up! If that happened, I'd probably pee myself!

As we made our way along the corridor, we had to be careful not to run into the abandoned gurneys and wheelchairs that littered the hallways and turned them into obstacle courses.

Working toward the end of the first-floor hallway, we stumbled upon the Waverly Hills morgue. So much for easing my way into this. I could only imagine what kinds of energies we were about to find in there!

The Morgue

R emnants of the once busy Waverly Hills morgue remained, including operating tables, rusted gurneys, and
even a three-body upright cooler once used to store
corpses awaiting pick up. The owners removed the doors from
their hinges to prevent anyone from getting trapped inside,
much like people do with abandoned refrigerators. With the
doors missing, the cooler looked like a mausoleum raided by
grave robbers. I shined my flashlight inside the gaping holes in
the cooler, revealing rusted slide-out trays where the dead once
lay.

Being inside the abandoned morgue was both terrifying and
exhilarating. I'd never done anything like this before. But that's
why I was here; I wanted to try something different to challenge
my abilities. After doing readings for people and connecting
them to their lost loved ones, I'd begun to wonder what would
happen if I opened myself up somewhere like this, where such
massive amounts of energy surrounded me. Sure, I'd experienced individual energies many times, but this was a whole
other level.

Looking at the open mortuary cooler, I had this wild idea—
what would happen if I crawled inside one of those drawers?
What kind of reading would I get if I lay where dozens, maybe
even hundreds of the dead had lain before me? It would be wild,
right?

"You should totally try it," the lead investigator said.

"I don't know..." I backpedaled, wishing I hadn't brought it up.

"You said you wanted to challenge yourself," he said. "What better way than that? With your abilities, it should be easy to pick something up inside one of those drawers."

I hated to admit it, but he was right. I came down here to push myself and test the extent of my psychic abilities. If I couldn't connect with the spirits here, then what did that say about those abilities? After some coaxing, I finally broke down and agreed to be their guinea pig.

The lead investigator pulled the bottom tray out from the incapacitated cooler, the rusted rollers screeching in defiance. Filled with nervous excitement, I climbed onto the dusty body tray, its corroded surface rough under my hands. I tried not to think about the bodily fluids that must've oozed onto the trays to rust them like this.

Sliding my legs inside, I lay on my back and tried to get comfortable. The fit was going to be much tighter than I feared. The drawer wasn't much bigger than a coffin.

As I lay on the tray in the dark, I crossed my hands over my chest. Realizing that I was mimicking a corpse, I quickly dropped my hands to my sides. The feel of the rusty tray creeped me out so badly that I reconsidered and folded my hands at my waist instead.

"Are you ready?" the lead investigator asked.

"As ready as I'll ever be!" I replied.

"Okay, here we go..." he said with a smile.

He slid me slowly into the mortuary cooler, the rollers again shrieking their protest. As he pushed me inside, the cooler swallowed me whole. The narrow compartment felt terribly claustrophobic, the shelf above me only inches from my face. Thank

God the doors were removed. There's no way I would ever want to be trapped in one of those narrow, casket-like compartments!

I closed my eyes and took a deep breath, trying to relax. I couldn't believe I was doing this. I slowed my breathing and tried to concentrate, gradually opening myself up to whatever spirits might be in the room.

Before long, I felt a female presence somewhere overhead. Oh, God, was she lying in the drawer directly above me? My heart beat faster.

I felt the disembodied spirit reaching out to me.

"Is there somebody in here?" I called out.

The female energy above me intensified.

"Is there anything you'd like to tell me?" I asked aloud, hoping the quiver in my voice wasn't too noticeable. Suddenly, the female spirit lying in drawer number two gradually descended through the shelf that separated us. As she drew closer, her body rotated 180 degrees until we were eye to eye, her face hovering mere inches above mine! It was like she was staring directly into my soul!

I thought I was going to have a heart attack! Who was this woman, and what did she want? As if I wasn't claustrophobic enough, having this spirit float mere inches above me was enough to drive anyone insane! I cried out to the other investigators, begging them to pull me from this frigid tomb.

The lead investigator quickly grabbed the tray and yanked me out. In my panic, I forgot I could block spirit energy. As they pulled me from the cooler, I remembered and quickly blocked the meddling spirit. Once clear, I jumped off the slab and brushed myself off as if covered in spiders.

After the harrowing experience in the morgue, I checked over my shoulder constantly on the way up to the next floor. I

sensed the spirits here taking notice of me. And now they knew
I could see and hear them, too.

Since I'd survived the morgue, I figured the rest of the investigation would all be downhill. Boy, was I wrong. The party was
just getting started.

Morgue Cooler

Ghost Children

A s we wandered from floor to floor, there were several places where I heard children giggling and saw shadows popping in and out of the doorways. Could those shadows be ghost children playing hide and seek with us? When I asked the others, they confirmed what I was experiencing. Apparently, one of the entities that haunted the third floor was the ghost of a little girl who liked to run up and down the hallway. But the most famous child known to roam Waverly Hills was a boy named Timmy.

I encountered Timmy's spirit when we reached the fifth floor. I heard him running around and giggling as if playing with unseen playmates. Paranormal investigators have reported interacting with Timmy on multiple occasions. These encounters usually entailed rolling a ball in one of the fifth-floor rooms or down the hallway, then having it roll back to them as if Timmy was playing catch!

During its peak, Waverly Hills housed hundreds of tuberculosis patients, many of them children. In addition to patients, there were also the children of patients or staff. The children were encouraged to play on the fifth floor to avoid disturbing the other patients. They even built a playset on the roof with swings and a slide to keep them occupied.

After my visit here, I looked into the history of Waverly Hills and discovered that there actually was a boy named Timmy who once resided here. His full name was Timmy O'Shea.

The story of Timmy O'Shea is a depressing one. It's said that Timmy had a red rubber ball that he constantly bounced wherever he went. Well-loved by the staff, he frequently played catch with them when he wasn't running around with the other kids. And that's where the story turned tragic.

According to a newspaper report of the time, Timmy had been on the roof playing with his ball when it got away from him. He chased after his ball, trying to catch it before it went over the edge. Tragically, not only did the ball go over the edge, but so did Timmy, tumbling five stories to his death.

When police investigated the cause of the young boy's demise, detectives looked into the possibility of foul play. One of the patients quarantined at Waverly Hills was a convict from a local prison who was on the rooftop when Timmy fell off the roof. Unable to find sufficient evidence to prove that the convict was involved in the boy's death, the investigators determined that the boy had indeed been chasing his ball when he accidentally tripped near the roof's edge, causing him to plummet to his death.

While we investigated the fifth floor, we tried our luck interacting with Timmy by rolling a ball around and even blowing bubbles, but unfortunately, he didn't seem to be in the mood to play with us that night.

The tragic death of Timmy O'Shea

Fifth Floor Nurse

Although the fifth floor of Waverly Hills only spans a small portion of the top center of the building, it possesses more than its share of spirits haunting its abandoned halls. As we explored the rest of the top floor, I quickly discovered that Timmy wasn't the only person whose death was linked to this area.

The upper level of the sanitorium used to house the psychiatric ward as well as the nurse's headquarters. As we wandered through the nurse's area, I skid to a stop in front of Room 502. The moment I reached that doorway, a tremendous wave of sadness struck me. The emotion was so overwhelming that I began to cry.

At first, I couldn't understand why this was happening. I eventually determined that it must be an empathic reaction. I decided to open myself up to see what was causing such melancholy emotions. It wasn't long before I felt a presence in Room 502. As I opened myself up more, an image began to materialize, like a photograph developing in a darkroom. The spirit gradually manifested itself, revealing a woman wearing an old-fashioned, starched-white nurse's uniform. Her mousy brown hair was curled tight to her head and topped with a petite, white nurse's cap.

I suddenly doubled over with mysterious, gut-wrenching abdominal pains.

"Are you okay?" somebody asked, noticing my obvious discomfort.

"Something bad happened here," I said, holding my stomach.

I barely got the words out before my throat tightened. My airway continued to constrict as if someone was strangling me; I could hardly breathe! I knew I needed to escape from whatever was choking me before I passed out! The other investigators ran over to me, worried looks on their faces, realizing something was seriously wrong.

"I need to get some air," I wheezed.

One of the investigators ushered me out onto the children's play area on the roof, where Timmy met his untimely demise. Once outside, inhaling the fresh night air, I could finally breathe normally again.

The lead investigator asked me how I was doing and what I'd just experienced inside. When I told them about my impression of the nurse, the stomach pains, and the choking sensation, his eyes grew wide. He said he thought he might know the cause.

Legend has it that one of the head nurses who worked at the sanatorium had gotten pregnant by one of the doctors who, once he found out, refused to take responsibility for the child or even have anything to do with her anymore. Distraught, the nurse reportedly hanged herself from a light fixture in Room 502! That would certainly explain the emotions I felt, the abdominal pains, as well as the choking sensation.

Another tragic tale relating to Room 502 was regarding another nurse who leaped from the window of the same room the head nurse hanged herself in and plummeted to her death five stories below. The reason she made that leap to end her life was still unknown. It's no wonder the negative energy in this room was so powerful!

As we stood outside, enjoying the cool night air, I suddenly felt a group of children run past me, giggling. They seemed headed toward the swingset where the children of the TB patients and staff used to play. My thoughts returned to Timmy. I looked to the edge where the boy had likely gone over. Although a wall ran along the perimeter, it wasn't very high. I could see where a boy, running after his ball and not focusing on where he was going, could easily have tripped and gone over the edge. As a mother, the thought of losing a child tore at my heart.

With all of the activity on the fifth floor, it was getting too much for me. We'd already spent a good deal of time up here, so our group agreed that we would start working our way back downstairs.

After we reached the first floor, we strolled down a long, dark hallway. The farther we progressed, the stronger the feeling of dread grew inside me. It felt like someone placed a heavy weight on my chest. My psychic alarms went off, and I immediately went into defensive mode. It was as if my guardian angels were trying to warn me to put my guard up. I know better than to question that feeling, so I quickly put up my psychic shield to protect myself from the dark energy. Little did I know that we were headed toward the most disturbing area of all – a place more affectionately known as... the "Body Chute."

Waverly Hills Body Chute

The Body Chute

As we neared the opening, I was struck by an overwhelming sense of impending doom. A shiver of goosebumps spread up my arms to my neck, making the hairs stand on end. Everything inside me told me to turn around. Once I caught a glimpse of the Body Chute, I understood why.

The Body Chute, also known as the "Death Tunnel," was an enclosed concrete tunnel that led roughly 500 feet down the hill to the outside. On one side, there was a set of stairs employees used to enter and exit the building. On the other was a flat concrete ramp where staff transported food and supplies using a cart powered by a motorized cable system. Except, that wasn't the only thing transported down this tunnel.

As the "white plague" spread across the nation and more and more people were sent to Waverly Hills for tuberculosis treatment, the death toll at the sanatorium began to rise. It was devastating for patient morale to see the dead wheeled out day after day. At its peak, it's said that one patient died every hour!

The doctors became just as concerned about the patient's mental health as their physical health. Seeing how many of their fellow patients were dying and being carted away couldn't have been beneficial for the remaining patients' recovery efforts. The staff decided it would be better to utilize the tunnel to transport the dead down the hill and out of sight of the other patients. The Body Chute eventually emptied out near a set of railroad tracks at the bottom of the hill, where the deceased were then taken away to their final resting place.

When we arrived at the opening of the body chute, I stared down into the pitch-black abyss, and the abyss stared back. Without any lighting in the tunnel, aside from our meager flashlights, it was like staring into the pits of hell. A few of us trained our flashlight beams down the tunnel, but the void seemed to just swallow them up.

Being the only psychic medium in our party, they wanted me to go down to the bottom to see what I might detect. Since this was my first time here at Waverly Hills and my first time investigating any haunted location, there was no way I was going down that dark tunnel by myself. I told them I would only go down there if somebody who knew the place took point and someone else walked behind me the whole time. I was too afraid of what I might stumble across down there, and I definitely didn't want something sneaking up behind me.

To be honest, I really didn't want to go down there. But I also didn't want to be the only one to chicken out. Once the others agreed to create a hedge of protection around me as we filed down the tunnel, I couldn't back out.

We inched our way down the body chute, our flashlights nervously exploring the darkness. The concrete tunnel was like an echo chamber, amplifying every footstep. We were all on edge, half-expecting some phantom or demon to manifest itself any moment. I couldn't believe I let them talk me into this.

Our probing flashlight beams created shifting shadows on the walls and ceiling, heightening the paranoia. And the way sound bounced around in the body chute made it hard to tell if we were hearing disembodied whispers, the skittering of startled rats, or just the echoes of our own shuffling footsteps.

No one seemed to be in a hurry, whether they were afraid of tripping down the seemingly endless flight of concrete steps or just afraid, period. I was in the dark in more ways than one. I decided to open myself up just enough to determine what was happening around me but kept myself about 95% blocked. It was kind of like going to a scary movie and peeking between your fingers.

By the time we'd ventured about halfway down the body chute, two of our team members had lost their nerve and turned back. I thought about heading back with them, but I didn't want to let the rest of the team down since the main reason they invited me was to have a psychic medium help them investigate.

Even with the flashlight, I still couldn't see the bottom.

"How much farther down does this go?" I asked, hoping to get out of there as soon as possible.

"It shouldn't be too much farther," they assured me.

The deeper we descended, the thicker the energy around us grew. I tried lowering my guard a little at a time, testing the waters. It felt like we were wading through a murky swamp, knowing that somewhere beneath the surface, an alligator was lurking. And then, when you least expected, it would select its victim and pull them under.

The heaviness seemed to follow us the length of the pitch-black tunnel. I wished we had more than a few flashlights to dispel the all-consuming darkness. With our tentative pace, it probably took us about ten minutes to make it to the bottom, though it seemed like an eternity.

When we finally reached the end of the body chute, we encountered a locked, wrought iron gate. I peered through the bars only to see that someone had boarded up the entrance. That's when it struck me; we'd reached a dead end. The only way out of the death tunnel would be to go back the way we came.

The other investigators decided we should start a recording session at the bottom to see if we could capture any EVPs (Electronic Voice Phenomenon). For anyone unfamiliar with the term, an EVP is the audio recording of spirit interaction. Whether through a digital recorder or just an old-fashioned cassette recorder, there are times when playing back an audio recording will reveal spirit communication that wasn't audible at the time it was recorded.

We set a flashlight on the floor, pointing up, creating an eerie glow like the embers of a dying campfire. Those with digital recorders started recording as we took turns asking the spirits questions and then pausing for the spirits to answer. In total, we likely spent about fifteen minutes at the bottom of the body chute recording EVPs.

Suddenly, I noticed an anomaly farther up the tunnel at the far reaches of the flashlight's glow. Something I would later come to know as... The Creeper.

The Creeper

At first, it was just movement out of the corner of my eye, a shifting shadow quickly dismissed. I wrote the anomaly off as just our shadows cast by the flashlight. But then I realized that the strange shadow continued its descent even when we weren't moving. What kind of being was so black that you could still see its silhouette even in a dark tunnel?

Each time I looked up, it seemed to be in a different location.

"Do you guys see that?" I asked.

I tried describing it to the others as they surveyed the dark, but no one else could see what I did.

I felt a low, negative energy inching toward us from deep in the tunnel. A solid black form slithered down the ramp of the body chute where the cadavers were lowered during the pandemic.

Then, it disappeared.

I looked away for a moment to concentrate on our EVP session. When I glanced back up the tunnel, the black mass manifested again and crawled up the wall. I gasped. The negative energy in the tunnel continued to intensify, driving a spike of fear into my chest. Something else was in the tunnel with us. And it wasn't human.

Spooked by my reaction, the remaining team members shined their flashlights around the tunnel, trying to locate the anomaly. Up ahead, the thick, black shadow crept up the wall and onto the ceiling, defying gravity as it crawled toward us, upside down!

The creeper seemed to single me out and crawled toward me. I could see its features more clearly as it drew closer to the light. To the others, it appeared as just a black shadow mass, but as a psychic medium, I could see its true form. And it was hideous.

The entity crawled on all fours with spider-like appendages, its long, sharp claws scrabbling across the ceiling. It advanced in jerky, unnatural fits and starts. The creature's gray, hairless body crawled toward me, its pitch-black eyes fixed on me. The elongated mouth reminded me of a snake when it unhinged its jaw to swallow a much larger prey.

I suddenly felt nauseated. The creeper's negative energy seeped into me, filling me with an overwhelming sense of hopelessness and dread. I had never felt anything this dark before. I retreated cautiously. What the hell was this thing, and what did it want?

The creeper descended along the wall until it reached the floor again and continued toward me. Was it hunting me? Backpedaling, I nearly lost my footing. I knew I couldn't retreat much further, or I would crash into the wrought iron gate behind me. It had me cornered. There was nowhere to run.

It was only fifteen feet away now. I considered my options and all of them were bad. I could try standing my ground, but I'd never faced anything like this before, and I had no idea what it was capable of. I couldn't retreat because we'd reached a dead end. The creeper had blocked our only other means of escape and continued to close on me.

Then, it disappeared again.

Just when I thought it was gone for good, it reappeared, crawling along the wall at shoulder height. I grabbed one of the gals and pointed at the thing, but she still couldn't see it. Even with my full guard up, it continued to hone in on me. Once it crawled to within ten feet of me, it vanished again. I screamed.

Terrified of what it would do if it reached me, I knew I had to take advantage of this brief window where the creeper had blinked back to the underworld.

"Fuck it, I'm outta here!" I shouted, "And I'm not going alone."

My terror rubbed off on the gal next to me, and she agreed to go back up the tunnel with me. I shoved her in front of me and hid behind her, using her as a human shield. I tried not to look around, terrified the creeper would reappear just as we reached the spot where it blinked out of existence. I pushed her up the tunnel until I was sure we'd gone far enough and finally let her go.

"What did you see?" she asked.

"Trust me, you don't want to know."

I heard footsteps behind me as we reached the halfway point. I felt someone catching up to us. I breathed a sigh of relief, knowing someone finally had my back. I turned around to say something and screamed. There was nobody there! The rest of the remaining investigators were still at the bottom. *Then, what was following me?*

Hearing me scream, the other gal sprinted for the exit without looking back to find out why.

Fearing the presence behind me was the creeper, I bolted too, praying I could outrun it. I may not look like it, but when I'm scared, I can really move. In no time, I caught up to the other gal and stuck to her like glue until we reached the top. Neither of us stopped until we got to the first-floor hallway.

After regrouping on the first floor, everyone wanted to know what I had seen in the body chute. How do you describe the indescribable? I'm no H.P. Lovecraft, but I did my best. After hearing my description, they told me they believed I had encountered something known around Waverly Hills as "The Creeper."

Apparently, we weren't the first to see this thing. The Creeper was infamous for haunting the body chute as well as some of the other floors, primarily the third. Others who encountered the creeper also described it as a non-human energy form. Some believed it was created by all the pain and suffering that occurred at Waverly Hills over the years. Others theorized that the pain and suffering attracted these unusual entities from the underworld.

Whatever they are and wherever they come from, I hoped I'd never run into one of those things again. Unfortunately, my first encounter with the creeper energy wouldn't be my last. The good news is that they are extremely rare. I've only encountered creepers at a couple of locations in all my years of investigating. And each of those places possessed an extremely negative history or had seen a lot of deaths. Like Waverly Hills.

We decided to head back upstairs since we still had some time. As we wandered the hallways, we continued to hear children giggling and playing. It was like something out of a horror movie!

Bats!

Toward the end of the investigation, we decided to check out the outer hallway. The front of the sanitorium featured a hallway with large windows that gave patients access to fresh air and sunshine. Back in the day, netting or screens covered the windows to keep out the bugs. Now, the screens were all gone, with nothing separating the hallway from the outdoors. The cool night air felt terrific after spending all that time in the stifling tunnel.

The only light available here in the boondocks came from the sliver of a moon. The hallway was cloaked in menacing shadows. All of a sudden, something flew past my head. What in the world was that? Did a bird just try and attack me? But what would a bird be doing flying around this late at night?

Soon, another bird flew past our heads. We started screaming and ran for cover. But instead of escaping them, the sound of my flip-flops slapping at my heels and our flashlight beams waving around seemed to draw more of them to us.

Somebody yelled, "Bats!"

Now we were really screaming, male and female alike! We did our best to duck their attacks, but they continued to dive-bomb us. I could feel them brushing against my arms and legs. We panicked and bolted for the door. It was so dark I could hardly see anything, making it even more terrifying. I never knew where they were coming from next. Dozens of them attacked us from every direction!

Once we made it inside, we all burst out laughing, realizing we had probably scared them as badly as they'd scared us! To this day, I am deathly afraid of bats, thanks to this experience.

We finally left around 2 a.m. to return to the hotel. Waverly Hills was such an overwhelming experience for my first investigation. I wasn't sure if I ever wanted to do this kind of thing again after all of this. But, of course, I did. I absolutely love the historical aspect of these investigations and the adrenaline rush of seeing and communicating with the other side. So, it wasn't long before I gave it another shot.

Jeepers Creepers –
Old South Pittsburgh Hospital

O ne of the most terrifying places I've ever investigated also possessed a creeper energy — the abandoned Old South Pittsburgh Hospital in Tennessee. The facility, which closed in 1998, is arguably the most actively haunted location in the entire state.

The hospital rests on land that once belonged to the Chiaha Indian Tribe. During the Civil War, this Native American tribe allowed Union soldiers to store their supplies on their reservation until the Confederate army invaded and massacred both Union soldiers and tribe members alike.

A dark cloud still seemed to loom over the property today. Whether that's because of the tremendous loss of life on this land during the Civil War, the many people who died in the hospital, or something to do with the Native land it was built on was uncertain. But what was certain was that Old South Pittsburgh Hospital was haunted by a host of dark energies.

Paranormal investigators and former employees claim to have seen dark shadows creeping through the hospital's halls and objects moving around on their own. The most notorious spirit at the hospital was a seven-foot-tall ghost that haunted the third floor and tried to scare off trespassers by hollering at them to leave him be. I discovered the hard way that this abandoned hospital also possessed multiple creeper energies.

In 2016, a local paranormal society extended an invitation for me and several other paranormal investigation teams to spend the night investigating the abandoned hospital. Among those they invited were my friends Jay Lynch and his wife, Teresa. It's always a pleasure to investigate with people I know. I gave my very first interview on the Lynch's podcast.

After all the groups arrived, the host of the paranormal society gave introductions and laid out our agenda for the evening. Some of the more experienced investigators got up and spoke for a while, and then our host came back up and announced that they heard a couple of people were celebrating birthdays, including me. They had even gotten us a cake to celebrate. Everyone sang Happy Birthday to us, and then we cut the cake.

As everyone was digging into the birthday cake and getting to know each other, it was obvious that we were all antsy to start investigating. The person in charge went over the house rules and said that we could pretty much have free reign of the place and investigate wherever we wanted unless it was blocked off or locked.

Once they gave us the go, the various teams split up, and we each got to do our own thing. I investigated with the Lynches and one other investigator I'd just met. Only part of the old hospital had electricity, so the lights were only on in the main lobby area and the rooms where we planned to spend the night. When investigating the other parts of the hospital, we would have to use our flashlights to navigate.

During the early part of the evening, we heard a few suspicious noises as we wandered the halls, but none that we could definitively identify where they came from. About three-quarters of the way through the evening, we ventured into the unlit area to investigate a place nicknamed *The Mirror Room*.

When we shined our flashlights into The Mirror Room, we caught a faint reflection from a large, dusty mirror hanging on the wall to the right, apparently what inspired the room's name. To the left of the entrance was an old metal office desk positioned lengthwise. Behind the desk hung a large blackboard someone had mounted to the wall sideways and secured with a padlock.

I stared at the bizarre arrangement, wondering why someone would hang a blackboard like that. Had this been a classroom at one time? If so, it still wouldn't explain why anyone would padlock the blackboard to the wall. Were they afraid someone was going to steal it?

Jay explained that the current owner of the building hung the blackboard door to cover up a second mirror. Apparently, other investigators had been exploring the building when they discovered that the two mirrors, when facing each other, created some kind of portal between them that enabled spirits to travel from the underworld into our dimension!

Just as I thought about how grateful I was that the owner had blocked off the portal, Jay held up a key. He and Teresa explained that they planned to unlock the second mirror and expose its surface to the other mirror to create a kind of infinite reflection between the two. Their goal was to open up a portal to encourage archangels to pass through and form a circle of protection in the room for us.

It was an intriguing concept, but having heard horror stories about mirror portals, I knew it wasn't good angels that came out of them but those of the fallen variety. I'd also seen my share of bizarre phenomena relating to mirrors over the years. Looking back, I should've just left the room right then. But I didn't want to be the only chicken. Plus, at some level, I was curious to see if they could actually pull it off. I should've followed my first instinct.

I sat back on the edge of the desk facing the middle of the room, careful to avoid sitting in the direct path of the two mirrors. Teresa, also a sensitive and adept at detecting energies, stood with her back to me, acting like a human shield. Seeing how frightened this bizarre experiment made me, she told me she would use her psychic energy to protect me as best she could.

The room was pitch dark except for Jay's flashlight, which he set on the floor. He placed it in the middle of the room, the beam facing the ceiling, hoping it would help us see anything that passed between the mirrors. Then, they turned on their digital recorder to catch any EVPs generated during the experiment.

"Is everyone ready?" the other investigator asked.

The Lynches announced that they were. Then everyone looked at me. I hesitantly nodded. The room seemed eerily silent, like the calm before the storm.

Jay slipped the key into the padlock and unlocked it with a loud click. Removing the lock, he glanced back at us one last time. Not hearing any objections, he swung the makeshift door open, and the rusted hinges cried out a warning. My body tensed.

The flashlight beam created a thick shadow as the blackboard swung away from the wall, exposing the second mirror. The mirrors now faced each other, the two ends of the portal now complete. As soon as Jay revealed the second mirror, I heard the number eleven repeating over and over in my head.

The once boarded-up mirror seemed to waver, like a ripple caused by a rock tossed into a still pond. Then, the most terrifying creatures I've ever seen floated out of the uncovered mirror. The beings were humanoid in appearance, like a person with all the life sucked out of them. Their hairless, gray flesh appeared corpse-like, almost translucent, revealing a roadmap of blue veins all over their face and body. Their empty eye sockets were like bottomless pits.

There was something disturbingly familiar about these creatures. I suddenly flashed back to Waverly Hills, remembering The Creeper.

Unlike the creeper from the death tunnel, they didn't crawl out of the mirror. Instead, they seemed to float through the air, their bodies visible only from the waist up.

And unlike Waverly Hills, there wasn't only one of them.

As these abominations flew out of the mirror, one after another, they reached out to me with their long, bony fingers. There had to be at least ten of these things, I thought. Then I heard the voice in my head again.

"Eleven."

Seeing all those hideous creatures floating through the air, grasping for me, was so terrifying that I screamed bloody murder and jumped off the desk, burying my face into Teresa's back, muffling my screams.

Jay yelled, "Get her out of here, quick!"

Teresa grabbed ahold of me and practically carried me out of the room.

Once in the hallway, I covered my face, bawling. Teresa tried her best to calm me down.

"Look at me," she said.

I raised my head, hoping to find the reassuring gaze of my friend. Instead, I recoiled at the horrifying creatures floating up behind her. Once they saw me, they screeched this high-pitched sound like angry banshees. The sound was so shrill it was ear-piercing, the way they all shrieked in unison. I quickly covered my ears, afraid their siren's call might drive me insane. I buried my face in Teresa's shoulder and sobbed uncontrollably.

Teresa put her arm around me and practically dragged me down the hallway. Too terrified to look back in case the creepers were chasing us, we didn't stop until we made it out of the building and felt the fresh night air. Once outside, Teresa grounded herself and proceeded to help cleanse my energy and remove anything that may have attached itself to me.

After ten minutes or so, I finally began to relax. The calm was quickly shattered when the doors burst open, and several people came running out of the building, terrified. After we opened the portal, the creepers started flying around the hospital, terrorizing the others. Some claimed to have seen creepers all the way on the other side of the building. I felt terrible that our team had released something so dark and potentially dangerous. If I had known this would happen, I would've tried to stop them.

As the frightened investigators paced outside, Teresa and I tried to help them figure out how to put the genie back in the bottle. That's when it hit me; we were supposed to spend the night in this place!

I'd reached the point where I was ready to quit. Let the others figure out how to close Pandora's box. There was no way I was going back into that Mirror Room. Hell, I didn't even want to go back into the building! But after much coaxing, I reluctantly let Teresa talk me into going back into the lobby where everyone else was hanging out by the front desk. After all, it was probably safer in the light, surrounded by other people.

We stood around the lobby and recounted our teams' experiences seeing shadow figures, crazy dark energies, and flying creepers. The investigators were all abuzz with excitement. But when the topic of the mirror room came up, I had no desire to engage in whatever was going on in there.

The only other lighted areas besides the lobby were the former hospital rooms where we were supposed to sleep. After all I'd just experienced, I was emotionally and physically drained. And with it now being so late, all I wanted to do was lie down.

I made my way along the lighted corridor to the old hospital room where I'd been assigned to sleep. Since I was the first one in the room, I left the lights on, hoping to keep the dark energies at bay. Crawling into my sleeping bag, I pulled it up as far as possible in case one of the creepers flew into the room. I didn't want to see anything, and I definitely didn't want anything to see me.

Hiding inside my sleeping bag, I scrolled on my phone, happy for the distraction. About a half hour later, my roommates wandered into the room. Since I signed up late, my two roommates and I were randomly assigned. We talked for a few minutes to get acquainted as they readied themselves for bed. Finally, they closed the door and turned the lights off in the room. The hallway lights were left on, leaving a slash of light under the door.

I climbed back inside my sleeping bag cocoon and distracted myself with my smartphone, trying to block out any energies that might try to get my attention. Before long, I could hear the deep breathing of my roommates as they drifted off to sleep.

Moments later, I heard footsteps echoing in the hallway as if someone was pacing outside our door. I started getting nervous again. Was it just the residual haunting of a former nurse making her rounds or the spirit of a prior patient pacing in front of the door, unable to figure out how to get back into their room? Or, worse yet, was it one of those things from the mirror trying to find a way to get at me?

"Do you hear that?" I cried, waking up my roommates.

"Hear what?" one of them said, sounding annoyed.

"Footsteps. Like someone is right outside our door!"

They mumbled something groggily, reluctant to get out of their beds to check.

"How do you not hear that?" I asked, still hearing the persistent pacing outside our door. The others just ignored me and went back to sleep.

I stared at the door and watched a shadow pass underneath. Screw this, I thought, and pulled the sleeping bag over my head like I did when I was little, as if whatever I couldn't see couldn't hurt me. Believe it or not, I still do that today. My fiancé teases me about always having the covers pulled up or a pillow over my face when I sleep. I don't even let my feet poke out under the covers for fear something will grab them.

My anxiety levels rising, I focused back on my smartphone, trying to ignore the constant pacing outside our room. Finally, my eyes grew so tired from staring at the screen that I eventually fell asleep.

Ohio State Reformatory

A few local Michigan paranormal teams gathered at the end of summer 2014 to investigate the former Ohio State Reformatory in Mansfield, Ohio. Built between 1886 and 1910, the prison operated until 1990, when the state finally closed it down.

The Ohio State Reformatory has a long and storied history. The land where they built the reformatory previously contained a training camp for Civil War soldiers. The iconic limestone structure is an architectural marvel blending three unique styles, including Victorian Gothic, Queen Anne, and Richardsonian Romanesque. The reformatory looks more like a medieval castle than a prison.

More than 200 people have died at the facility over the years, including two guards who prisoners killed during various escape attempts. Most supporting buildings and the 25-foot stone wall that once surrounded the facility have been demolished. Fortunately, the beautiful architecture of the reformatory and offices remain. Ohio State Reformatory has since been converted into a museum dedicated to the former prison, and what it's most famous for, the location of the film *The Shawshank Redemption*.

In addition to daily guided tours dedicated to *The Shawshank Redemption* filming locations, Ohio State Reformatory offers evening public ghost tours and private overnight paranormal investigations.

The first paranormal investigation group I belonged to pooled resources with three other Michigan paranormal teams to book the facility overnight, so we had it all to ourselves.

Being only my second paranormal investigation, I was extremely nervous about spending the night at a site with such a violent history. But I was also excited to explore the historic prison and see what we might be able to connect with.

When we first arrived, the various groups assembled outside and introduced themselves. Some of us knew each other only by name, whether by reputation or social media. I didn't know any paranormal investigators outside my group, so everyone was new to me.

One of the guys from another team, Todd Bonner, kept looking over at me as if he knew me. I was pretty sure we had never met before, but once we started talking, it was like we'd known each other for years. Todd had come with his friend and partner, Jeff Adkins, and I soon discovered they both lived nearby. Maybe I'd seen them around town before.

I believe there were a total of four teams from Michigan that came together that night to investigate Ohio State Reformatory. Once we were let in and given our instructions, the teams split up and pretty much did their own thing. My team investigated the East Cell Block prison area. Throughout the night, the various teams crossed paths with each other, exchanged a smile or a nod, and asked if anyone had experienced anything uncanny. The East Cell Block is incredible. It's six tiers high, each with rows of rusted prison cells. To this day, it remains the largest free-standing steel cell block in the world.

Not all of the prison cells were accessible, though. Some sections were gated off or locked. But for the most part, we had free reign from the bottom, where prisoners were kept in solitary, and all the way up to the top. I couldn't imagine being locked in one of those tiny cells surrounded by nothing but cold steel and concrete and no view of the outside. The metal bars, stairs, and catwalks all bore scars, with paint chipped away revealing a time capsule of colors and underlying rusted metal as the facility had fallen into decay.

My team started their investigation on the fourth tier of the East Cell Block. The long hallway on one side was locked and gated off, but the other was open to explore. As we passed the off-limits area, I felt something strange coming from the other side. I kept telling the lead investigator on my team that something just didn't feel right. He started an EVP session with his digital recorder to see if we could catch supernatural audio messages.

As I opened myself up, I sensed a strong male energy down prisoner's row. And with it came this growing feeling of white-hot rage. Suddenly, a disembodied woman's voice shouted, "He's coming... He's coming!"

Raging energy charged toward me. A deep baritone voice from far away seemed to grow louder as the presence closed on me, but I couldn't make out what it was shouting. Caught up in the moment, I panicked and picked up my friend by her collar, spun around, and placed her between me and the rushing energy just as the energy reached its peak.

And then, it vanished.

I'm not proud of my reaction, but I still do the same thing today. I can't help it; it's just my natural reaction. So, if you think you want to go on an investigation with me, be prepared to become a human shield!

As my friend struggled to get her bearings after I spun her around, she braced herself against the wall with one hand. I didn't realize it when it happened, but I was holding my smartphone when I hoisted her in front of me and accidentally snapped a photo. It wasn't until we got back to the hotel and I scrolled through the pictures that I discovered what I had captured.

The image was oddly warped, and in the bottom left-hand corner, there appears to be a semi-translucent man's hand grasping for us. The creepiest part is how the skin looked jaundiced and bruised like a corpse. It still gives me shudders when I look at it.

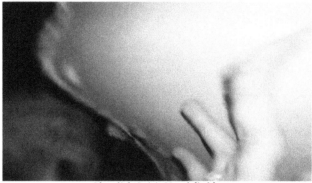

Ghoulish Spirit Hand (left)

The most notorious inmate housed on the fourth tier of the prison was a man named James Lockhart. He was in cell #13, serving time for assault with intent to kill. Faced with the prospect of doing up to fifteen years in this bleak prison, the distraught inmate chose the most extreme method of escape – the permanent kind. In a fit of despair, Lockhart doused himself with lighter fluid and lit himself on fire, burning himself alive.

By the time the guards arrived and attempted to extinguish the flames, his skin had already begun to melt. When they finally dragged him out of his cell, his skin stuck to the floor and pulled away from his body.

I can't imagine how distraught and hopeless someone would have to be to do something as horrific as that. Could Lockhart's ghost have been the rage-filled energy I felt charge at me?

We heard footsteps and other strange noises the rest of the evening, but nothing we could definitively confirm as paranormal. Once our investigation of the Ohio State Reformatory concluded, the teams gathered for a group photo. By the time I got home, I discovered that the group picture was already trending on Facebook. I was surprised to see how many other paranormal investigators were out there. It was nice to know that I wasn't alone in my interests.

* * *

Five months later, on a cold February day, I asked my son Austin what he wanted to do for his fourteenth birthday. He said he'd like to go on a tour of the Ohio State Reformatory. He heard me talk about how amazing the place was, plus The Shawshank Redemption was his favorite movie at the time.

With all my kids having psychic mediumship abilities, I figured I should take Austin on one of the public day tours since it would likely be less active and safer. The Ohio State Reformatory was only about a two-and-a-half-hour drive from our house, and I'd already fallen in love with the place, so I had no problem saying yes. A part of me was also a little curious if Austin would pick up on anything there.

When we first arrived, my son was blown away by how enormous the place was. He was so excited to see the locations where they filmed The Shawshank Redemption. During the self-guided tour, I took photos of Austin at some of the most memorable filming locations.

Next to the warden's office, where his wife and kids used to stay, I sensed a strong male energy near one of the doorways. I couldn't see what it was, but the feeling was so intense I thought I would try to catch something with my camera. Like EVPs, where you can occasionally catch auditory phenomena with an audio recorder that weren't heard in real-time, sometimes you can capture images with a camera that are invisible to the naked eye. Like the decomposing hand that I caught the last time here.

Just for the heck of it, I decided to aim my camera at the doorway where I felt the energy coming from and snapped a couple of pictures. By this time, Austin had already moved on, so I hurried to catch up with him, not bothering to check my camera.

When I went through the reformatory pictures at home later, I discovered the shots I'd taken of the doorway. To my surprise, I noticed an anomaly to the left of the door that looked like a Civil War soldier running. At first, I couldn't believe it, but then I remembered what I'd heard during the tour about how the property the reformatory was built on once hosted a Civil War training camp. It finally made sense. I later showed the picture to the director of the Ohio State Reformatory, and he asked for permission to use my photo for their archives, claiming it was the best visual evidence they had seen yet!

Ghost of Civil War soldier (left)

After Austin and I finished our tour of the Warden's area, we moved on to the prison. The East Cell Block was freezing, with its open architecture and everything made of steel and concrete. We worked our way up to the old chapel, where they used to allow up to 1,900 inmates to attend their church services. Back in its prime, I'm sure the chapel was magnificent with its tiled floor, stately pillars, varnished pews, and hand-painted murals. But now, it was in shambles, marred by chipped floor tiles, peeling walls, scarred wooden pews, and its dust-covered pulpit. It was sad to see how it had become just a shadow of its former splendor.

A worn metal staircase next to the former chapel led to the boiler room area that was now chained off. Austin wandered over and seemed to just stare off into space, looking sad. Did he see something?

"Austin, are you okay?" I asked.

Looking a bit confused, he didn't respond at first. When I asked him what he was staring at in the boiler area, he described the spirit of a man with dirt or soot on his face, wearing overalls, a striped shirt, and a cabbie hat. When I pressed him about what he felt, the best way he could explain it was just an overwhelming sense of sadness.

Overall, Austin's first paranormal investigation was a success. He picked up on the spirit by the boiler room and handled it quite well for a first-timer. Much better than I usually do!

Goodbye, Mom

D espite our hair-raising experiences with the shadow figures, our time living in the single-story house wasn't all doom and gloom. I still have many wonderful memories of our time there. Especially when my mom used to come over and stay for days, sometimes even a week at a time. Despite some rocky times during my teen years, my mother and I were extremely close. She wasn't just a parent; she was also my best friend. We were kindred spirits in so many ways. And she loved her grandchildren more than life itself, spending time with them whenever possible.

My kids loved it whenever Nanna came over. Anthony liked it because if he was grounded, Nanna would sneak him candy, or if I left to go shopping, she'd let him out. Grandmas do love to spoil their grandkids!

My daughter Autumn loved having Nanna visit because whenever we sat and watched TV, they would play with each other's hair, brushing and braiding and trying out fun new hairstyles.

My mom enjoyed getting down on the floor with the twins, and they could play with trains and cars for hours. She also loved to play-scare them, telling them she was going to get them, and then they would run, screaming and laughing.

Whenever Austin stayed the night with her, my mom would make him his favorite food: crab legs with garlic butter sauce. I told you Nanna delighted in spoiling her grandkids!

Of course, I cherished having her stay at our house, too. We made dinners together and watched movies, she would help clean, and it was always nice to get a break, including free babysitting!

Sadly, my mom's health had been deteriorating for years. It all started one winter when she slipped on the ice and fell, shattering her ankle. The damage was so bad it took multiple surgeries to repair the damage. But for some reason, it would never heal. After nineteen surgeries, they finally told her that part of her right leg would have to be amputated.

The news was devastating for all of us. Not long after that surgery, the doctors had to go back and amputate her leg even higher. After spending time in a wheelchair, she was finally fitted with a prosthetic leg. Amazingly, my mom was a real trouper through it all and never let her disability slow her down.

During this time, my mother lived in a double-wide mobile home with her boyfriend and his father, who she helped care for. A month before my mom passed away, she confided in me that she saw dark figures running through her bedroom and darting into the bathroom.

When I asked her what she thought they were, she said she couldn't tell whether they were male or female or even what they were. It didn't surprise me, though. My kids and I never liked the feeling in her hallway, and my mom admitted she felt something disturbing about the hall, too.

I inherited my psychic abilities from my mom's side of the family. Being raised strict Catholics, there was a major stigma attached to anything that could be associated with the occult. My mom explained to me that my grandmother and great-grandmother had the gift of second sight and would often see shadow figures and spirits but were unable to hone in on them.

Having suppressed their gift for so long, they found it difficult to communicate with these supernatural visitors.

That Catholic guilt was passed down to my mother, so even though she occasionally saw things she couldn't explain, she did her best to ignore them. She also confessed that she mostly suppressed her gifts and blocked the spirits out of fear. And I can't say I blame her!

People who know me from my TV appearances and paranormal investigation events are often surprised to learn that I get just as scared by the things I see as they do. When I come in contact with a demon or a particularly dangerous entity, I'm out of there! Unfortunately, once I committed to being locked down for the Netflix series *28 Days Haunted*, I had no choice but to face them. But more on that later.

Mom's Boyfriend's father lived in the first bedroom on the left at the front of their mobile home. Not long after they moved in, the father died in that bedroom. Then, only two years later, my mom awakened one morning to find her boyfriend dead on the couch. Once again, she found herself alone.

After my mom told me about seeing the dark figures in her bedroom, I put out my psychic feelers to see what I might discover about the dark entities haunting her home. The one thing that kept coming back to me was a single word... *Death.*

Why death? God knows this home saw its fair share of it. But could it be something more systemic? Were these shadows harbingers of death, warning or preparing the living for what was to come? Or were they active agents of death, expediting the residents' demise?

Not long after moving into that mobile home, my mom started experiencing health problems. But after the terrible experience with her leg, she no longer trusted doctors. When I finally convinced her to get checked out, they initially diagnosed her with cervical cancer. The news hit me like a sledgehammer. After the initial shock subsided, I mustered up the hope that, after all my mom had been through, she would overcome this obstacle, too.

After a period of grieving her boyfriend's death, my mom eventually reunited with an old flame who moved into her mobile home with her. Not long after, my mom called and told me that she'd had a strange dream about her father, who had died a year prior, coming to her and holding out his hand as if he was there to help guide her to the other side.

Her dream turned out to be an omen one week later when the Grim Reaper came knocking again. This time, for my mom.

Still not satisfied, the angel of death visited that same mobile home only a few months later to claim the life of her new boyfriend as well. There must be something seriously wrong with that place. It seems to attract death.

I was gutted by the loss of my mom. Needless to say, so were my kids. None of my children had ever lost a close family member, so losing someone this close was devastating. But one good thing about psychic abilities running in our family was that we knew this wouldn't be the last time we'd see her.

At the time of her death, my mom was battling a nasty cough, which we later discovered was actually pneumonia. And the cervical cancer she thought she had turned out to be lung cancer that had already spread throughout her body. We didn't find out about either of these until after the autopsy. It's no wonder my mom didn't trust doctors.

The last time I talked to my mother was the night before she died. When I called her, she was coughing like crazy and kept complaining that her lungs hurt. I told her it might be pneumonia and that she needed to go to the hospital. She promised to go to Urgent Care if she didn't feel better in the morning. Then, as we always ended every call, we told each other, "I love you."

The following morning, I awakened around 11:00 a.m., lit a cigarette, and turned on my computer. Scrolling through my Facebook feed, I suddenly felt a sharp pain in my chest. It felt like I was having a heart attack! I stubbed out my cigarette and took a few deep breaths, hoping to lower my pulse rate.

Once the feeling passed, I navigated to my mom's timeline and posted a short message: "I love you, Mom!" I'll never know if my mom saw my post before she passed, but I'm so glad I got to talk to her the night before to tell her I loved her one last time.

I continued on with my busy day, expecting to hear from her at any time, thinking she was finally getting some rest. Finally, at 3:48 in the afternoon, my phone rang. Excited to see my mom's name come up on the display, I answered the call only to be surprised by a man's voice. At first, I thought it was her boyfriend.

"Is this Brandy Marie Miller?"

I knew something was wrong from the official tone and the use of my middle name.

"This is the Warren Police Department calling to tell you that your mother is dead."

The cold, matter-of-fact way he said, "Your mother is dead," stunned me at first. His voice had no more sense of empathy than if he'd been casually discussing the weather. It took a moment for the words to sink in. The next sentence snapped me out of my stupor.

"We'll need you to come and identify the body."

I fell to my knees and bawled like a baby. The kids were still with their father, Mike, but were due home at four. I was left to grieve alone.

After I managed to collect myself, I called my brother and broke the devastating news. He was equally shocked. Neither of us could believe she was gone. We had no idea how sick she was. I guess everyone thinks their parents will live forever. After letting the news sink in a moment, he told me he would meet me at Mom's house.

I checked the clock, and the kids were due home any minute. I ran around like a madwoman gathering the kids' things since I knew I'd have to leave them with their grandparents while we went to identify my mom's body.

Hearing the sound of Mike's truck pulling into the driveway, I rushed outside. Before I could reach Mike to tell him, my knees buckled, and I fell to the ground in tears. I screamed, "My mom is dead!"

Mike helped me up and hugged me, trying to calm me down. The kids all started crying as the realization hit them that their Nanna had died. They rushed to my side and wrapped themselves around me in one big sobbing embrace.

Still numb, I packed up the kids, and we dropped them off at Mike's mother's house. While Mike drove me to my mom's, I called my dad and broke the news to him. He didn't say anything at first. Then, in a small voice, my dad asked if we could pick him up on our way. Even though they were no longer married, I knew he still loved her.

When the three of us pulled up to my mom's mobile home, my brother was waiting outside. He thought we should both go in together. We mounted the porch steps and stood at the threshold for a moment. None of us wanted to go in. A policeman noticed us standing there and opened the door before ushering us in.

I asked who discovered my mother's body and was told that a kindly neighbor had come over to check on her hours earlier.

When she didn't respond, he called the police. Once the officers arrived, they found my mom lying on the couch, unresponsive. The police summoned the paramedics, who examined her before pronouncing her dead.

When we entered the living room, we found my mom lying on a gurney covered with a sheet. I tried to steel myself for what I was about to see, but there's no preparing for a moment like this.

An officer pulled back the white sheet, and there she was, her head poking out of a body bag. She had one eye closed, the other staring at nothing, winking as if she were letting me in on some sort of morbid secret. I was so numb; all I could do was just stare back.

After a moment that seemed like a lifetime, one of the officers broke the silence and asked us to confirm that what was lying on the gurney was Susan Renee Miller. My first thought was, No! That's not my mom! What lay in repose before me was nothing more than an empty shell. Her debilitated body might still be on that gurney, but her beautiful spirit was now free.

Fortunately, my brother stepped up and confirmed her identity. All I could do was robotically nod in agreement. One of the paramedics reached to pull up the sheet, but I held up my hand to stop him. My throat was so tight I couldn't speak, but I knew I wanted to say farewell to my mom somehow. I leaned in and caressed her hair, then kissed her cold forehead for the last time.

After the paramedics covered her back up, they wheeled her body out to the ambulance while the rest of us muddled around as if in a trance. Watching them take my mother's body away, I knew we'd see her again.

✳ ✳ ✳

Losing my mother further spurred my interest in communicating with the spirit realm, providing a pivotal stage in my growth as a psychic medium. The thought of speaking with my mom again was a great comfort, but it also challenged my faith in my psychic abilities. Would I be able to correspond with her on the other side?

About a week after my mom's funeral, I sat at my computer in the living room, posting and commenting with others in my spiritualist group. I kept sensing someone behind me. At first, I just ignored it. When you're a psychic medium like me, you get used to it.

A voice behind me shouted, "Turn around."

I wasn't sure what to think at first. But the voice was insistent, repeatedly telling me to turn around. Finally, I couldn't resist the call. And I turned.

I didn't see anything at first, but something inside told me I should start recording. I grabbed my smartphone and started recording. At first, nothing happened. Then, all of a sudden, I sensed my mom's presence. Her energy felt as if she were still earthbound. Earthbound energies feel the same as if the person were still here, alive. But once someone has passed on, their energy seems lighter, ethereal. I knew then that my mom hadn't crossed over yet.

I believe it can take weeks or even a month for someone to cross over once they die. I missed my mom so much and wanted to see her, to feel her presence again. I reached out to her and said, "Mom, if you're here, I need you to come to me. Let me know you're here."

Still recording, I panned the phone around the room, hoping to capture some sign that might corroborate the presence I was feeling. When I swung my phone back toward the kitchen, a bright orb came flying out of the kitchen, right at me. The brilliant orb of light zig-zagged a bit, then flew right up to me as I continued to record. (*See photos at end of chapter.*)

I felt the energy grow as the light approached me. The energy felt positive and light, not dark like all the shadow figures we'd dealt with in this house. In my heart, I knew this was her. Tears streamed down my face. Not tears of sadness, but love, for my mom and best friend.

Two weeks after this incident, I had another encounter with my mom's spirit. We were barbecuing in the backyard like we often did. And as I carried the food outside to place on the grill, I heard my mom's voice.

"Everything moves so fast here!"

I knew then that she had crossed over.

Her comment didn't surprise me, though. Once we enter eternity, time is no longer relevant. A day is like a thousand years, and a thousand years is but a day. Our spirits are pure energy, and energy moves at the speed of light. No longer weighed down by her mortal body, her spirit was finally free to soar.

Mom pays me a visit

Turning the Page

Five months after my mom passed, I felt it was time for a change. I had finally had enough of living with shadow figures terrorizing our house and a basement portal churning out dark entities from the underworld. It was time to look for a new home. One that wasn't steeped in negative energy and, with five kids, a place with a lot more rooms.

With the loss of my mother, it was time to turn a new page in my life. Although she lived in her own home before she died, my mom probably spent more time at our place than hers. Our single-story house held more than just dark shadows; it was also full of fond memories of my mom doting over her grandchildren. But with her gone, those memories became bitter-sweet.

After a good bit of searching, I found a quad-level home for sale with enough room for our family of six. Quad-level homes are basically tri-level homes, with the main floor containing the living room, dining room, and kitchen halfway between the basement and the second-story bedrooms. It's a less expensive way to maximize space while maintaining a smaller footprint.

The older kids liked the new house since they each got their own bedroom and more space for everyone to spread out. Austin decided to forego the basement this time and chose a bedroom on the main floor next to the living room. Unfortunately, he later discovered the main floor of our new home wasn't immune from shadow figures either.

Shortly after moving into the new house, we had our first supernatural visitor. It was a familiar presence, although deceased.

We were all sitting in the living room, watching television, when my five-year-old, Carter, looked toward me and cried, "Nanna!"

That was strange, I thought. Why would he call me Nanna? Did he mean to say, Mamma? Then I realized he wasn't looking at me but next to me. Although he was excited to see his grandmother, he was a little confused. After all, she was dead.

"Can you tell me what she looks like?" I asked, hoping to confirm it was Mom.

"Nanna is really tall now,' he said, amazed. "And she has both her legs. She's standing!"

My youngest kids had never seen their grandma with both of her legs intact. She had been in a wheelchair their whole life.

I turned to where he was looking but couldn't see anything. It may sound strange, but sometimes, spirits only reveal themselves to certain people. Or, if you're not in the right place mentally, you might unintentionally block the spirit world from connecting with you. Also, the younger we are, the more open we are to the spirit world.

I said, "I love you, mom!"

I asked Carter if Nanna had said anything to him. He smiled, then said something that brought a tear to my eye.

"She says that she loves you, too!"

That's when I knew for sure my mom was with us. That was kind of our thing, my mom and me. We never separated or ended a call without saying, "I love you." My mom always told me that you never know when you're going to leave this earth, so be sure to let your loved ones know how much you love them whenever possible.

Carter wasn't the only one of the twins who saw their Nanna while we lived in the quad house. A few months later, his twin brother, Lucas, saw her, too.

Come bath time, Lucas was the last to get into the shower. After he finished washing, he grabbed a towel and stepped out on the rug to dry himself off. The mirror was foggy from the steamy shower, so Lucas used a towel to wipe off the condensation. As he lowered the towel, he noticed a second face in the mirror.

"Mom! Mom!" he yelled.

Hearing Lucas shouting and thumping down the stairs gave me a start. He bounded toward me, his towel barely wrapped around his waist, eyes wide.

"Mom!"

I wondered what he could possibly be so worked up about.

"I saw Nanna! In the mirror!"

His expression was more shock and excitement than fear. He was thrilled that his beloved Nanna had come to see him.

"Go finish drying off," I said, giving him a big hug. With tears welling in my eyes, I added, "And if you see Nanna again, tell her I love her!"

But not all the visits to our new home were pleasant ones.

Austin, now thirteen, had hoped that by moving into a new house and avoiding the basement, he might escape the shadow figures that haunted him in the old house.

He was wrong.

When we moved to the new quad-level house, Austin chose a bedroom on the main floor. From his room, he could see the bathroom and living room to the left. To the right, a set of stairs leading up to the kitchen.

One night, around 2 a.m., I awoke to Austin screaming bloody murder. I jumped out of bed and ran downstairs to see what was going on. When I reached his room, I found my son curled up in the fetal position, clutching his blanket around himself.

Once I got him to calm down, he told me what had happened.

Austin had gotten up to go to the bathroom when he encountered a towering, black shadow! It darted from the living room and down the hallway toward the kitchen. The shadowy entity was so tall it had to duck to go up the stairs. That would make the thing at least 7 feet tall!

He was so shaken by the confrontation that I had to sleep downstairs with him for the rest of the night.

But Austin wasn't alone. His younger brother Anthony had his own terrifying run-ins. For Anthony, it started with his closet. When lying in bed at night, he often heard the slow creak of unoiled hinges as his closet door slowly swung open. He tried to ignore the phenomenon, but it continued night after night. It got to the point where he had to double-check his closet door each night to make sure it was closed securely before turning out the lights and crawling into bed. But then, as he tried to fall asleep, he would inevitably hear his closet door slowly creak open again.

Anthony also saw shadow figures in the new house while doing his laundry in the basement utility room. A shadow figure used to stand in the corner and watch him. He found himself constantly glancing over at the dark figure, afraid to take his eye off it for too long in case it decided to sneak up on him while his back was turned.

As the dark entity watched him, it subtly jerked and twitched, almost as if it were fighting to remain in the physical realm. As soon as the wash cycle started, Anthony hightailed it up the stairs and waited there until he heard the bell signal that the load had finished. Then, he would cautiously venture back down into the basement to start the frightening process all over again.

Although Anthony primarily saw the shadow in the basement, it wasn't the only place. On several occasions, while walking along the hallway upstairs, he caught the shadow figure out of the corner of his eye, lurking in Autumn's room.

The first time he saw it, he stopped dead in his tracks. Peering into Autumn's bedroom, he noticed the sinister apparition lying in wait in a shadowy corner of her room. A feeling of dread fell over him. The eerie silhouette creeped him out so badly that he did his best to avoid his sister's room whenever possible. But, whenever he found himself walking past Autumn's room alone, he would inadvertently glance into her room and see the shadow waiting for her to return.

As Anthony grew, so did his supernatural abilities. Once, when one of my girlfriends came over for a chat, the conversation turned to the paranormal. Anthony, who was in the living room with us, repeatedly glanced toward the stairs. He didn't want to say anything at first, but he finally broke his silence.

"Mom, I see an old woman standing over by the stairs."

My friend asked him to describe the old woman to her. He was hesitant at first but finally told her what he saw. As he conveyed what the elderly woman looked like, her jaw dropped. Anthony had just described her grandmother to a tee.

She started crying. But they were tears of joy. She thanked Anthony, and he smiled, proud of what he'd been able to accomplish.

One of the benefits of working on this book has been talking to my children about some of their paranormal experiences. To my surprise, they began sharing stories I'd never heard! One of these stories came from Anthony. When asked to share, he shocked us by producing a recording of the event on his smartphone I didn't even know existed.

Anthony recounted the story about the evening when he and his brother were in the living room of the quad-level house, and Carter had fallen asleep on the couch. Out of the blue, Carter just sat up, dropped to the floor, and started running across the room on all fours like a dog!

Surprised by his brother's unusual behavior, Anthony asked him what in the world he was doing. Carter eventually stopped and knelt at the foot of the steps leading upstairs. He remained there, head bowed as if he were genuflecting. But who or what could he be paying homage to?

Anthony quickly grabbed his smartphone and started recording. The video showed Carter on one knee, head bowed for a moment. Anthony kept calling to his brother, asking him why he was acting so weird. But Carter still didn't respond.

Then, Carter slowly looked up at the top of the stairs as if awaiting further instructions. Finally, he seemed to snap out of whatever trance he was in. It was almost as if whatever was at the top of the stairs chose to release him. After lowering his head one last time, Carter stood, put his hand on the side of his head, and went back into the living room.

Anthony continued questioning his brother's bizarre behavior. But Carter ignored him like he wasn't even there and shambled back to the couch. Anthony asked him one more time why he was acting so weird. Carter said he just wanted to be left alone and climbed back onto the sofa, covered himself with the blanket, and went back to sleep.

Anthony stopped the recording, shaking his head. Our dog then picked up where Carter left off and stared into space. Anthony followed the dog's gaze and then jumped, seeing a shadow figure rush up the stairs and disappear down the hallway.

Left: Carter genuflecting   Right: Carter gazes at shadow upstairs

Autumn's Awakening

My daughter Autumn was a little late to the paranormal party. But once she discovered her abilities, she became one of the most gifted of us all. And it all began after we moved to the quad-level house.

As my only daughter, Autumn naturally developed a special relationship with her Nanna. My mom loved buying her girly clothes, and they were always playing with each other's hair. That inseparable bond continued even after Nanna died.

Autumn took it extremely hard when she lost her grandmother, so it was bitter-sweet when Nanna started visiting her in her dreams. As much as Autumn loved Nanna's nightly visits, waking in the morning only to remember that Nanna was gone was heartbreaking. It was like scratching a wound that itched, knowing you were preventing it from healing.

Eventually, I had to step in. I reached out to my mom's spirit and told her to step back. Her granddaughter needed time to heal. She needed closure. I believe my mom had the best intentions and just wanted to bring peace and comfort to her granddaughter and to let her know she was fine on the other side. But it was having the opposite effect.

Since talking with my mom, Autumn has only had a couple of dreams where Nanna visited her.

Autumn had her first run-in with the dark side of the spirit realm when she was twelve. It took place in the same upstairs bedroom where Anthony saw the shadowy figure lurking in the corner.

Late one night, while she lay in bed sleeping, she was awakened by the spine-chilling sensation of long, icy fingers crawling up the back of her neck. Terrified, she sat straight up and started freaking out, screaming at the top of her lungs.

I can't say I blame her. I also wouldn't blame you if you were to check for a gap between your headboard and mattress before you crawled into bed tonight. Or wonder if the dark shadow in the corner of your bedroom might be staring at you, waiting for you to fall asleep.

Autumn's bedroom developed into a hotspot for paranormal activity. One of the most terrifying experiences took place after she turned eighteen. Once again, it occurred while she was sleeping. After experiencing icy fingers crawling up her neck, Autumn started sleeping as close to the foot of the bed as possible. Unfortunately, the plan didn't work.

One night, Autumn jolted awake. She moaned. Then, another jolt. Autumn blinked her eyes open half-mast, wondering what woke her. Lying there in a daze, she listened, but all she heard was the sounds of the night.

Just as her eyes drifted closed again, she felt icy hands grab her ankles and pull! Autumn panicked, grasping for anything to prevent her from being dragged from her bed. She rolled over onto her stomach and clawed desperately at her bedding. She clutched the fitted sheets, but they only pulled away from the mattress. Despite her frantic efforts, Autumn was losing the battle with her mystery attacker.

In a last-ditch effort, she screamed and kicked her legs, terrified of what awaited her at the foot of the bed. With one last flurry of kicks, Autumn shouted, "Leave me alone!"

And with that, the unseen force released her.

Another one of Autumn's supernatural encounters happened when she awoke with a full bladder in the middle of the night.

Half asleep, she shuffled down the hallway and into the bathroom. After she finished relieving herself, she stepped out of the bathroom doorway and something caught her eye in the dining room.

Someone was sitting at the dining room table.

She thought it was odd that somebody would be up this late, but it wouldn't be the first time one of her brothers had snuck into the kitchen for a late-night snack.

Autumn rubbed her eyes and squinted into the dark to see who it was. But something wasn't right. The figure sitting at the table was too big to be one of her brothers. It looked like a man. She studied the silhouette but couldn't make out the features. The mysterious figure was solid black, seemingly absorbing any moonlight filtering into the room.

The shadow man's head slowly turned and gazed up at her. Autumn's heart fluttered erratically, her head buzzing with static. What was happening? Was he trying to communicate with her?

Wanting nothing to do with the shadowy intruder, Autumn quickly turned on her heel, hurried back to her bedroom, and shut the door behind her. Diving into bed, she yanked the covers over her head and prayed that the shadow man hadn't followed her into her bedroom.

Although it might seem like it, especially if you watch lots of paranormal shows or horror movies, not every supernatural experience happens at night. Spirits are active even during the day. Autumn discovered this the hard way one day while kicking back on the living room couch. From the corner of her eye, she noticed two figures standing in the corner by the stairs.

Glancing over, Autumn saw what appeared to be an elderly couple. She looked away, hoping if she ignored them, they might disappear. After several minutes passed, Autumn sensed they were still in the room. Her curiosity getting the better of her, she slowly turned back and discovered the elderly couple was still in the same spot. Except now they were staring at her.

Their expressions darkened. Their gaze was so intense it felt like they were staring into her very soul. It was as if they were willing Autumn to acknowledge them so they could share some dark secret with her.

Autumn learned from her mother and siblings that the best thing to do with encounters like this was to just ignore them and try to mentally block them. And that is precisely what she did. Eventually, she felt their energy gradually fade back into the ether.

Dead People See Me

Our house wasn't the only place where we saw the spirits of the dearly departed. I see the dead everywhere I go. And they also see me. Even in a grocery store or just walking around town, I'll see the spirits of lost loved ones shadowing the living. Once they realize I can see them, they're drawn to me like a death's head moth to a flame. The spirits are often frustrated by their inability to communicate with the living and will try to convince me to convey a message to those they've left behind.

Once, when dining at a Bob Evans Restaurant with the kids, I sensed a spirit's presence in the room. Scanning the dining area, I noticed an adult couple sitting with their children and the family patriarch. Next to the elderly man stood his deceased wife. She glanced over at me, and our eyes met. She realized that I could see her. Then, as if to explain why she was here, she told me she had come to help guide her husband to the other side.

"It's almost his time."

I never know what to do in these situations. Do I go over to their table and tell them that Grandma came back from the dead to tell them that Grandpa won't be around much longer? Can you imagine their reaction?

Instead of worrying about people calling me a witch or siccing the manager on me, I usually just let it go and try to ignore the spirits, hoping they will eventually leave me alone.

But not all messages from the deceased are as dire as someone's impending death. Sometimes, it's something more mundane, like someone's grandmother wanting their daughter to get out her old recipes and start cooking them instead of eating out all the time. Other times, the messages are more direct and blunt, like "Quit slacking off!" or "Stop being such a bitch!"

Spirit energies are not always so grim, either. They can often be playful. Oftentimes, I will see spirits joking and laughing. I even have dead old men flirting with me, if you can imagine! The cool thing is that after people die, their personalities appear to remain intact.

My gifts may seem incredible to others, but to me, they are both a blessing and a curse. It's rewarding for me to help provide closure and healing for those struggling after losing a loved one. Easily, 85% of my readings deal with people wanting to connect with a loved one. But as an empath, I often feel their pain and hurt as strongly as they do, which can be incredibly draining emotionally. But I consider it a calling, and I can't imagine living any other way.

Dad Comes Around

Although I come from a long line of psychic mediums on my mom's side of the family, my father has always been a skeptic. Growing up, he was never supportive of my abilities. My dad often made fun of me whenever I told him of things I'd seen or experienced. He'd say something like, "You're crazy" or "Okay, Sylvia Brown." (Brown was an author and acclaimed psychic medium who appeared regularly on television and radio programs but had a sketchy reputation with her accuracy.)

His lack of acceptance, compounded by my parents' divorce, put a strain on our relationship. We didn't really reconnect until I was 16. My dad did become more open-minded after my mom died. The man who had always been so closed-minded suddenly became interested in the spirit world and the possibility of an afterlife.

My dad's belief in the supernatural also seemed to develop as his belief in me grew. When he saw how my abilities were being recognized by others and that I was appearing on all these different TV programs, he couldn't help but think that maybe there was something to it. He gradually progressed from a non-believer to a skeptic. But what turned my dad from a skeptic to a believer, like most people, was when he had his first supernatural encounter.

I went to the grocery store one day and left my dad back at the house. While I was gone, he kicked back in the living room. From where he sat, he had a clear view of the stairs leading up to the second floor. Noticing something out of the corner of his eye, he turned and saw his grandson, Anthony, peeking through the railing. Dad gave him a little wave, and Anthony retreated. My father didn't think any more of it until I returned with the groceries.

"When did Anthony get here?" he asked.

"He's not here, Dad. He's at his friend's house," I replied.

"I just saw him sitting on the stairs, peeking through the railing."

"That's impossible," I assured him. "Are you sure you didn't nod off and dream it?"

He was adamant that he'd been awake the entire time. Then he looked at me, dead serious, and said, "I know what I saw, Brandy. I swear on my mother's grave. I saw him plain as day, peeking at me through the railing."

Confused, I went upstairs to look around, just in case Anthony had come home early. But he was nowhere to be found. A little while later, I went to pick Anthony up at his friend's house. When I walked back in the door with him, my dad shook his head, totally bewildered.

This strange phenomenon is what's called *doppelgänger energy*. Doppelgänger is a German word that literally means double-goer and describes the ghostly duplicate of a living person. A doppelganger energy is an entity that mimics another. Negative in nature, this non-human energy can take the form of anything it wants to get you to open up, so it can influence you or potentially even take over your body. According to folklore, seeing your own doppelganger foreshadows your imminent death.

Since that experience, my dad now watches all the ghost shows and has become my biggest fan, following my career as closely as anyone. And it means the world to me.

Detroit Paranormal Expeditions

After my first time investigating Ohio State Reformatory, I received several friend requests from the other investigators who participated in that event. I accepted all the friend requests but didn't interact much with them at first. One of those requests came from a paranormal investigator named Todd Bonner, who became not just a Facebook friend but a real friend and one of my mentors in the field of paranormal investigation.

Todd and I followed each other passively on Facebook until my mom died in 2015. I was so devastated after my mother's death that I locked myself away and avoided anything to do with the paranormal for almost two years. No investigations, no readings, nothing. After losing my mother and best friend, I slipped into a deep depression.

As I tried to process the immeasurable loss, I began posting on Facebook again. Todd responded to my gloomy posts with great compassion and stayed in touch with me, regularly checking to see how I was doing and if I was ready to investigate again. To his credit, Todd never gave up on me. He encouraged me to get back out there and told me that just because my mother's life ended didn't mean mine had to. And he was right. I know my mom would want me to keep moving ahead with my life.

But I continued to make excuses whenever Todd invited me to go on investigations. I just didn't feel ready yet. Finally, in 2016, Todd contacted me again, asking if I wanted to join him for an investigation he was planning with his partner, Jeff

Adkins, and a new investigator, Matt McCoy. Looking for something to do to help get me out of my depression, I finally agreed.

Todd's obsession with the paranormal began at a young age after two life-altering, near-death experiences left him searching for answers. His investigating partner, Jeff Adkins, became fascinated by the supernatural as a boy when his family began experiencing paranormal activity in their home. Todd and Jeff were a big help in getting me to where I am today, and I'm forever grateful for their influence and support.

Todd, Jeff, Matt, and I agreed to meet at an old infirmary in Winchester, Indiana, that was reportedly haunted. We decided to conduct an old-school style investigation using only three essential tools: A K-2 meter to measure Electromagnetic Fields (EMFs), which many believe can be produced by spirit energies; a Sony digital recorder in hopes of catching Electronic Voice Phenomenon (EVPs); and flashlights to see our way around in the dark since most abandoned locations do not have electricity.

Our first investigation together, although fun, failed to produce any serious evidence. We didn't capture any EVPs, and I didn't detect any spirits trying to contact us. As a matter of fact, I didn't sense any supernatural energies at the infirmary while we were there. Naturally, we were somewhat disappointed by the results, especially after the incredible responses I got on my first two investigations. But that's the reality when it comes to paranormal investigating. You can't just get ghosts to perform on demand. It takes patience, finding the right location, and a bit of luck.

Although we didn't capture any evidence on our first investigation, I felt we meshed well together as investigators. We hit it off immediately, and everybody got along. There was no drama, just people of like minds pursuing our shared interest in the supernatural.

Todd also liked the dynamic of the four of us and asked if we might be interested in forming a paranormal investigation team of our own. I quit my first paranormal group when my mother died, and Todd and Jeff had been considering striking out on their own for a while to pursue more ambitious investigations. Matt was just getting started and was excited to be a part of a group with a good amount of experience.

So, the four of us banded together to form a new paranormal investigation team under the banner *Detroit Paranormal Expeditions,* or DPX for short. I was nervous at first, but Todd told me to just give it a try and see how it went. There was no pressure, and I could leave whenever I wanted. I still go on investigations with DPX from time to time, though I also freelance with several other teams.

Left: Brandy & Jeff investigating. Right: Brandy & Todd at Eloise Psychiatric Hospital

6th Precinct

The first place the newly formed DPX team investigated was in the winter of 2016. Todd called and told me he wanted to investigate Detroit's 6th Precinct in downtown Detroit, an old building with lots of dark history. He didn't want to reveal too much because he wanted to see what I could discern without any outside influences or previous knowledge of the location. I always prefer to go into investigations blind for the same reason.

For our trip to the 6th Precinct, we were joined by fellow psychic medium Teena Pare-Duchesne, who Todd had connected with on social media. She was part of a paranormal team across the river in Canada. On our drive downtown, Teena and I chatted and just tried to get to know each other, discussing each other's abilities to see what gifts we had in common. We were both curious to see what it would be like to join forces and how that might affect our investigation. Would we be able to feed off each other's energy? Could we maybe even combine energies to amplify our abilities?

The closer we got to the location, the more nervous I became, knowing the city's reputation. Why did we have to come to Detroit at night? But as we drew near, I realized that my cousins lived not too far from there, which made me feel a little better.

When we pulled up to the red brick building, it looked similar to the other abandoned buildings in the area, with plywood covering the broken-out windows. We parked on the street and strolled toward the abandoned precinct. A siren wailed nearby, reminding us what kind of neighborhood we were in. I glanced around, trying to be mindful of our surroundings.

Teena and I were both on edge, sensing the negative energy emanating from the place. We reached the entrance just as the bearded owner, Ed Steele, loped around the corner. Ed was a large man with the heart to match. We introduced ourselves, and I was struck by Ed's boyish grin. I could tell that he was as excited as we were. Pulling out a giant, crowded keyring, he unlocked the door and let us in.

As soon as we entered, I tensed, my guard immediately going up. Something didn't feel right. People died here. Teena and I glanced at each other, and I could tell she felt it, too.

Ed gave us a quick tour of the precinct, describing his plans for the place and a little about its history. I told him I didn't want to know which areas he thought were active because I didn't want to be influenced and preferred to discover that for myself. Although I like to go into new locations blind, it's hard not to notice jail cells, so some aspects were obvious. I do my best to just open myself up to the energies around me without letting my surroundings impact my judgment.

Ed explained that he had recently purchased the precinct from the city, hoping to turn it into a secure data center. He also wanted to build a small museum in the lobby dedicated to the precinct's history so he could display some of the interesting artifacts and historical documents he'd discovered there.

The 6th Precinct has a long and storied history in Detroit. It served the community as a police station and jail from 1930 until 1986, when the gang squad took it over. It was finally closed in 2005 when they basically just boarded the place up, turned out the lights, and left. It sat abandoned for decades, just as they'd left it, until Ed acquired the building from the city.

Notorious for corruption, the 6th Precinct saw its share of violence. In 1943, a five-hundred-person mob surrounded the building, broke their way in, and released all the prisoners. Then, in 1967, the precinct became the epicenter of Detroit's race riots, where the police and National Guard were forced to shoot it out with the rioters. During its operation, there were people killed right on the front doorstep. Inside, several people committed suicide, both inmates and officers.

With all the death and violent history surrounding the 6th Precinct, there's no wonder it's so haunted. The most active areas we discovered during our many investigations there were the jail cells and the basement—primarily the evidence room and the shooting range next to it. There's also a gymnasium upstairs, which is pretty active.

The place was definitely still a work in progress, with the main room stacked to the ceiling with furniture. Up until Ed's purchase, it was only being used for storage. The walls were covered with badly peeling paint and graffiti. The ceiling was crumbling down due to severe water damage over the years. Ed explained that the roof was the first thing he had to take care of to prevent further damage to the interior.

Although there was some overhead lighting, it was dim and sparse due to the ceiling damage, which added to the gloomy atmosphere. I asked Ed if he ever got scared coming here at night. Ed admitted that he'd heard and felt things here that gave him pause. Then he added, "But they know me, and I know them. We're good."

We free-roamed a bit to get a better lay of the place, then decided to begin our investigation down in the basement. I let Todd and Jeff go first. The banister was little more than a length of iron pipe bolted to the roughly plastered wall. As we descended the staircase, we left footprints in the thick dust blanketing the steps. It had obviously been quite a while since anyone had been down there.

The basement floor was carpeted with decades of dirt and broken pieces of concrete. We shined our flashlights around what used to be the evidence/records room, illuminating empty shelves and graffiti-tagged walls. The air was stale and full of negative energy.

Standing in the middle of the room, the boys started an EVP session to see if they might catch any voice phenomena.

"If anyone is here, can you let us know by making a sound?"

We waited quietly for a response. Suddenly, the silence was broken by the sound of a rock striking the wall and bouncing across the concrete floor. I dismissed it at first, thinking it was probably just a piece of the ceiling falling onto the floor.

Then, the energy around us grew heavier. It felt like we were surrounded by a gang of prisoners, intent on sending the message that we weren't welcome there.

I sensed a male voice ask, "Why are you here?"

I was beginning to wonder the same thing myself.

Then, another rock or chunk of concrete ricocheted off one of the walls.

"Did you hear that?" Teena asked.

I realized then that it wasn't just my imagination.

"Ow!' Todd shouted. "Something just hit me!"

Hoping to confirm whether this was truly a paranormal event, I called out, "Can whatever threw the rock at us do it again?"

Sure enough, we heard more rocks ricocheting off the walls. The assault continued with Todd, Jeff, and myself all getting pelted by flying debris. We shined our flashlights around, inspecting the shadowy corners to ensure there wasn't anyone else down here with us. But all we found were spiderwebs. None of us had ever experienced a physical encounter like this before. It was crazy!

Finally, the onslaught stopped. Either the spirits ran out of energy or realized that we weren't going to be scared off that easily.

Once everything calmed down, we decided to move on to the shooting range. It was attached to the records room by a single, open doorway. The floor was thick with layers of dirt and crumbled concrete debris. A dim light bulb hung from the ceiling midway down the long, narrow range. Todd and Jeff shined their flashlights toward the far end where the targets used to be to make sure the rock thrower hadn't hidden in there. Again, we confirmed that we were the only ones in the basement.

I opened myself up and sensed a powerful male energy. Sadly, we found out later that at least four officers ended their lives in the shooting range over the years. Teena warned that she felt something terrible was going to happen to us in there and for us to be on guard.

All of a sudden, I felt someone grab my rear end! I screamed and ran behind Teena. By this time, Todd, Jeff, and Matt had already ventured to the other end of the shooting range to examine the target area, leaving us by ourselves. And with Ed still upstairs, I knew that it wasn't any of them getting fresh.

With the energies in the basement getting more and more aggressive, I decided that was it. I was getting out of there. Teena and I bolted upstairs and went outside to grab a smoke and calm our nerves. While we were out there, we grounded our energies and recounted what we'd just experienced. It's rare to find a place with intelligent energy that can lash out physically like that. We knew then that we'd uncovered an extremely dangerous place.

Once we finished our cigarettes and the nicotine had a chance to calm our nerves, Teena and I went back inside just as the guys came upstairs to check on us. We told Ed what had happened in the basement, and he confirmed that he felt really uncomfortable whenever he was down there, like something didn't want him there either.

DPX must've investigated the 6th Precinct dozens of times over the years. We led tours whenever possible to raise money to help Ed restore the historic building and realize his dream of turning the place into a data center and museum.

One of our most terrifying encounters at the 6th Precinct occurred about a year after our first visit. The DPX team was investigating the basement when I sensed we were not alone. Standing in the doorway between the records room and where the boys were in the shooting range, I opened myself up to see if any spirits were with us. Suddenly, three hulking prisoners appeared in the shooting range with us! For some reason, they seemed to be fixated on Todd and Jeff and were getting right up in their faces!

"Todd, I'm telling you, they don't like us being down here," I told him. "They're saying that they want you to leave."

Because they can't see what I'm seeing, Todd and Jeff didn't realize the danger they were in. I finally coaxed Todd into going into the evidence room with me to continue investigating there while Jeff and Matt stayed in the shooting range. I yelled for them to be careful because I could see the angry spirits still in their faces like they wanted to fight.

After I turned my back, a loud noise shattered the silence. Jeff cried out from the shooting range, feeling an invisible hand grab ahold of him. Then, a dark mass of energy rushed through the doorway toward me and Todd. This time, Todd also saw the shadowy figure charging toward us and quickly turned heel and ran for the exit.

I wasn't about to let him leave me down there, so I caught up to him and jumped on his back. He carried me for a few strides before glancing over his shoulder.

"What the hell are you doing?" He asked.

"I'm not staying down here!" I yelled.

I finally let go as we reached the staircase. Freed from my body weight, Todd bolted up the steps with me hot on his heels. At this point, we were done. Neither of us looked back until we were both outside, huffing and puffing, our hearts beating out of our chests.

The only other place that DPX has investigated more times than the 6th precinct would have to be Eloise Psychiatric Hospital in Westland, Michigan. Eloise was the place that put us on the map as paranormal investigators. It was also the place that got us on television.

Brandy and Ed Steele

Eloise Psychiatric Hospital

If you mention "Eloise" to anyone who grew up in Southeastern Michigan, you will likely get *the look*. There is something about that name that unsettles people and even evokes fear—fear of those once committed to the legendary asylum and fear of being committed there themselves.

Eloise began as a poor house back in 1839. Over the years, the facility grew to rival many small cities. At its peak in the 1920s, Eloise encompassed over 900 acres with 78 buildings, including a hospital and a mental institution that housed 10,000 patients and 2,000 staff members. Eloise eventually expanded to become completely self-sufficient with its own farm that included dairy cows, pigs, and a variety of crops. They also had their own bakery, post office, power plant, and police and fire departments. Eloise even had a potter's field cemetery across the street, now overgrown with weeds and mostly forgotten.

Eloise Psychiatric Hospital was a pioneer in its time, being one of the first hospitals to use X-rays and open-air treatment for tuberculosis patients. They also introduced Music therapy to help patients suffering from anxiety and depression.

Treatment of psychiatric patients continued to evolve throughout the years to include hydrotherapy, as well as more extreme methods such as electroshock and insulin shock therapy. But, like many sanitoriums of its day, budget cuts and understaffing led to reports of questionable conditions, violence, financial misconduct, and patient neglect.

Like many other mental institutions nationwide, Eloise began shutting down its psychiatric operations in the late 1970s and finally closed the last of its facilities for good in 1982.

The "D Building," also known as the Kay Beard Building, is the last building standing. When it closed, it was primarily used for administration purposes. But remnants of its psychiatric practice remain, including the hydrotherapy tubs on the upper floors and a piano in the basement once used for music therapy.

After years of neglect, the D Building fell into major disrepair. Curious teens and homeless vagrants did a number on the interior, as did the Michigan weather. Finally, in 2018, the County sold off the former Eloise grounds to developers for one dollar, hoping to see the dilapidated property rejuvenated.

In August of 2018, Todd called to tell me he'd been speaking with the new owner of Eloise about how we might help him raise money to repair the historic administration building by doing paranormal tours like we did for the 6th Precinct. Like many others, Todd remembered sneaking in to explore the abandoned psychiatric hospital with some of his friends as a teen.

We needed to keep the deal hush-hush so other paranormal teams didn't find out and get the jump on us. About a month later, Todd called me back, all excited. We got permission to go in and check the place out. I couldn't believe how lucky we were! This was a huge deal to be the first paranormal team allowed to officially investigate this notoriously haunted, abandoned asylum. It brought back memories of investigating Waverly Hills. I couldn't wait to see what we might unearth.

I called my dad to tell him the big news, figuring he would know the place. To my surprise, he revealed that our family had our own connection to Eloise: my great, great grandfather, Albert Eugene Miller, died in Eloise back in 1954 from pneumonia and complications from dementia. Now, I was even more intrigued. What if I could make contact with my great, great grandfather here at Eloise?

The DPX crew, Todd, Jeff, Matt, and I, rallied at Eloise's Building D to check it out. Since there was no electricity, we went during the day. We were like kids in a candy store with five floors of abandoned asylum to explore.

The inside reminded me of Waverly Hills, with its institutional green paint peeling from the walls and ceiling, the broken-out windows, and random graffiti. I could tell the place had been abandoned a long time by how the dust swirled in the air as we wandered the desolate hallways.

Soaking in the scenery and energy of the place, I visualized how everything looked back in the 40s and 50s. I could feel the doctors and nurses rushing past, almost as if we were in their way as they tried to carry out their duties.

We stumbled across the common area where the psychiatric patients once gathered to play cards or sat in a semi-circle of mismatched chairs to watch the television bolted to the wall above them. It looked like a scene right out of *One Flew Over the Cuckoo's Nest*.

As I entered the space, I could feel the patients in the room. But I had to be careful not to draw their attention. It's always a fine line when doing a paranormal investigation. I want to open myself up enough to see the spirits but not enough for them to notice me. Once we establish a connection, it can be hard to close it.

I forced myself to keep moving so I didn't draw any undue attention from the troubled spirits still haunting this area. As we wandered from floor to floor, I opened myself up more, repeating my mantra, "Be the building, fill the building." It's my way of connecting with a location and the energies lingering there.

I could still feel the former nursing staff hustling past me on their way to some important assignment, punctuated by moments of irrational fear or unrelenting sadness from former patients. It was like the place was alive!

We worked our way from the basement to the fifth floor, getting the lay of the building and familiarizing ourselves with this incredible, abandoned time capsule. As we explored the various floors and remaining artifacts, we envisioned how we might conduct tours, where the best places to stop and perform spirit box sessions might be, and the most likely locations to capture something with our cameras or EVPs. I made mental notes of the areas where I sensed the most active energy.

Before we knew it, it was getting dark out. I could feel the negative energy growing as the sun set. Eloise becomes an entirely different place at night when the dark energies take over. I could feel the spirits that had previously been hiding in the shadows come alive.

My body tensed and my guard went up as the confused thoughts and random babblings of the insane filled my head. It was so disorienting I had all I could do to concentrate.

As we continued to explore the psychiatric hospital, my mind wandered back to my great, great grandfather and what he must've endured during his time here as dementia clouded his mind and stole his memories. What did they do to him here? What kind of experimental therapy did they try out on him?

My emotions overtook me and I became overwhelmed with anger and sadness. The roller-coaster of emotions that an empath like myself can experience in a place like this is almost debilitating. So many disturbed minds have come through here over the sanitorium's decades of operation that waves of confused psychic energies left me disoriented and exhausted, forcing me to shut down.

It took me days to recover from my first experience at Eloise. I felt completely drained. But I also knew that I had to go back. There was so much to explore at Eloise, and it was such an excellent opportunity to challenge myself and expand my abilities.

Once Todd worked out all the details of the business arrangement with the new owner, DPX started conducting private and public investigations and tours for the next couple of years. We took advantage of our exclusive arrangement for as long as we could. Soon, DPX became the first paranormal team to conduct an overnight investigation at Eloise.

Eventually, our exclusive contract ended and the property was sold to another investment group. I'll never forget all the uncanny and startling paranormal encounters we experienced at Eloise.

Our work at Eloise Psychiatric Hospital really drew attention to the place and brought other paranormal teams from around the world to investigate. It also put DPX on the map. After posting some of our findings on YouTube and Facebook Live, we were contacted by a production company to develop a limited series on Eloise that they planned to pitch to various networks. They flew out a cameraman and their director of development to shoot footage of us investigating Eloise, which they edited together for a pitch reel they sent around to Travel Channel and other cable networks.

Unfortunately, the series did not get picked up. I've learned over the years that most of these opportunities never see the light of day. But it's always exciting, and we try not to get our hopes up, but it's hard not to. Even though the Eloise series wasn't greenlit, it didn't stop us from doing what we love—exploring historically haunted places and sharing those experiences with others. It also didn't stop Hollywood from calling on us again.

Even though we didn't land the Eloise series, some of the extraordinary evidence we captured there did end up getting featured on such paranormal series as *Fright Club, Paranormal Caught on Camera,* and *Destination Fear,* who came and did their own overnight investigation. As recently as 2023, *Expedition X* with Josh Gates filmed a two-part series at Eloise, adding further evidence to the haunted lore of the legendary asylum.

The Elevator

One of the most disturbing encounters we experienced while investigating Eloise occurred when Todd and I set up cameras in the basement as we prepared for our first-ever Facebook Live event. Todd decided to put a camera in the elevator, thinking it might be an excellent place to capture spirit activity. While he mounted the camera, I told him I sensed something in the elevator with him.

He confirmed that he felt a strange presence in there, too.

As he fiddled with the camera, I noticed what looked like a female psychiatric patient in a loose-hanging cotton gown standing in the elevator with him. The ghostly figure reminded me of the female spirit in the film *The Grudge*, with her long, dark, greasy hair hanging in strips across her face. Her head was tilted down in a deadlock stare focused on Todd as if she wanted to hurt him in unimaginable ways.

"Todd, you better hurry up!" I warned.

He didn't need much coaxing. The ghostly presence exuded such creepy energy that it chilled him to the bone. Todd couldn't get out of that elevator quickly enough. Once he secured the camera sufficiently, he high-tailed it out of the elevator. We booked it down the hall and up the stairs, neither of us looking back.

One for the Record

T he third and fifth floors of Eloise Psychiatric Hospital have always felt the heaviest to me, ever since my first walkthrough. Although, I've had experiences on other levels, too. One particular encounter on the third floor stands out to me, and I'm glad I had the foresight to record it because this was one of the encounters that's been shown on multiple paranormal shows, including Travel Channel's *Paranormal Caught on Camera*.

I invited my friend Jenny and her sister to join us for one of our public tours at Eloise. But before the tour with the general public started, I wanted to give them a private tour without all the noise and distractions of the big group tours. I decided to take them to the floor where I'd experienced the most activity. Since neither of them had psychic abilities, I brought Todd's custom Geobox along to hopefully capture some spirit communication for them to hear.

With us being the first ones there and no one else allowed up without a tour guide, I knew it was just the three of us on the third floor. I started recording a video on my smartphone as I led them down the third-floor hallway. We strolled past the common area with the TV and a couple of five-foot-tall filing cabinets with dust-covered folders and vinyl records stacked on top.

I took a deep breath and opened myself up to the spirits.

Suddenly, Jenny gasped and pointed ahead, where we saw a tall, black silhouette peek around the corner of one of the doorways and then retreat. She stopped dead in her tracks.

"Did you see that?" Jenny asked.

"What did you see?" I asked, verifying she had seen the same thing I had.

"It looked like a tall... black guy. Right there, peeking out of the doorway."

I had to break the news to her. "That was no black guy."

She looked at me, confused. Then, the realization slowly sunk in when I explained that we didn't have any tall black guys leading tours today. But before I could convince her that what she'd seen had been a shadow figure, there came a loud CRASH! We all screamed and practically jumped out of our skins.

"What was that?" Jenny's sister asked, her voice rising in fear.

"Okay, time to go," I said, doing my best to calmly escort the girls out of danger.

On our way out, I glanced at the floor and discovered the vinyl record I heard shatter a moment ago. It was as if someone had thrown it on the ground in a fit of anger. Or had something in here been targeting us and just missed?

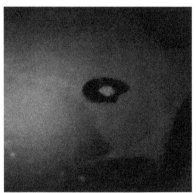

The shattered record at Eloise
See video at: www.youtube.com/shorts/XqYl3Mv0WXA

"Okay, we're going..." Jenny said, hoping to pacify the angry spirit.

"We're leaving," I added, apologizing to the dark energy we had inadvertently provoked.

Our hearts racing like mad, the three of us hurried down the hallway to the stairs and hoofed it out of the building before things could get any worse.

Shirt Pull

Arguably, the most compelling evidence we caught on camera occurred on the first floor of Eloise Psychiatric Hospital. We had just set up a tripod in one of the rooms in preparation for one of our Facebook Live events. Todd, Jeff, and I were joined by a couple of our friends for that evening's investigation. I sat on one side of an old metal desk while one of my guy friends sat on the other. The other gal stood behind us, leaning on the desk.

Once we went live, I turned on the spirit box and asked if any resident spirits wanted to communicate with us. After a few minutes, I felt an intense male energy in the room. As the entity drew nearer, I grew more and more uncomfortable.

A tingle shot up my leg as I felt something poke me, and I jumped.

The energy then circled around the desk behind me.

Fearing for the safety of the female investigator behind me, I glanced over my shoulder and said to her, "You need to come over here, please."

I motioned for her to come around and stand in front of me so I could see her and to get her away from the threatening male presence creeping up behind her. Something told me I needed to protect her back because the dark entity wanted to get at her, thinking she was vulnerable.

When it comes to attachments, in my experience, dark entities usually like to attack at the nape of your neck. I'm not sure if we're more vulnerable there or if it's easier for them to manipulate us by attacking us near our brain stem or what.

Just as the other gal came around in front of the desk, the entity crept up behind me. The hostile energy then attempted to go through me to get to her. I quickly put up a white energy shield to protect myself and her, blocking the energy and sending it back where it came from.

It might sound strange, but I didn't fully realize what had happened to me until we watched the video back. That's when we all witnessed an invisible hand grasp hold of my sleeve and give it a pull. The video evidence is so clear that many think we somehow faked it with a fishing line or something. But I swear the video is legit. I have never, and will never, fake anything in an investigation. I challenge you to watch the video in slow motion, zoom in, or whatever you want to try, and you will see the natural movement of my sweater being grabbed and pulled. If you don't believe me, believe your own eyes.

This evidence was so compelling that a producer from Jack Osbourne's series, *Fright Club,* contacted us and asked if Todd and I would come on an episode to show the video and discuss our experiences at Eloise.

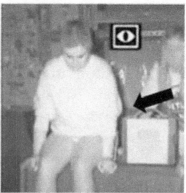

Brandy's shirt pulled by an unseen force
To watch the full video, visit: youtu.be/NiBWnFTw5aU

The Whistler

When you spend as much time in an actively haunted location as I have, you often get to know certain lingering spirits. Some are from a residual haunting of a specific event played over and over as if on a loop. Others are intelligent spirits you can interact with and even become comfortable with, as long as they are the non-threatening type. Then there are those who make it clear they do not want you there. With a place like Eloise, most of the energies are likely former staff members or patients of the psychiatric hospital.

One of the personalities that I came to appreciate was *The Whistler*. I first noticed this phenomenon while investigating with my friends Joe and Tanya Posey from *Unknown Paranormal of Detroit*. When we conduct tours with larger groups, we often split up, with part of our team leading a group on one floor while another team member leads another group somewhere else. The smaller the groups, the better, because if you have too many people together at one time, there are too many distractions and excess noise pollution. Plus, you have to worry about people photo-bombing your pictures.

On this particular occasion, Tanya was on the 4th floor while I took the 3rd. We carried walkie-talkies for safety and to communicate with the other team leads. As I walked down the hall, I heard the sound of someone whistling, followed by a woman humming. I glanced around at the people in my group, but it wasn't any of them.

145

I got on the walkie-talkie and radioed the other team members to tell them I thought someone else was on the 3rd floor with us. A couple of the guys came up and did a complete sweep of all the rooms but were unable to find any party crashers.

Whenever I explored the 3rd floor at Eloise, I'd often hear the same whistling tune or a woman humming. It reminded me of people who like to whistle while they work. Unlike the occasional blood-curdling scream of a madman, this felt more like I had come across a nurse or a member of the cleaning staff merrily doing their job.

While I experienced the phantom whistling and humming on the 3rd floor, Joe and Tanya dealt with their own phenomena on the 4th. Tanya swore she heard the sound of running water. After shushing everyone, she and Joe went to investigate. At first, Tanya thought that maybe one of the members of their tour group had wandered off and gotten into the janitor's area, looking for a restroom.

Tanya went to check out the area where the cleaning staff used to rinse out the buckets, but by the time she got there, the water sounds had stopped. She checked the drains, but everything looked dry. And it should be dry because Eloise no longer has running water.

Brandy in a hydrotherapy tub at Eloise

Rose

Of all the ghostly personalities I've come to know at Eloise Psychiatric Hospital, my favorite would have to be Rose. I grew attached to Rose through her melodious singing that occasionally drifted through the spirit box. I always knew it was her because of the angelic lilt in her voice. It was unlike anything I've ever heard.

When performing spirit box sessions at Eloise, I often heard the name Rose come through, accompanied by that angelic singing. It turned into a regular thing whenever I investigated Eloise. If I thought I detected the name Rose come through the spirit box, I'd ask her to do that thing she does for me so I would know it was her. Before long, I would hear her melodic singing drift out of the spirit box.

I got the impression that Rose was an older woman, maybe in her 70s, who might have worked in music therapy at Eloise. Her singing was so comforting I thought of her as my protector whenever I was there.

My relationship with Rose soon extended beyond Eloise. The first place where Rose and I connected outside Eloise was at the 6th precinct during a spirit box session. I was surprised to hear the name Rose come through at a completely different location. On a hunch, I asked the spirit to do her thing. Moments later, I heard her unmistakable, angelic voice float through the air.

At first, I assumed Rose came through at the 6th precinct because Detroit wasn't far from Westland, where Eloise is located. For all I knew, her husband could've worked at the precinct. But later, when investigating places in Ohio, Rose's name came through there, too. It seemed that no matter where I went, whenever I used the spirit box, Rose would pay me a visit.

After our exclusive arrangement with Eloise ended and word got out about the things DPX had discovered there, tons of other groups started visiting Eloise, trying to duplicate our paranormal findings. I also learned through the grapevine that other groups were trying to communicate with Rose, too.

It may sound weird, but I kind of felt a special relationship with Rose's spirit, and it bothered me to think that others with less-than-honorable intentions might be trying to contact her. Not all groups approach paranormal investigation the same way. My friends and I at DPX never go into locations to provoke or anger spirits just to get a reaction and say we captured some evidence.

We always approach destinations with respect. If the spirits have something they want to communicate, we want to give them a chance to be heard. If they don't, then we don't force it. Besides, if you come at the spirit world with a negative attitude, trying to provoke a response, you're more likely to stir up a negative reaction. Not all energies are the same. There is some dark and scary shit on the other side that you don't want to provoke. Trust me!

I decided when I went back to visit Eloise, I would intercede on behalf of Rose. I told her that if she didn't want to stay at Eloise, she didn't have to. She could move on. I'll never know whether Rose closed herself off because of what others did, or if she chose to move on. But after my last conversation with Rose, I haven't heard from her since. My hope is that she moved on and added her beautiful voice to heaven's angelic choir.

* * *

I have investigated so many amazing, historic haunted locations, from Savannah, GA, to the upper peninsula of Michigan, from underground tunnels to towering lighthouses, from bars to seminaries. Far too many places and experiences to document in one book.

My friends at DPX and I have posted volumes of paranormal evidence we've collected over the years on Facebook and YouTube. Some of our EVPs and video recordings have even been featured on various TV shows, including *Destination Fear*, *Fright Club*, and *Paranormal Caught on Camera* (multiple times). But the biggest opportunity of all, the chance to star in our own series, didn't come until 2021.

Jeff, Brandy, and Todd on Destination Fear: Eloise episode.

28 DAYS HAUNTED

In the Beginning

It all started with a phone call from my close friend and co-founder of DPX (Detroit Paranormal Expeditions), Todd Bonner, in April of 2021. A casting director had just contacted him looking for experienced teams of 2-4 people to participate in a potential paranormal investigation series for a major streaming platform. She had come across our work online and thought that, based on our credentials, we could be an ideal fit for their series.

She attached a flyer to her email spelling out what they were looking for and what we could expect. How's this for a Help Wanted ad?

```
"Are you a paranormal expert?
Do you love working with others to investigate
haunted spaces and demonic presences?
Are you an adrenaline junkie who thrives on de-
coding messages from spirits?
If so, we want to hear from YOU!
This hair-raising, exciting new series will fol-
low teams of paranormal experts as they immerse
themselves in one of the most haunted locations
in the country! Each team will use their own
style of paranormal investigation they've honed
```

over the years to decode the terrifying mysteries of the entities tormenting the location.
If you think you and your team have what it takes
to embark on this journey for up to 28 days,
please send an email with your phone number,
social media links, photos, names, and contact
info for each team member, and a brief bio."

Todd immediately called partner and DPX co-founder Jeff Adkins to see if he was interested. After Jeff said he was on board, Todd called me to see if I'd be willing to lend my psychic medium abilities and audition with him and Jeff for the show.

Once I said I was in, Todd replied to the casting director and told her our team was interested in trying out. They asked for our contact information, social media links, photos, and bios.

A month passed without a word from anyone. With my busy schedule, I kind of forgot about the show. In the television business, people are always pitching shows that never get produced, let alone picked up by a network. So, when they contacted me to get on a Zoom call, I was shocked.

I didn't have a computer at the time, so I went over to Todd's house. The casting director ended up conducting separate Zoom calls with Todd, Jeff, and me. She asked us each a bunch of questions about our paranormal investigation experience to see how we responded and to get a feel for our personalities to see if she thought we might be good on camera.

Todd and Jeff sensed my nervousness, and since Todd was contacted first, he and Jeff felt the need to talk me up and sell the producers on me and my abilities. They spent so much time building me up on their calls that they didn't focus enough on selling themselves.

When it came to my Zoom call, I was super nervous. I had no idea what they were going to ask me, and I didn't want to blow it for us, knowing what a huge opportunity this was to co-star in a series for a major network. But once we got going, I started to relax more and just be myself.

The casting director asked me questions about my abilities, what my specialty was, and when I first recognized that I had these gifts. The questions then turned to how I met Todd and Jeff and who I looked up to in the paranormal field. I didn't know the show would center on Ed and Lorraine Warren's theories then, but looking back, I think they were looking to see if I mentioned them as inspirations. Fortunately, I did.

A few weeks later, Todd received an email from the production company saying how much they loved our interviews/auditions, then added, "...especially Brandy." I was shocked! Like many times before, we were told that the head of the production company would contact us if we made the final cut. But the casting director sounded highly optimistic about our chances. I tried not to get too excited, but it was impossible not to.

More weeks passed until we finally got word that we had made the final four. I practically squealed. This could be our big break! But there was one problem. The series only called for three teams. Although we'd been a guest on other people's shows many times before, we'd never been the leads on a series. And we had no idea who our competition was.

After the exciting news, we texted each other back and forth every day.

"Did you hear anything yet?"

"No, you?"

"No."

The more time that passed, the more nervous we became. That's one of the worst things about show business. It's always hurry up and wait. And as Tom Petty sang, the waiting is the hardest part.

But then, it finally happened. I got an email from the production company saying they were very interested in me being part of the show and wanted to schedule another Zoom call. I was so stoked! It was starting to look as if this might actually happen!

I called Todd and asked if he'd seen the email. He replied that he hadn't while quickly checking his phone. No emails from them yet. We figured it would just be a matter of time since we knew they had at least a dozen people to contact.

Todd checked with Jeff, but he hadn't gotten an email yet either. Todd kept checking his email throughout the day, but still, nothing.

A few more days passed, and they still hadn't heard anything. Surely, if one team member was contacted, the others would be too, right? The more time that passed, the more doubt began to creep in. Finally, the casting director called and broke the news to them that I was the only member of the team that made the final cut.

I was shocked, confused, and totally heartbroken for Todd and Jeff. After all, I wouldn't even be in this position if it hadn't been for them. At first, I seriously considered not doing it. In the past, we'd always agreed that if we weren't all three picked for a show, we wouldn't do it. But Todd told me it was way too good of an opportunity to pass up and argued that I deserved it.

I worried about working on the show with people I didn't know and hadn't worked with before. I trusted Todd and Jeff, but would the others have my back if things went south? Plus, the idea of being locked down for 28 days with people I'd never even met was nerve-wracking, to say the least. What if we didn't get along? Or what if they were jerks?

After thinking it over for a while, I knew that Todd was right. This opportunity was way too important to pass up. If the show got picked up by one of the major cable networks or streaming services and was a hit, it could be life-changing. Also, the better things went for me on this project, the more it helped the chances of the three of us to get our own show in the future. So, after much deliberation, I signed the contract.

* * *

As with all productions, there are always tons of things producers need to do to prepare for a show. One of the most critical is casting. For 28 Days Haunted, they planned to cast three teams of 3-4 people. Each cast member had to undergo an extensive background check and psychological evaluation since we had to be isolated in one location for 28 days straight, away from family, friends, and all contact from the outside world.

My second Zoom call was scheduled with the director of development, one of the producers, and my prospective teammates. This is when I first met Jereme Leonard, star of the series *Ghosts of Morgan City* and better known as *The Cajun Demonologist*. In addition to Jereme, a pair of paranormal investigators from Las Vegas were also on the call and slated to join us.

After our Zoom audition, it was determined that the Las Vegas guys just weren't the right fit for me and Jereme, so the producers decided to replace them with a tech guy named Chris. Chris had lots of experience with spirit boxes, cameras, and other paranormal equipment.

I was surprised to find out later that I was the only person chosen for the series that the production company hadn't worked with before in some capacity, which was probably a big reason they balked at hiring all three of us from DPX or teaming me up with two new guys from Vegas.

I was flattered they were willing to take a chance on me, but it also made me more nervous. I've never been the lead investigator before. Whenever DPX performed investigations or hosted events, Todd and Jeff were always the leads, and I was like the sidekick, doing my thing as the resident psychic medium. Imagine having to be one of the leads on a TV series that people all over the country or even the world might see! That put extra pressure on me to figure everything out quickly.

Finally, our team looked to be set. We had a demonologist (Jereme), a psychic medium (me), and an investigator/tech guy (Chris) to balance out the team. Unfortunately, the background checks weren't conducted until late in the process, and our tech guy ended up failing his background check.

Even if it was a mistake, there wouldn't be time to sort it out or to vet anyone new. That meant Jereme and I would be the only group with just two members. And now, this newbie would have to carry half of the load! What do I do if something happens to my only team member? I could be stuck in an insanely haunted location all by myself!

And as fate would have it, two and a half weeks into shooting, that's exactly what happened.

28 Days

28 Days Haunted was the brainchild of Tony Spera, son-in-law of Ed and Lorraine Warren, who became famous for their investigation of *The Amityville Horror* house and their pioneering work in the paranormal field; and Host Aaron Sagers, a journalist best known for *Paranormal Caught on Camera* and his paranormal pop culture podcast, *Talking Strange*.

The idea for conducting a twenty-eight-day investigation derived from a theory developed by Ed and Lorraine Warren. The Warren's *28 Day Cycle Theory* suggested that it can take up to 28 days to reach total spiritual immersion at a haunted location and to pierce the veil between the living and the dead. 28 days also happened to be the length of time the Lutz family lived in the Amityville house.

But none of the show's cast knew we were testing a theory connected to the Warrens. The producers didn't want anything to influence our investigation, not even the theory we were testing.

Another hypothesis developed by the Warrens suggested that the longer you stayed in a haunted location, the more activity you were likely to experience. Yet, the longest most paranormal investigations lasted, like the ones you typically see on television, were no longer than 2-3 days due to cost and scheduling. Hell, some only last 2-3 hours!

The most time I had ever spent at any haunted destination was overnight. Could I handle 28 days straight locked down in an actively haunted location? And what about being away from my family and friends for an entire month?

Being confined in one location for 28 days turned into as much of a social experiment as it did a test of the Warren's theories. We would not be allowed to communicate with anyone from the outside except in an emergency. Even then, we would have to use a walkie-talkie to contact one of the producers first.

I never imagined that, before the 28 days were up, I would have to use one of those walkie-talkies to call for help.

With the production staff having to edit 28 days of raw footage, times three locations, down to only three and a half hours of air time, there would inevitably be a lot edited out that the viewers would never get to see. Although I can only speak for what my team experienced at our location, I can assure you it was insane!

Now it's time to pull back the curtain and show you what it was like to film a paranormal investigation series, give you an insider's look at the most dramatic moments from *28 Days Haunted*, and share never-before-revealed secrets of what occurred behind the scenes but never aired on Netflix.

DAY 1 – Going in Blind

Before production began on 28 Days Haunted, the producers intentionally kept us in the dark to ensure we wouldn't be influenced by our location's history. The goal was to test not only the Warren's 28-Day-Theory but also our psychic and investigative abilities to see if we could unravel the mystery behind the hauntings.

The only clue about our mystery location was a plane ticket revealing the state we were flying to. In my case, it was North Carolina. But that was it. I didn't know the city, let alone the haunted location. I usually like to go into investigations with as little information as possible anyway, so my observations and intuition aren't falsely influenced.

After I arrived in North Carolina, one of the production assistants picked me up from the airport and drove me to my hotel. The hotel's location didn't offer any clues since I'd never been to this area, and for all I knew, our destination was hours away.

Once settled in at the hotel, I met my new investigation partner, Jereme Leonard, in the lobby. Up until now, we had never met in person. Our only communication was our Zoom audition and a few text exchanges once we discovered we'd been selected for the series. I hoped getting to know Jereme a little better over dinner might make me more comfortable working with him. At least, as comfortable as one could be, quarantined in a haunted place for 28 days straight with a demonologist.

We were both excited about our upcoming adventure, and a little anxious, not knowing what we were getting ourselves into. We discussed our similar beliefs in God and the afterlife over dinner. We agreed it was essential to be on the same page with our approach to paranormal investigation since we had no idea what kind of supernatural forces we might face. Jereme advised how crucial it was to work in God's name when dealing with dark entities or demons and not to confront them under our own power. We also agreed to respect each other's boundaries and strengths. But most of all, we determined that, no matter what happened, we would have each other's backs.

After our dinner, I felt better about my new teammate since we seemed to be on the same page. With all the uncertainties ahead and not getting to choose my partner, I felt that I got pretty lucky when they paired me with Jereme.

That night, as I lay in my hotel bed, I began seeing visions of a dark-haired woman standing at the top of a long staircase flanked by two children. The woman's shabby dress had a dingy apron skirt tied around it. She kept pointing to the room on her left, warning me not to go in there. Little did I know then, but the room she pointed to would soon become our new living quarters.

When I say that I went into this investigation blind, I mean it literally. After one of the producers picked us up from the hotel, they shot some B-roll of Jereme and me getting blindfolded and loaded into a van.

Once inside the vehicle, our phones were confiscated and placed in Ziploc bags. We were then told we'd have to wear the blindfolds until we reached our destination. It wasn't until we arrived and were guided to the front door that we were finally allowed to take off our blindfolds.

First Impressions

During the ride to our haunted location, I attempted to tune into the woman from my vision. It wasn't long before I connected to her spirit. I was struck by a sense of heaviness as if something tragic had happened to her. I soon discovered that the events that befell her and her family were far more tragic than anything I could've imagined.

As I opened myself up further, I felt other spirits coming through. They revealed a brown, two-story wood cabin with a brick fireplace chimney running up the side that looked like someone built themselves. It was like I was a drone hovering outside the house that someone else was controlling. Just as I zoomed into the porch and approached the front door, our driver interrupted the vision, announcing we were two minutes away from our destination.

With the connection terminated, I closed myself off and focused on preparing for what lay ahead. For better or worse, the adventure was about to begin.

The van slowed and came to a stop.

"Here we are," said the driver.

I heard the van door slide open, and we were both guided out the passenger side, presumably for the camera guy to capture us arriving.

Still blindfolded, I heard the van drive off. My heart sank. This was actually happening! 28 days locked in a haunted location. Hopefully, I hadn't made the biggest mistake of my life.

The cameraman signaled for us to take off our blindfolds. As I removed my mask, the blinding early afternoon sun stung my eyes. The building finally came into focus, and I was shocked that we weren't in some backwoods town in front of the two-story cabin from my vision. Instead, we were standing in front of a small-town Main Street storefront. On the window was painted the name *Madison Dry Goods*.

Wait, the scary location they are locking us down in is a quaint little country store? Was this a joke? Where was the haunted house I was expecting?

We gawked at the place for a moment, not sure what to think. Could this really be our final destination? Or did they just drop us off here for someone else to collect and take someplace scarier? My question was quickly answered when I felt a powerful energy emanating from the building, hungry to draw me in. I carefully opened myself up just enough to get a sense of what the place was trying to tell me. The message was clear.

Something incredibly tragic happened here.

I inched my way up to the storefront window and peeked inside. At first, it looked just like an old country store. But as I looked around inside, my heart skipped a beat. There it was, the staircase I'd seen in my vision! This was definitely the place.

Jereme and I shared a nervous glance. I told him about the overpowering feeling we were in for way more than we bargained for.

My body tensed. Was it too late to back out? Then, I noticed something shiny at my feet. I got choked up seeing the dime there on the sidewalk. Before my mom died, I asked her to give me a sign to let me know if she ever visited me from the afterlife. The sign we agreed on? A dime placed heads up.

I bent down and looked at the coin and saw the face of Franklin D. Roosevelt shining up at me. I believed my mom was letting me know she had my back.

Taking a deep breath, I nervously grabbed the tarnished brass door handle and pulled. The hinges creaked, and a brass bell sounded the alarm, alerting the spirits that we had arrived. But who were we kidding? They already knew. They'd been waiting for us.

The First Floor

It was like stepping back in time. The air inside was thick with negative energy. I jumped as the door shut and was locked behind us. The cameraman smiled and waved good-bye, letting us know there was no turning back now.

We were surrounded by all the trappings of an old country store. Some items on the shelves were new, but all had a down-home country flavor. They still had some of the original furniture, scales, and a vintage cash register.

Jereme and I briefly explored the ground floor to get our bearings and better understand our surroundings. As we perused the store, I was overwhelmed by all the energy attached to this place. I sensed a lot of activity occurred in the old country store section and that sometimes items on the shelves moved or shifted around during the night.

We ventured deeper into the store. The hair on the nape of my neck bristled as I sensed the woman from my vision following us around.

When we reached the second-floor staircase, I gasped. It was identical to the one the spirit showed me last night at the hotel. I half expected to see the mother-like figure standing at the top with her kids. But that would come soon enough.

The Second Floor

My curiosity peaked, I took a deep breath and headed up the stairs. The old wooden steps groaned beneath our feet. With every step, the boards creaked as if resisting our intrusion. Reaching the top, I turned to the right, where the woman had been pointing in my vision.

"You have to be kidding me!" I shouted, startling Jereme.

The room the spirit had warned me about contained a pair of beds separated by a partition. That's right, the room the mysterious woman warned us about was our new sleeping quarters! What does that say about the rest of this place?

Jereme and I dropped our stuff and plopped down on our beds. I looked around the room until my gaze returned to Jereme, and his eyes met mine. Now what? We just got there and already we were bored. We decided we might as well explore the rest of the second floor since we were already there. And you know what they say about curiosity and cats.

Madison Dry Goods second-floor display room

Across the hallway, catercorner from our bedroom, one of the rooms was decorated in the period. It was like we were back in the early 1900s with the old wooden furniture, manual washing machine with hand-crank wringer, and wooden ironing board. A twin iron bed was placed against the wall beside a beautiful old steamer trunk. On the other side of the room, a glass-doored cabinet displayed vintage glass jars and antique tins.

At the end of the hall, we found another room with dried tobacco leaves hanging on the wall above an antique scale surrounded by old feed sacks and farming tools. I love vintage artifacts like these! It was as if we had just stepped out of a time machine.

We turned around and headed back up the hallway to explore the area on the other side of the staircase. That's where we discovered the setup for our base camp. It was a large room with tables, a couch, and upholstered chairs. Someone installed a whiteboard for us to plan our daily investigations and document any sightings, noises, or voice phenomena we might witness. The whiteboard also came in handy when connecting the dots as we strove to solve the mystery behind the hauntings.

A separate room was set aside for us to record our daily video diaries that contained a camera and microphone. They also provided us with one computer, without access to the internet, which we used to copy over the digital audio and photos we captured. The only time it was connected to the internet was when we did a video interview near the end of our investigation. But that was it. And since they confiscated our smartphones, we were completely disconnected from the outside world.

We continued exploring the second floor and found another sizeable room next to our base camp. Nothing could've prepared us for what we saw in that room. This was the moment we knew that Madison Dry Goods was much more than just an old general store.

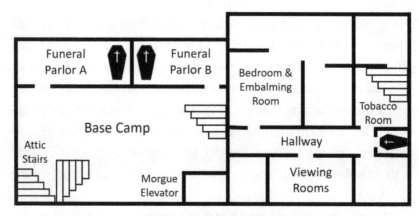

SECOND FLOOR

Funeral Parlor?

Y ou've got to be shitting me!" Jereme cried out.

My heart practically skipped a beat as we entered what looked like an old-fashioned funeral parlor, coffins and all! I couldn't believe my eyes. Investigating a funeral parlor was one thing, but did they seriously expect me to live in one?

We later found out that nearly a century ago, this building was more than just a dry goods store. It was also a funeral home. No wonder the woman in my vision was trying to warn me about this place!

The negative energy on the upper levels eclipsed anything I felt on the first floor, making me even more nervous. There was something extremely dark lurking up there. Something that made me glad I had a demonologist with me.

While examining the funeral parlor, we came across an old family portrait. In the black-and-white photo, a couple posed with their seven children. The parents stood in the back row, the mother holding her baby. Next to them, the two oldest siblings looked to be in their late teens or maybe early twenties. The four youngest children were all crammed together in the front row, seated on a wicker bench.

As I looked closer, my mind reeled. The woman and the two kids I'd seen in my vision the night before were all in the photo I held in my hands! But what did it mean? What was she trying to tell me?

Lawson Family Portrait

The longer I stared at the photo, the more I was filled with dread. Somehow, I knew that something horrible had happened to those kids. My voice nearly cracked as I told Jereme, "I think they were murdered!"

Shaken, I returned the photo to where I found it and headed back to our sleeping quarters. As we settled in, Jereme quipped, "Well, tonight's sure gonna be entertaining!"

* * *

Jereme and I discussed ideas for our first night's investigation as I tried to shake the thoughts of murdered children from my mind. But that's easier said than done.

We decided to use a REM pod to help communicate with the spirits here. For those unfamiliar with these, a REM pod creates an electromagnetic field around the antenna to help detect spirit energies in the vicinity. The theory is that if spirits want to communicate with us, they can break the electromagnetic field around the antenna to signal investigators. When they do, the device lights up and beeps to alert us.

This REM pod also reacts to temperature changes. It's common for spirit energies to produce a cold spot around them as they draw from the ambient heat around them for energy and use it to communicate or even materialize.

As we put together the plan, Jereme shocked me with a disturbing suggestion.

"Brandy, I'm gonna put you in a coffin tonight!"

"Are you serious?" I asked him, incredulous.

"Oh yeah," he said. "I'm gonna put you in that coffin and pretend I'm giving you your last rights."

Jereme theorized that the coffin on the second floor was somehow associated with the tragedy that had befallen the children in the photo, or at least symbolized it. He thought it would help to use the coffin to provoke or trigger the spirits.

Funeral Parlor

"If you're too scared, I'll understand," he said with a snarky grin.

Was I scared? Hell yeah! But was I going to let this guy know that? Hell no! And I had to admit, it would make for good television.

"I'll do it," I conceded, afraid that the waver in my voice belied the confidence I hoped to project. I later admitted to Jereme that I was a little freaked out by the idea of getting in that coffin.

He said he wanted to challenge the spirits in this place immediately to stir up raw, paranormal activity. If that coffin had any relation to the tragedy or the ghosts that haunted this place, then putting me inside it could provoke those spirits to make contact.

Great. What did I sign up for?

Our First Investigation

We began investigating the room where we felt the most energy during our initial walkthrough... the coffin room. I have to admit, Jereme's coffin experiment made me extremely nervous. I'd never done anything like that before. Sure, it might give us answers quicker, but at what cost? What if an evil energy attacked me while I was lying in the coffin? The casket wasn't much bigger than me, and I could easily break my neck trying to escape. What am I supposed to do, just fly out of the room?

If this was what Jereme came up with for the first day, what was day 28 going to bring? Too proud to chicken out on the very first investigation, I reluctantly climbed into the casket. A disturbing thought occurred to me. Was I the first body to occupy this coffin?

Once I got settled inside the coffin, Jereme handed me a set of headphones and the blindfold I arrived here in. He suggested we start our paranormal discovery using the *Estes Method*. The Estes Method is a paranormal investigation technique invented by Karl Pfeiffer, Connor Randall, and Michelle Tate and was named after Estes Park, CO, which is the home of the infamous Stanley Hotel—the inspiration for Stephen King's book, *The Shining.*

These Stanley Hotel ghost-tour guides pioneered the technique in an effort to better communicate with the spirits there. Since some questioned the validity of spirit boxes, the team wanted to remove all doubt about whether the messages they heard coming from the other side were legitimate or not.

The Estes Method required one person (the receiver) to wear a blindfold and noise-canceling headphones to block out any outside stimulus while another person (the questioner) asked the spirits questions. The receiver's job was to verbalize any sights, sounds, or impressions they received directly from the spirits. Since the receiver had no idea what the questioner was asking, any potential bias from the questioner was eliminated. After testing this new investigative method at The Stanley Hotel, the team was shocked at how often the impressions the receiver reported matched the prompts from the questioner.

Acting as the receiver, I donned the blindfold. The thought of not seeing what was happening around me was terrifying. After putting on the headphones, I couldn't make out what Jereme was saying. I was shaking as I lay inside that coffin, knowing the sensory deprivation would only heighten my sixth sense. I could only imagine what kind of messed up energies might inhabit a funeral home!

What was I thinking, letting Jereme use me for bait? I tried to relax as dark thoughts swirled through my head. Then, my partner turned out the lights.

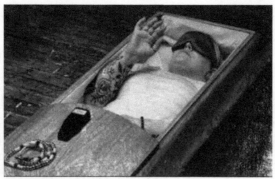

Brandy's Funeral Experiment

Brandy's Funeral

Jereme began reciting my eulogy. I can't believe I agreed to attend my own funeral! With the headphones on, I couldn't make out the words, but as he spoke, I felt the presence of children draw near. The REM pod suddenly pierced the air with a loud BEEEEP! The device's alarm was so shrill it was the only sound that clearly penetrated my headphones.

As if on cue, I detected a younger female energy descend from the ceiling and hover over me, reminiscent of my experience in the cooler at Waverly Hills. Opening myself up more, a deep melancholy washed over me. I sensed that something traumatic had happened to her. And the perpetrator was male.

I called out, "Who are you?"

A startling vision of blood flashed in my mind's eye. So much blood! Blood-soaked beds and blood-splattered walls dripping with gore. It was a veritable slaughterhouse. I had to force myself not to look away, to try and uncover as much as possible about the mysterious tragedy. I needed to know what we were dealing with here.

There were multiple victims, including children. My heart ached with hers.

Floorboards creaked around me as Jereme paced the room. The REM pod continued to scream.

I put my hand over my chest to calm my racing heart as the energy above me drew closer and closer until the young woman's face was mere inches away from mine, staring right into my eyes! To my surprise, it was the older daughter from the photo who I saw in my initial vision. What could be so important to make her come to me a second time?

I listened carefully, hoping she would reveal why she was here.

But she was silent.

The spirit above me didn't seem malevolent. Instead, she felt more like a lost soul seeking help. I reached out to her, trying to communicate. Although she didn't speak, she was able to relay the message that something tragic had happened, not just to her but to her family.

I tried to probe for more details, but our communication was suddenly cut short when a strong male presence neared the casket. Although I couldn't see him, I could sense the darkness in his soul. A fiery anger lurked just beneath the surface. I did not like this new energy at all.

Then he came closer.

The REM pod shrieked again and the female spirit flew toward the ceiling and faded away.

"Jereme, somebody is standing at the head of the coffin," I shouted.

My pulse quickened as the REM pod went berserk. Did the gentle female energy that floated above me get scared off by this powerful male energy? The child spirits that I felt earlier also seemed to have vanished.

"Something just touched the top of my head!" I shouted.

It's bad enough when I hear or see otherworldly things, but I hate to be touched by supernatural entities. If something can do that, then what can't they do?

The ominous male presence multiplied. Was he summoning other dark entities from the underworld? I felt them all around me. In my mind's eye, I saw these men in black suits and black Quaker-style hats encircling me, tightening the noose. There must've been fifteen or more! Most of them had lengthy beards, and one had shoulder-length hair. I could tell they were together, like members of some kind of order or even a cult.

My sense of claustrophobia heightened, and I began to hyperventilate.

I cried out to Jereme.

But just when I thought I might lose my mind, the Men in Black began to retreat, as did the powerful male presence at the head of the coffin who touched me. Jereme told me afterward that the exact moment the energies backed off was when he started praying.

As he called upon God's highest protection, I suddenly felt three of the most angelic beings hovering over me, surrounded by blinding white light, like guardian angels. The divine beings were so beautiful and comforting it brought tears to my eyes. God had answered Jereme's prayer for protection.

It was like I was five again, and the Man in White and the Dingy Man were dueling over my soul. The Men in Black continued their retreat but didn't leave willingly or entirely. I could still hear them repeating a two-word mantra over and over again.

"Get out. Get out!"

The dark spirits surrounding me made it abundantly clear that they wanted us to leave this place and never return. This was *their* domain, and *we* were the intruders.

"Why do you want us out?" I shouted.

Hearing the fear in my voice, Jereme finally made the call to end the experiment for my safety.

"That's it," he said, "Let's get you out of there."

He turned on the lights and came over to help me out of the coffin.

Removing my blindfold and headphones, I wiped the tears from my face. After a deep breath, I let it out slowly, trying to calm my anxious breathing and racing heart. That was one of the most intense experiences I'd ever had investigating. I was still shaking when Jereme pulled me out of the coffin.

Although the experience was terribly stressful, it did give me better clarity about the family haunting this location. It also proved that a potent force did not want us here.

I later found out that everything I had sensed during our investigation mirrored experiences others have had here. Visitors have reported hearing faint whispers that grow deafening the longer they stay. Many have also reported being touched or poked by the ghosts of disfigured women or children.

Having survived our first emotionally exhausting investigation, I readied for bed. Opening my journal, I started documenting the experiences and discoveries of our 28-day experiment.

My first night's sleep at Madison Dry Goods was horrible. Our "bedrooms" were no more than mattresses on the floor, separated by a cubicle partition to give us each some semblance of privacy. Privacy is nice, but I told Jereme I couldn't sleep like this. It made me nervous not being able to see what was going on around me. It didn't help having just been stuffed into a coffin.

Jereme agreed, and we removed the partitions. As we lay there, we talked into the night about what we'd just experienced and what spiritual battles might still lie ahead. I tried to fall asleep, but every time I closed my eyes, I'd get visions of blood and bodies lying on autopsy tables. At the time, I didn't understand why I saw dead bodies splayed open on tables, but my visions made sense once I found out that the room we were sleeping in used to be the funeral home's embalming room!

We stayed awake practically all night until we both finally passed out from sheer exhaustion.

DAY 2 – Buried Secrets

Unknown to us at the time, a crucial part of the 28 Day Cycle occurs on days two through seven. Once the dark entities realize that visitors are not going away, the activity ramps up in an attempt to force the intruders to leave. This is when many psychological and spiritual attacks happen.

It's been reported that during this period, spirits will take advantage of any moments of vulnerability, like when people become exhausted, scared, emotional, and when they are most vulnerable—once they fall asleep. Unlike typical investigations where teams might only spend a few hours at a location, we were locked down for 28 days straight and had to sleep here, too!

The longer I stayed here, the more I became convinced that the family in the photo and their story were connected to this place. After last night's experience in the coffin and seeing the young woman floating above me, I retrieved the photograph to examine the family again. As soon as I laid eyes on the picture, I knew I was right. The oldest daughter in the photo was the same face I saw hovering over me in the coffin!

As I held the photo, the oldest daughter showed me visions of blood *everywhere*. There was a sense of shock that something traumatic had transpired. She was weeping. I empathically felt her depression, as well as the fear and pain coming from the children. It was so overwhelming.

Moved by their distress, I desperately wanted to help this family. And if that wasn't incentive enough, as an empath, their pain becomes my pain. If I have to deal with these bleak emotions every day for the next 28 days, I'll go mad.

There was another energy here that did not want us prying into the violent mystery behind the haunting. And the energy was powerful. I sensed additional energies who didn't want us poking around here either. And quite frankly, I was scared because I didn't know if I could handle one, let alone a dozen or more!

As I thought about last night's investigation, I recalled feeling that the oldest daughter wanted to tell her story. Because of her strong desire to communicate, I thought it would be a good idea to use my mediumship abilities to reach out to her tonight to see what we could uncover.

When I commune with spirits, it's more than just interrogating them. It's about building an emotional connection. I hoped that if I could do that with the oldest daughter and make her feel safe with me, then she might be more willing to divulge their family secrets, how they relate to the tragedy that occurred, and why those dark entities are trying so hard to keep those secrets buried.

* * *

On our second night investigating Madison Dry Goods, we returned to the funeral parlor. With our initial success here, it only made sense. But this time, I was not getting inside a coffin. I sat and took a deep, cleansing breath. Clearing my mind, I reached out to the oldest daughter and asked her to come to me.

"It's okay, you don't have to be scared," I assured her.

After a few minutes of trying to connect with her, I heard the oldest daughter say, "We always had to pretend that everything was happy and okay at home." And that "We always needed to put on our best faces whenever we went out."

She went on to tell me that she was tired of the charade. I thanked her for opening up to me. The next thing she said, however, gave me the chills.

"The baby."

I kept hearing those words over and over, as if on a loop.

"The baby. The baby."

Was the young woman's spirit telling me that she was with child? I got the impression she was hiding a family secret she wasn't allowed to tell anyone. She projected a sense of total helplessness.

"But why," I asked?

"I told my dad I was pregnant."

She began showing me a vision of her father stomping up the stairs, anger in his eyes. Then, all of a sudden, I saw blood splattered everywhere.

As I relayed all this to Jereme, a dark energy crept toward me from my right. Then came another from my left. Then another. The Men In Black were surrounding me again. I must be getting close to something.

Their circle continued to close in around me. They seemed intent on preventing the young woman from exposing their secrets to me.

I switched my focus to the Men in Black. These dark entities seemed to descend from the attic. I also detected that they had some kind of connection to the father. I swear, those beings possessed some of the darkest energy I'd ever felt.

The spirits here had likely held onto these secrets for over a hundred years. And the dark energies did not want those hidden truths to come out. But how far would they go to keep me from uncovering their dark secrets?

Suddenly, my back was on fire! It was like someone had pulled a white-hot poker from a fireplace and shoved it into my back. Or was it a branding iron? I cried out to Jereme.

But he was struggling with his own issues. Jereme described it as goosebumps crawling all over his skin. His head began to throb like he was coming down with a migraine.

Then, as soon as it began, the pain was gone.

I knew now that there had to be more to the story than what had been revealed to me so far. I also knew that I needed to continue strengthening my connection with the oldest daughter if I was ever going to find out what that was.

Throughout our time at Madison Dry Goods, whenever Jereme and I investigated the connection between this place and the family in the photo, I would feel those same shadowy forces creep downstairs from the attic.

I told Jereme my suspicions about where the dark entities seemed to be originating from. He suggested that before we did anything else, we should focus on investigating the attic.

That's easy for him to say. He wasn't seeing what I was seeing.

I knew we'd have to explore the attic eventually, but I wasn't ready. I was still trying to recover from my funeral! As much as I dreaded going up there, I knew it was just a matter of time before I found myself in the attic. But, God help me, not today.

DAY 3 – Sleepless in Madison

I t was 4 a.m. and I still couldn't sleep. My energy was high from the full moon. The place was extremely restless to-night. The biggest challenge so far was just trying to sleep with all the paranormal activity around me. I'm not used to sleeping without the radio, TV, or some sort of white noise to block out the voices and the whispering spirits trying to contact me. Especially since we were sleeping in a former funeral home!

I finally managed to doze until about 6 a.m. when something startled me awake. I glanced around the room, not sure what had interrupted my sleep. I looked over at Jereme but he was fast asleep.

Since I couldn't sleep, I figured I'd tune into my surround-ings, hoping to gain some additional insight into the mystery we were brought here to solve.

Be the building, fill the building.

As I listened, I was surrounded by random noises: floor-boards creaking, heavy, disembodied footsteps, women whis-pering. Were these voices quietly gossiping about the dark secrets they didn't dare share publicly? I heightened my focus, hoping to glean something about this tragic mystery.

I heard more chattering, some male, some female, all indeci-pherable.

The walkie-talkie abruptly erupted in a blast of white noise. It startled me so badly that I nearly fell out of bed! I was defi-nitely awake now.

Somehow, Jereme had managed to sleep through the squawk from the walkie-talkie, so I decided to let him continue sleeping since he was awake most of the night, too. With my heart still racing from the walkie-talkie, I thought it might be safer to wait for Jereme to wake before opening myself up to the spirits. There was no way I wanted to face them alone.

I got out of bed and tiptoed over to the makeshift shower they provided for us. They chose this second-floor area for the shower because it already had a drain in the floor. Why, you may ask? This area used to be the embalming room, and the former funeral home used this drain to empty the bodily fluids from the deceased as they prepared them for burial.

If I had known this when we arrived, I probably wouldn't have showered until I got home!

After my shower, I grabbed a quick bite, kicked back in our base camp, and let my mind wander. Before long, I felt something reaching out to me, drawing me toward the area I'd been avoiding... the attic.

The door to the attic was in the corner of the big room used as our base camp. A door we always kept closed. Subconsciously, I felt that if I kept the door shut, the evil entity hiding up there wouldn't come down from the attic. But realistically, I knew supernatural beings couldn't be restrained by doors or even walls.

Since the very beginning, I felt a dark and possibly demonic energy lurking up in the attic. That old wooden door was like the elephant in the room. In a way, it reminded me of the portal I had in my former basement. Even when I wasn't looking at the door, I felt something watching me.

I thought about what Jereme said. And I knew he was right about our need to investigate the attic. I nervously glanced over at the door. Was it curiosity or a sense of duty drawing me to the attic entrance? Or something on the other side? The thought made me shudder.

Despite the pull from the other side, I resisted the urge to open the attic door. We had 28 days to finish our investigation, right? Plenty of time to investigate the attic.

And I was in no hurry.

It felt like it had been two weeks already, but we'd only been here 3 days. North Carolina in August was miserably hot. At least they gave us two AC units and a fan. But since we were constantly being recorded, we could only have the air on when we weren't investigating or talking, so pretty much only when we were sleeping. Or at least trying to. Welcome to the glamor of Hollywood!

DAY 4 – Ghosts Never Sleep

I t was 3 a.m. as I lay in bed, staring at the ceiling. Sadly, this was becoming the new norm. My mind drifted back to my family. I couldn't believe how homesick I was already. In some ways, it was nice to get away from my part-time job and taking care of the kids, but I missed my babies so much!

At 6 a.m. I was still awake. The whisperers had returned. I listened intently but still couldn't make out what they were saying.

Around 7 a.m., I heard heavy boots clomping across the hardwood floor. I glanced around to see if Jereme had gotten up... but he was still in bed, sleeping.

I closed my weary eyes again, trying to shut out the voices. As I lay there, I saw a vision of the mother in the photograph, her tears raining down on the baby in her arms. A lump formed in my throat as she gently kissed her baby's forehead.

"Hey!" I jumped, hearing an angry man's shout.

My eyes popped open, and I sat upright. I glanced around the room, but no one was there except me and my sleeping partner. My heart was practically beating out of my chest as I called Jereme and woke him up.

"Did you hear that?" I asked.

"Hear what?"

"You didn't just hear that man yell?"

Jereme looked at me with his sleepy eyes. "The only person I heard yelling was you," he said, giving me one of his signature smirks.

I shot him a dirty look.

Now that we were both awake, we decided to get up and go outside to grab a smoke together. I surveyed the street, hoping to spot a man out on an early morning walk who could have been the one who shouted earlier. But no one else was around. Looking up and down the empty main street, I felt as if we were dropped in the middle of a ghost town. The town we were in dated back to 1818, and it showed.

Jereme said he felt like somebody kicked his butt. He plopped down onto the bench with a sigh. I knew how he felt. This lack of sleep and constant onslaught of negative energy was taking its toll on both of us.

After we finished our cigarettes, we went upstairs and lay back down. I desperately needed to get some sleep. Closing my eyes, I took a deep breath and let it out slowly, trying to clear my mind.

We couldn't have been lying there for more than five minutes when I heard a man and woman arguing. The woman's voice seemed to be the more prominent. Frustrated, I determined to see if I could debunk the disembodied voices I kept hearing.

After searching the whole second floor, I still came up empty. No radio. No television. No hidden speakers. The walkie-talkie and spirit box were off. I looked out the window but couldn't see anyone milling around. I couldn't find any natural explanation for what could've generated those voices. The only answer left was something... supernatural.

Jereme and I decided that doing a quick spirit box session might provide some clues. I powered on the spirit box and listened as it scanned through the frequency spectrum. The speaker hissed static, punctuated by occasional cracks and pops but no coherent messages, at least at first.

"Is there anything that you'd like to tell us?" I asked.

Just then, a voice interrupted the static.

"Help!"

I glanced at Jereme to see if he heard that. Then another voice came through.

"Murder!"

Great, now we're getting paranormal activity during the day, too! Despite what you see on TV and in the movies, where supernatural events only seem to manifest at night, if a place is haunted, you can experience activity any time of day.

The disturbing truth is that *ghosts never sleep.*

People, however, do need sleep. It's 8 a.m., and Jereme and I are both wiped out. We're having a terrible time figuring out how to handle all this negative energy around us. We knew we'd be watched/recorded by the cameras 24/7. But we soon discovered that they weren't the only watchers.

I desperately needed to get some sleep or else I was going to lose my mind. We turned off the spirit box and I did my best to block out the energies around me. I thought that if I turned the fan back on, the white noise might help drown out some of the voices and other uncanny activity.

Somehow, we managed to crawl back into bed and fall asleep for a few hours. Since we'd been investigating every night, we usually didn't wake up and start our days until around eleven. Since I didn't get to sleep until eight this morning, we slept until about 2 p.m. After that, I got up, ate some cereal, and stepped outside for a smoke.

The energies here seemed to be getting stronger by the day. I spotted shadow figures lurking in one of the rooms, where I later discovered they used to perform autopsies.

Now, on our fourth day of no phone, no TV, no internet, and no sleep, I was mentally drained. None of the walls had a clock on them, and we were starting to lose track of what day it was. The only way to mark time was to monitor the rising and setting of the sun.

At this point, all we did each day was eat, sleep, plan, and investigate. Since we investigated every night, we tried to brainstorm during the day, hoping to find some new approach that might help us solve the mystery of these strange hauntings.

I wasn't eating much by now. The anxiety made my stomach hurt and stole my appetite.

The walls seemed to be closing in. We felt isolated even when we stepped outside the front door for a smoke. We'd been told not to leave the area in front of Madison Dry Goods. They wanted us to stay by the windows because cameras were aimed at us even out there.

We learned later that we had a crew of about 13 producers & workers behind the scenes. But we didn't see any of them unless they were changing batteries or needed to fix the remote cameras or microphones. Even that didn't last long as they quickly decided to just drop off batteries and train us how to change them. After that, we couldn't expect to see another living soul!

They asked us to make a weekly grocery list and leave it at the front door. Then, our note would disappear, and a little while later, boxes of food would magically appear on our doorstep. I wish I could get this kind of service at home!

As I began to reflect on our time here, I realized how much I'd pushed myself already. I'd spent the night in a funeral home, lain in a coffin, and even acted out my own funeral. I was nervous to see what lay in store for me next!

The producers were fantastic throughout our 28 days here, though. I heard that one of the Netflix producers came and watched us for the first 3 days from another building. No pressure! Fortunately, she said that she thought what Jereme and I were doing was fantastic!

The producers contacted us today and asked that we take a break for about three hours to do a video diary session. They wanted to review what we had experienced so far and have us explain some things they had seen and heard on the recordings. They designated a separate room for this, but we were only allowed in there for special calls and video-logging sessions.

After our call, Jereme and I brainstormed what to do for tonight's investigation. The hard work and late-night hours were already beginning to pay off.

Tonight's investigation was especially fruitful. I received confirmation from the spirits about many of the things that I intuited. During this session, the spirits revealed that multiple people died during the violent events I'd only seen flashes of in my visions. I also sensed that there had been sexual abuse among all the other tragedies.

Today was so overwhelming and exhausting that I finally fell asleep before sunrise for a change.

DAY 5 — The Vampires

oday, we slept a lot. I reached out to the oldest daughter again for a while. I feel like I'm really beginning to gain her trust. I get to know her a little better each day, it seems.

We're now adding daytime investigations since the activity here isn't confined to after dark. This was new to me as I usually performed paranormal investigations at night.

Now that we'd been here for almost a week, I kind of forgot that we were constantly being watched and recorded 24 hours a day. Noticing a red LED from one of the cameras reminded me that cameras and microphones were mounted in every single room of the building except the bathroom.

When I mentioned it to Jereme, he laughed and said, "Yeah, they're even filming my damn ass crack!"

I laughed so hard I snorted like a pig!

We started to refer to the night producers as vampires since we never saw them, but we knew they could see us.

We ended up sleeping most of the day today and mostly took it easy. I guess you could say that we took a mental health day. We desperately needed some time off to rest. This was our first night without an investigation and it felt good to take a break. I'm sure the vampires were glad to take a break, too.

DAY 6 – New Nightmares

I was now experiencing strange dreams every night, and it was driving me crazy! It's like the spirits here were invading my thoughts day and night. There was no escape!

In tonight's dream, I dreamt I was in a rowboat with the oldest son from the photograph. I was relaxing in the back of the boat and enjoying the warm sun as he rowed down a slow-moving river. It was weird; it kind of felt like we were on a date. I gazed at the sun reflecting off the water and delighted at the fish breaking the surface and flipping their tails in the air.

Then, the mood changed. Dark clouds gradually formed overhead, choking out the sun. The sunbeams peeking through the trees were replaced by ominous shadows. The sun's reflection on the river's glittering surface faded, and the crystal-clear water grew dark and stagnant. Suddenly, fish began breaking the surface all around us, floating belly up, judging me with their dead, milky eyes.

A man shouted from the bank of the river, chastising us for wasting our time out here. He berated the young man for flittering away his afternoons, lecturing him that he needed to focus on his schooling and not be distracted by giddy young girls.

The eldest son paddled away from the man shouting from the riverbank, trying to put distance between us. The man continued shouting after us. Who was this angry man, and why did he care what we were doing? I glanced back at the shore and my heart almost stopped cold when I suddenly realized the person chasing us was the father from the photograph!

191

DAY 7 – Making Contact

I have to admit, I wasn't sure I would last a week here. But here we were on day seven, down but not out. We had made some progress, but we knew we had to keep pushing if we were going to get to the bottom of this mystery.

After breakfast, Jereme asked what I thought we should do tonight. The direction my energy drew me to most was the second floor, particularly the former funeral home's viewing room at the end of the hallway. And I needed to know why.

By now, I was confident the father had killed his family. But what I didn't know was why? There seemed to be a dark presence in this place, blocking me.

I decided it was best to focus on the mother's energy next. If I could communicate with her, she might be able to assist me in understanding why the father killed his family and enable me to help her and her children find peace. As a mother myself, our maternal bond may help the mother spirit trust me enough to reveal what happened to her family.

Before I opened myself up, I could already tell the spirits would be very active tonight.

I decided to incorporate the REM pod again to make it easier to communicate with the spirits. Jereme wanted to wait outside in the hallway and let me work one-on-one with the mother's energy. He was concerned that a male presence might hinder my efforts to communicate with her if her husband had indeed massacred his family.

While in the hallway, Jereme offered up prayers to make the mother feel safer and more willing to connect. Jereme liked to use scripture as a form of protection for us. On the flip side, reading from the Bible often provoked evil entities, so he cautioned me to be on guard. He stressed the importance of putting any evil spirits here on notice to let them know that we have no intention of backing down or leaving until we get the answers we came for.

Reading scripture helps differentiate whether we're dealing with spirits of light or spirits of darkness based on their reaction. If these were dark spirits, they usually either lash out at you or leave immediately. I hoped it would be the latter.

As Jereme began reading from John 14:27, the REM pod triggered, lighting up and sounding the alarm.

"My peace I give to you; not as the world gives do I give to you. Let not your heart be troubled, neither let it be afraid. Amen."

This seemed to do the trick, letting the family's spirits know we were there to help them. The mother's spirit came near and sat next to me. A feeling of peace washed over me. All of a sudden, I felt her hold my hand!

Having made a psychic and physical connection, I felt confident she would answer my questions.

"What happened?" I asked her.

She didn't answer at first. Perhaps the question was too vague. I tried a different tack.

"Can you tell me why you are stuck here?"

I listened, but again, there was no response. Frustrated, I decided to just ask her directly.

"Did your family get murdered by their father?"

There came a loud thump, and the REM Pod screamed to life.

"Did you hear that Jereme?"

"Just keep doing what you're doing," he said. "I've got things under control out here."

"If you're the mother energy, can you turn that light off for me?

The light on the REM pod went off.

"Thank you. If you're the mother energy, turn that light back on for me."

Right on cue, the REM pod lit up and beeped again. I had my answer.

Jereme stepped into the room and sprinkled holy water as he made the sign of the cross to keep the evil spirits at bay so I could continue communicating with the mother.

Her spirit kept pointing me to the two children's caskets in the room.

"Were these your two small kids?" I asked. 'If so, please turn off—"

Before I could finish my sentence, the REM pod went silent.

"Are you keeping them safe from their father?"

The REM pod signaled again to confirm that her answer was yes. Now for the big question that I'd been struggling to get answered.

"Do you know *why* your husband killed your family?"

The REM pod lit up.

A vision of the oldest daughter flashed in my head. And she was pregnant. Was the mother trying to give me the final clue? I had to know for sure.

"Did the murders have something to do with your daughter being pregnant?" I asked.

A loud knock sounded in the room, making me jump. My throat began to tighten as if I was being choked by an invisible hand!

As the negative energy ramped up in the room, I felt the mother's energy fading.

Jereme began to pray. "Spirit of our God—"

Another resounding knock came from the other room, cutting him off.

I leaped to my feet and ran into the hallway with Jereme.

He prayed louder in a deep, commanding voice. "Spirit of our God: Father, Son, and Holy Spirit, most holy Trinity; descend upon me! Please, purify me, mold me, fill me with yourself, and use me."

My knees gave out, and I dropped into a nearby chair. The stranglehold finally released.

"Vanquish all forces of evil from this place!"

A loud boom shook the floor.

"Destroy them!" he shouted.

"Jereme," I yelled. "Don't you hear that?"

"Don't let me stop," he warned. He knew the prayer was working and didn't want to quench the Holy Spirit's work.

"Destroy them!" he continued. "Vanquish them!"

Bang! The room shook again, rocking my chair. I nearly tipped over. That was it. I was done. I jumped up and bolted down the hall as Jereme continued his prayer.

The closer I got to discovering the secrets about the fate of that family in the photograph, the more I became the target of the dark forces in this place. The secrets had been buried for so long that the prospect of us uncovering them seemed to make the evil spirits all the more hostile. And all the more dangerous.

I had to get out of the building for my own safety and sanity.

Once outside, I grabbed my cigarettes, lit one, and took a deep drag, hoping to calm my nerves. Several minutes later, Jereme joined me.

The bench outside the Madison Dry Goods building became the closest thing to a safe space I could find. Jereme and I came out here whenever we needed a break from the darkness inside. We must've smoked a pack a day out there.

As we smoked, we shared a bit of group therapy, trying to process the recent paranormal attacks. Don't get me wrong, I've experienced some crazy shit before. I've had vinyl records fly across the room and shatter next to me at an abandoned Psychiatric Hospital. I've had physical encounters with the spirit realm where I was pushed, had unseen hands yank on my clothes, and even choke me. Believe me, I've seen and heard many terrifying things.

But being on the front lines where Jereme engaged in spiritual warfare was incredible and frightening to watch. The way he used prayer and scripture to combat the dark forces. Then, to hear the loud knocks and feel the floor shake as the creatures of the night fought back against the light with the REM pod shrieking in the background became too much for me to handle. Mainly because I just didn't understand everything that was going on.

I knew that we were getting close to a deep, dark secret. And the closer we got, the more it seemed like something was doing everything in its power to keep us from uncovering the hidden truth. Whether this entity was the father or not, I don't know, but we needed to get to the bottom of this to understand what we were up against.

When Jereme utilized the power of prayer, the dark entities always seemed to increase their attacks on *me*. For some reason, they weren't going after Jereme. And each attack they waged against me appeared more potent than the last. The only reason I could come up with was that I must be getting close to some truth the dark energies didn't want revealed.

DAY 8 – Calling it Quits

I t was 1:00 a.m. and I'd had enough of this place. I'm becoming convinced that the energy tormenting us here is *not* human. Any time Jereme prayed in the name of Jesus, something made me feel sick and dizzy. There was no doubt in my mind that a spiritual battle was raging behind the scenes. I hated to be in any of the rooms alone for fear of being outnumbered and possibly getting jumped by an evil spirit.

Hours passed, but I still couldn't bring myself to go back inside.

Jereme and I remained outside the entire night, smoking and talking, trying to make sense of everything, and doing our best to convince ourselves to stay. It was so bad in there I wanted nothing more than to run screaming from this place and never return. I hadn't slept for days, and it had taken a major toll on me.

The lack of sleep had sapped all my energy, and my nerves were frazzled from living in a haunted funeral home from the 1800s. It was such a rollercoaster of emotions. Just when it felt like we were making progress and on the verge of a major revelation, dark forces would rise and shut us down.

I missed my home and my kids terribly. I never anticipated how hard this would be.

Last night was the worst experience yet. I seriously wondered whether I could handle all this, physically and mentally. I knew I needed to push myself, but it's so damn hard. And we still had 16? 17? 20 days left? I had lost track of time at this point.

197

It was all so disorienting. I had no idea what day it was. The days blurred together. Hell, everything had become a blur.

The sun rose slowly over Main Street, setting the rooftops afire. When the clock in the town square struck 8:00 a.m., I was still looking for answers to what I should do. I wasn't naive enough to believe that if I went back inside, their attacks would magically stop. If anything, they seemed to be progressively getting worse.

What seemed to be taking the greatest toll on me was the entity upstairs where we slept. The constant attacks robbed me of sleep and depleted my energy, which left me vulnerable to even more attacks.

Normally, once the sun rose and dispelled the darkness from the previous night, my mind was renewed with the hope of light and a new day. A chance to reset and start anew. But in this place, each day proved darker and more difficult than the last.

Exhausted from over a week of (not) sleeping on the second floor of Madison Dry Goods, dealing with the constant whispering, shouting, disembodied footsteps, and being touched by invisible hands, I finally went inside and told Jereme that I'd decided to tap out.

He was surprised and extremely disappointed, but he understood what I was going through.

"If you really don't think you can handle it anymore," he said, "you should do what you gotta do."

Without having a decent night's sleep in over a week, I was physically, emotionally, and mentally drained; I just didn't think I could go on. I finally broke down, grabbed one of the walkie-talkies they gave us in case of emergency, and told the person on the other end I wanted out.

The voice on the other end told me to sit tight and someone would come talk to us and try to work something out.

Before long, an SUV pulled up outside and producers Tom and Jeff got out. They came inside the shop and attempted to talk me off the ledge.

"I'm done," I told them. "I can't take it here anymore."

Worried I might bail on them, they decided to break out the big guns and got the head of their production company, Mark, on the phone.

"Listen," I told Mark, "you didn't tell me I would be locked in a funeral home! There's no way I can survive 28 days in this place without sleep."

Mark's voice was calm and soothing. He was honest and sympathetic to my situation.

"Brandy," he said, "I need you. Without you, we don't have a show. What can we do to help you?"

After I calmed down a bit, I felt terrible. I didn't want to ruin the show for Jereme and everyone else, but I also didn't feel like I could stay here any longer the way things were. The second floor (site of the former funeral home) was just too active for me to get any rest. The sleep deprivation was stealing my energy, my focus, and really messing with my head.

Not wanting to be the first one to tap out, I finally asked him if there was any way we could move our beds down to the first floor, where the energy was lighter. If we could sleep downstairs, there might be a chance that I could make it through the second half of the investigation.

"Will that make you feel better?" Mark asked.

I figured it was at least worth a shot. What did I have to lose, except for maybe my sanity? If they were willing to make this accommodation, I told them that I would try and stick it out.

The relief in Mark's voice was palpable. He thanked me profusely for hanging in there and told me to let him know if we ever needed anything.

I handed the phone back to the producers, who also looked relieved the drama was over.

For now.

We said our goodbyes, and once again, it was back to just me and Jereme... and the spirits haunting the place.

As I headed toward the stairs, I paused, realizing that Jereme wasn't following me.

"I ain't going upstairs by myself!" I told him.

Jereme just smirked and shook his head, "All right, Brandy." Then, he reluctantly accompanied me up the stairs.

I determined to stick it out here but swore I'd never do this again. Jereme and I headed upstairs to tackle the arduous job of moving our beds downstairs. We pushed the mattresses to the edge of the staircase but they were too wide to fit. We ended up having to flip them on their sides and then slide them down the stairs to the first floor.

After clearing space for our mattresses next to the staircase, we plopped down, hoping to finally get some sleep since we'd been up all night. Moving downstairs did seem to help. The energy felt much lighter on the first floor. For once, I wasn't hearing voices or footsteps all around me. But, with the large storefront window, it was also a lot brighter, making it harder to catch up on sleep during the day. Fortunately, I still had my trusty blindfold!

We rested for a few hours, then got up, ate, and just relaxed for the rest of the day. The last week had taken a major toll on us mentally and physically. We had investigated every single night so far and never got to sleep before 2 or 3 a.m. Hopefully, this recharge would help us recover and get back to investigating.

✳ ✳ ✳

After a good day's rest, Jereme and I felt recharged and ready to resume investigating again. With the rollercoaster emotions of quitting and then being convinced to stay to finish our investigation behind us, I was starting to feel better. It's amazing what some rest can do for you.

Tonight's investigation turned out to be a monumental one. The highlight was when Jeremey finally connected with the father's energy. Was it because they could speak man to man or father to father? Or did the energy identifying itself as the father think it could use the male connection to influence Jereme? I wondered who was actually manipulating whom?

By 2:30 a.m. Jereme and I had called it quits on the night's investigation. We returned to our home base on the second floor and sat at the table to review our recordings for any possible EVPs.

As we reviewed the audio and chatted, we ended up disagreeing over what we heard and the proper way to communicate with and dispel the negative energies haunting the building.

Jereme comes from a staunch Catholic background, unlike myself. Despite my belief in God, I'm not particularly religious. Early on, my mother instilled in me a faith in God. Every night at bedtime we prayed and thanked God for all he'd given us and asked for His guidance and protection. As a teenager, I connected with God on a deeper level, thanks to a good friend who invited me to her church. I can't imagine trying to combat evil spirits in a place like this without drawing upon the almighty creator of us all.

Jereme and I agreed to rely on the power of the Holy Spirit to fight our battle against the unholy spirits. But I'm not big on the traditions and practices of any particular religious denomination. I find those differing traditions, introduced by men over the centuries, end up dividing us more than uniting us. The power to overcome dark spirits and demons can only come from God, not a church. Without God, we are no match for Satan.

Whether it was our arguing that suddenly energized the negative energies around us or the other way around, I don't know, but I felt the atmosphere change in the room. Suddenly, a jolt of energy surged through me as if I'd stuck my finger in a light socket! It was almost paralyzing. A split second later, we watched in astonishment when something slid across the table!

Totally freaked out seeing things moving on their own; there was no way I was staying in that room another minute.

"I'm out of here!" I shouted and headed for the stairs. It was late, and we were both tired, so Jereme agreed to call it a night. He didn't want to admit it, but I think he was freaked out, too.

As we finally settled into our beds, closed our eyes, and prepared for a well-deserved night's sleep, I heard footsteps walking around above us. I did my best to ignore them, just grateful that we were downstairs now.

Just as I was about to finally doze off, the REM pod sounded upstairs. I cursed under my breath, realizing we'd left the REM pod on when we were investigating upstairs earlier.

Now that we were in our beds, neither of us wanted to go back to the second floor to turn the REM pod off. But we knew that if the spirits were restless again tonight, we would never get any sleep, with them continually triggering the alarm. We were also afraid of what we might find if we went back up there.

I made a deal with Jereme that I would go over to the stairs with him if he retrieved the REM pod. After he got halfway up the stairs, I chickened out and snuck back downstairs and into bed. He didn't realize what I did until he reached the top of the stairs and turned to talk to me.

"Damn it, Brandy!"

I couldn't help but bust out laughing, But then I started thinking. If Jereme turned off the REM pod, how would we know if any dangerous entities tried to sneak downstairs?

I'll admit, I was a bit nervous about our first night sleeping in the store area, not knowing what to expect down there. But with the lighter energy at street level, I did feel more at ease. It was as if we were surrounded by a bubble of protection.

I yelled up to Jereme and told him my concerns, and he agreed to leave the REM pod on the top step, just in case any evil spirits decided to follow him. Sure, it might not stop them, but it would at least give us an advanced warning if anything tried to creep downstairs and attack us in our sleep.

After tossing and turning for another hour, we finally fell asleep around 4:30 a.m. I guess it wasn't just the producers who had turned into vampires.

DAY 9 – Tragic News

At 5:30 a.m., the REM pod at the top of the stairs screamed to life. Jereme and I jumped out of our beds and hurried to the staircase to investigate. Just as we reached the bottom of the steps, the REM pod went silent. We stood there for a moment, watching and listening. Footsteps echoed across the wood floor above us.

As we stared up at the second floor, a shadow darted across the top of the landing as if something or someone had just run past, making me jump. The REM pod screamed, and so did I.

"Back off!" Jereme yelled upstairs. "You stay up there!"

The REM pod went silent again, but we remained on high alert.

Jereme and I waited at the bottom of the steps, expecting the REM pod to light up and sound the alarm again. But the restless spirits seemed to have calmed down. Perhaps Jereme's threat and the realization that they couldn't sneak up on us had warded them off.

With the activity seemingly over for now, we decided to head back to bed and catch up on our lost sleep. As I slept, I dreamed I'd written a book. The cover was dark navy blue and pink. Don't ask me why it was blue and pink! But it got me thinking. Maybe after this crazy experience, I could finally get around to writing the book I'd always dreamed of writing about my life as a psychic medium. Spending a month in a century-old funeral home would make a great addition to my life story!

It's so exciting to see this dream finally come true, with the help of my friend and author, Bryan Prince. I really couldn't have done this without him. But there was one thing he was adamant about when taking on this project: the book would not have a navy blue and pink cover. Whatever!

I finally awoke at two in the afternoon. The place was quiet except for Jereme's deep breathing. I got up and cleaned the kitchen before fixing myself a simple breakfast.

Heading to the front door to grab my morning smoke, I noticed that the *vampires* had brought us more groceries and some games. Was this a peace offering for agreeing to stick it out?

I finished my cigarette and took the supplies inside. Waking Jereme, I went through the groceries while he checked out the games. Jereme announced each item as he took it out of the box.

"Looks like they got us cards, Jenga, and…" he pulled out a colorful box and started laughing.

I glanced over and couldn't believe my eyes.

"Twister? You gotta be fucking kidding me!" I said, busting out laughing. One of the producers must have a really warped sense of humor. But I have to admit. It did help lighten the mood in here, even if it was only temporary.

Once we finished eating, we went outside for another smoke and chatted for a while. Finishing my cigarette, I stubbed it out and turned to go back inside when I discovered a gray and white feather on the sidewalk. It's been said that a gray and white feather represents a sign of change and an omen that new situations are coming and should be embraced, not feared. Maybe things were starting to look up after all!

❋ ❋ ❋

About an hour later, the producers surprised us again and came knocking at the door. Until now, they had stayed in the background to avoid interfering with our process. So why come out of hiding now?

Something didn't feel right. What if something terrible happened to one of my kids. I'd never be able to live with myself if something tragic occurred while I was away. It's my job to protect my children, and here I was chasing this silly dream when I should've been there, watching over them!

At first, I was afraid to let them in. But if the news was time-sensitive, the longer I delayed, the worse things could get. I nervously unlocked the door and let them in.

The serious looks on their faces made me even more nervous. I could tell they weren't here to bring us good news. My intuition soon proved to be correct.

They came to tell us that Jereme's wife called. A hurricane was ravaging the area in Louisiana where he lived, and there had been damage to his house. They gave Jereme his phone and allowed him fifteen minutes to talk to his wife.

Since Jereme was getting to speak with his wife, the producers felt it was only fair for me to get fifteen minutes of phone time, too. But when I turned my phone on, it practically blew up with all these text messages. Messages alerting me that my good friend and owner of the 6th Precinct in Detroit, Ed Steele, had died.

I burst into tears. Ed was the sweetest guy. We had developed such a wonderful friendship since we first met at the abandoned police station he was restoring. So many great memories flooded back to me.

Todd, Jeff, and I had investigated the 6th Precinct many times since forming Detroit Paranormal Expeditions. Ed was so passionate about that place. He'd devoted his life to restoring the historic landmark. What would happen to the 6th Precinct now that he was gone?

I managed to pull myself together and stared at my phone. Only 15 minutes to talk to everyone I missed and wanted to talk to? I felt like a prisoner whose jailer had given them their one phone call. I desperately wanted to call my kids, but I knew once I heard their sweet voices, it would be over. My heart hurt just thinking about them.

Ed's demise still weighed on my heart as I read through all the missed texts from my friends. The first message I read was from Austin Maynard, then Joe and Tonya Posey from Unknown Paranormal of Detroit. They were friends I met while conducting paranormal tours at Eloise Psychiatric Hospital. They all knew Ed well, having investigated the 6th Precinct with me many times. I decided to call them, knowing how much they must also be grieving. Hopefully, they could shed some light on Ed's passing, and we could comfort each other.

As soon as they answered the phone, I broke down in tears. I told them I didn't think I could finish the full 28 days here. With my separation anxiety, missing everyone so badly, all the frightening paranormal activity, and then to add the death of a close friend who I couldn't even mourn together with friends, I just didn't see a way through.

But as good friends do, they cried along with me. They also encouraged me, telling me how strong they knew me to be and made me believe I could see this to the end. And after much consoling and coaxing, they ultimately convinced me to stay.

Before I knew it, my time was up, and the producer was motioning for me to surrender my phone. I felt like a prisoner whose family visitation time was up. And with that, I was once again disconnected from everyone I held dear.

That night, Ed Steele came to me in a dream.

I dreamed of walking into the 6th Precinct for one of our many paranormal events. When I entered the jailhouse, Ed greeted me and smiled.

"How are you here?" I asked him, incredulous. "You're dead!"

His smile broadened, and he assured me, "Everything will be all right."

His message of hope brought me to tears. When I awoke from my dream, I sat up and discovered my cheeks were still wet.

DAY 10 — Attic Attack

O n day ten, I stood at the door leading up to the attic. I had purposely put off going into the attic as I sensed something evil lurking up there. But I knew that I couldn't avoid exploring the attic indefinitely. Eventually, I'd have to face my fear and investigate the final unexplored area of Madison Dry Goods. I took the family portrait with me as a trigger object, hoping it might help me connect with the oldest daughter's energy and possibly other family members who'd yet to come forward.

Jereme followed, carrying one of the digital video cameras. As I opened the attic door, the hinges shrieked, warning us not to proceed.

Whenever I investigate a location, I try to go wherever the energy leads me. And in the Madison Dry Goods building, the strongest, heaviest energy appeared to be emanating from the attic.

So, the attic it is.

The stairs creaked and groaned as we ascended, cautioning us with each step to beware of what awaited us above.

Reaching the dust-blanketed attic, I turned on my audio recorder to document any potential EVPs. Making my way to the center of the attic, I sat cross-legged on the wooden floor. The hot attic air was stale and suffocating. I wasn't sure how long I could tolerate it up there.

Closing my eyes, I reached out to whatever spirits might be in the attic. The energy around me was palpable.

BAM! I was startled by a loud knock to my left. I turned to look, and although I couldn't see anything, I definitely felt their presence.

"If you are over there," I announced nervously, "can you step forward, please?"

After a moment, I felt a female energy approach and sit next to me on the floor. It was the oldest daughter.

To my surprise, she began bringing members of her family forward, one after another, as if to introduce them to me. The youngest kids all lined up to my left. As I matched each of them with the photograph, I noticed that one family member was conspicuously missing. The father.

I extended my psychic feelers in search of the father until I finally detected his faint energy. It seemed afar off but gradually grew stronger as it drew closer.

Suddenly, the children scattered, running in a desperate effort to hide. But I got the awful feeling there was no escape.

Bright flashes in my mind as shots rang out. BLAM! BLAM! The children disappeared one by one with each blast. BLAM!

Everywhere I looked, there was blood. So much blood! It was as if someone was systematically murdering the whole family!

Suddenly, the smoking shotgun barrel was leveled at me. I traced the length of the barrel, up the shooter's weathered hands and blood-spattered sleeves, and finally up to the killer's scowling face. To my utter shock, I found myself staring at the father from the photograph.

BLAM!

I recoiled as a vision of the shotgun blasting me back into the wall flashed in my mind! I gasped, seeing the buckshot blow a gaping hole in my chest, painting the wall behind me red. Then, I watched in horror as my body slowly slid down the wall, leaving a bloody streak in its wake.

Was something trying to tell me it wanted to do that to me? Or was I vicariously reliving someone else's death?

The vision left me nauseated and shaking. After witnessing this family's bloody massacre, I took a deep breath to calm my nerves. But before I could relax, Jereme shouted.

"Oh, shit! There's someone coming up the stairs!"

Something to my left kept shouting, "Get out! Get out!"

I sensed that whatever was coming toward us was not in human form.

"I need you guys to come closer to me," I told the children's spirits, trying to gather and shelter them like a mother hen. "Don't let the energy push you back. Please, I need to communicate with you."

The negative energy in the attic continued to escalate. Something was trying to stop the family from talking to me.

Suddenly, an icy hand grabbed me by the throat! I forced out a choked, "Oh my God!"

Something evil had invaded the room. And it definitely was not human.

It took everything I had to repel the attack. Finally, I managed to push the entity away, releasing its chokehold on me. "What the fuck?" I shouted.

That was the last straw. I jumped to my feet. "I'm done," I told Jereme and bolted for the stairs. There was something much more dangerous in this attic than the family of spirits I'd been communicating with. Connecting with spirits was one thing, but demons? Hell no!

Some serious shit was going on in that attic, and I wanted no part of it. That's not what I signed up for. At this point, I didn't care what the producers said. I didn't even care if it meant I wouldn't get paid. You couldn't pay me enough to confront demons.

"This is the last time I come up here," I told Jereme. I realized then that we were dealing with something far more dangerous than the spirit of a homicidal father, as if that wasn't bad enough!

I was already exhausted and sick of the isolation and separation from my family and friends. I felt totally beaten down. This was a dangerous state to be in when dealing with evil entities that not only wish to manipulate you but to harm or even possess you.

The dark spirits in this place did not want any more secrets divulged. And I feared they would do whatever they could to mess with our heads to get us to leave. And this was after only ten days! What would it be like by day 28?

Once we returned to our sleeping quarters downstairs, Jereme managed to talk me down off the ledge and convinced me to stick it out a little longer. By this time, it was after midnight, and I was too tired to argue.

DAY 11 – Caged Animals

After ten days of persistent torment in this place, I was utterly exhausted. I've never felt so tired in my life. Do you have any idea how hard it is to sleep when you're constantly hearing voices? And then to be startled by mysterious footsteps creeping up on you? Frightened, you open your eyes... and nothing is there. You close your eyes and try to go back to sleep, only to be awakened by a disembodied spirit yelling at you.

I've struggled to sleep ever since the onslaught in the attic. I wanted to continue investigating the top floor, but the longer I stayed there, the more intense the spiritual energy grew and the more disturbing the visions. It finally got to be too much to endure. If I spent any more time up there, I feared for my safety and my sanity.

The family, who I'm now convinced was killed by their father, sees me as a beacon of light for them. Now that they knew they could communicate with me and finally be heard, they won't let up. The problem with ghosts is that they never sleep. Time's relative to them.

I wasn't sure if these spirits were stuck in a supernatural loop and reliving their murders over and over or if they were just trying to warn me about the dark tormenting them here. It was also possible that they just wanted their story told. As a psychic medium, I feel that's my job, so I'm reluctant to just ignore them.

I'm doing my best to push through for the sake of those victims, for Jereme and the other investigators, and for the sake of the show. There's so much riding on finishing what we started.

I've tried to sleep whenever possible because I need all my strength to deal with the spirits here. They are like psychic vampires, draining me of my energy to manifest themselves. But the stronger they get, the weaker I get. And that can be extremely dangerous. If my energy is depleted in any way, it can open the door for them to begin mentally and physically manipulating me. Or even worse, possess me, which is my biggest fear!

It was 6:00 a.m., the sun was coming up, and people were already walking around outside. With us investigating at night, our days and nights were flipped. During the day, people liked to walk the street and window shop. Now that we'd moved our beds downstairs, it was like we were in a zoo, and Jereme and I were the newest attraction.

Growing tired of feeling like caged animals, Jereme made a "Buy Me" sign and held it up to the window shoppers! I laughed so hard. These were the kinds of things we did to pass the time and to try and keep our sanity.

The producers scheduled another video interview with us to catch up and discuss how the investigation was going. The call lasted for about two hours. After that, we decided to take the rest of the day off.

Nearly two weeks into our lockdown, I missed my home more than ever. With all this downtime, I've had plenty of time to think about my life and where I'd like to take it next. I've become more determined than ever to write my book. I have a lot of other goals I'd like to achieve after this experience as well. My energy here was as good as it could be lately, especially now that we were downstairs.

This investigation has been the most challenging of my life. The unorthodox schedule is really taking some getting used to. It's difficult breaking up an investigation into daily sessions. It's a lot of stop-and-go instead of one continuous exploration like I'm used to. I'm accustomed to starting a paranormal investigation and working straight through until we finish inspecting a location, even if it takes until morning. But then we're done. It's hard keeping track of all the daily investigations and evidence, especially when it comes while we're trying to sleep!

Fortunately, we have a whiteboard to help us keep track of all the paranormal evidence and spirit interaction, so we can hopefully connect the dots and ultimately piece this mystery together.

Second floor Base Camp

DAY 12 – Reflections

I sat on the bench alone outside, writing in my journal and drinking coffee. It felt good to escape the haunted halls of Madison Dry Goods. It was also nice to experience a brief respite from being locked down with Jereme. No offense to my new friend and partner, but we're running out of things to talk about, and I miss my family and all my Michigan and Ohio friends.

I'm proud to be living out my dream to be more than just a mom, not that being a mom isn't one of the most important and fulfilling things any woman can do. But this has been, without a doubt, my greatest life challenge since losing my mother. It's been nearly a month since I've interacted with anyone or anything from the outside. This has definitely been an intriguing journey. I'm not used to spending so much time alone with my thoughts.

As I reflect on things, my thoughts always return to my kids, wondering if they are all right. The production team on this show has been great. I'm going to miss them once this is all over. But I won't miss this place.

I have no idea where this journey will take me next, but I'm always up for any challenge that will further me in life. It's important to me to show my kids that anything is possible if they believe and put in the necessary work. There's no limit to what you can do in life if you keep working toward your goals. I mean, look at me! I went from being a stay-at-home mom for 17 years to becoming a world-renowned psychic medium on TV. It all started when I stepped out of my comfort zone and risked putting myself out there as a paranormal investigator, and look where I am now!

Although I've been part of paranormal investigation teams before, here I was, stepping out on my own for the first time without a safety net or familiar friends to guide and help me through this adventure. It's wild to see myself here, filming a TV series. After binge-watching Netflix all these years, I never could've dreamed that one day I would be one of the stars of a Netflix series that would become one of the top 5 shows in America and the world!

It's so satisfying to reflect on all the haunted places I've investigated and the many TV appearances I've added to my resume. I'm forever grateful and humbled by all the fantastic opportunities that have come my way. And after this, I believe the sky is the limit!

When I get home, I have to visit Ed Steele's gravesite. I miss him already. I had a premonition that something terrible was going to happen while I was gone. But I didn't know what. When I learned that Ed had passed, it felt like my whole world came crashing down. He was my buddy. I used to call him "the handsome man." Whenever we investigated the 6th Precinct, he would come out to greet me with a big hug, and I'd always say to him, "There's that handsome man!" And he would give me the biggest smile. God, I miss him.

I cherish the time we spent together and the bond we developed. He was the sweetest man I've ever known. So generous and caring. I will always hold him close to my heart. Spending all this time here makes me miss and appreciate everything from my everyday life so much more.

In addition to getting confirmation from the spirits here of what I've intuited, getting positive feedback from the production team has really helped build my confidence. I wasn't sure what to expect, but everyone I've spoken with on the production has told me how much they loved my work. They especially liked how naturally I expressed my emotions and how authentic I seemed. I said to them that's just who I am. I don't know how to be any other way. I'm not an actress, believe me. And that's one of the things they liked best—I wasn't trying to put on a show or embellish things.

When I look scared, it's because I am! The reactions you see are genuine. That's not an act. I'm sure plenty of skeptics out there think all these paranormal shows are fake. But I'm telling the truth when I say everything I've done here has been the real deal. The same goes for every investigation and event I've ever done. I told the producers up front that I don't believe in faking things. And as a psychic medium, I don't need to. I experience crazy shit all the time. As I always say, my abilities are a gift from God, but they often feel more like a curse.

The producers complimented me on my work ethic and professionalism. They said they loved interviewing me because I spoke with raw emotion that others could feel and see. Of course, that's probably because I don't have a filter!

I doubt I will ever do another project like this again, even though it was a powerful learning experience. It's been extremely taxing on me, sequestered here for a month, away from everyone I love. I do want to do more shows, don't get me wrong, because I enjoy my work. But next time I travel for a TV project, I'd like to be able to take my kids with me.

It would be extra special for my skeptic father to see me in action and witness firsthand what a paranormal investigation was like. I know he would also enjoy the TV production side of things. Although, with 28 Days Haunted, the cameras and microphones were hidden, so it didn't feel like we were shooting a TV show.

I would love for my dad to see the woman I've become. For him to appreciate all I've accomplished as a professional psychic medium and realize that I am more than just a hobbyist. To finally see that I'm not just the little girl he's always seen me as.

Reflecting on my time here, I think about how much I'm anticipating the last day when I can finally go home. But at the same time, I'm already feeling a bit sentimental about leaving this place. It's been my home for so long now, 24/7. I look forward to taking whatever pictures we can before I go to help commemorate my time here. I'm sure it sounds strange after all the stress, terror, and discomfort I've been through, but I suspect that after I'm gone, I will look back on this place and my experience here fondly. Time seems to have that effect.

* * *

It was now 2:00 a.m., and once again, I couldn't sleep. I'm outside on the bench again, writing. My body's circadian rhythms are all off, and I'm still on the vampire shift. I love being outside at this time of night, though. With the scorching North Carolina weather in August, it's nice to get out of the stuffy building and enjoy the cool night air for a change. The streets are empty, and I'm alone with my thoughts. At least, I was until a black SUV slowly cruised down the street.

I looked up, a little nervous, until I saw the silver logo on the door. It was a police cruiser. Every night, the police came by, patrolling the area. I can't imagine they get a lot of crime or disturbances in a small southern town like this.

The cruiser rolled to a stop in front of Madison Dry Goods, and a policeman, who looked to be in his 60s, stepped out. He hitched up his gun belt, strode around his cruiser, and sauntered over to me.

"Evening, ma'am," he said in his thick, North Carolina accent.

"Evening, officer," I answered tentatively, wondering why he stopped.

"Mind if I ask you a question?"

"Sure," I said, my curiosity was piqued. And it wasn't like I had a lot going on at the moment.

"Are y'all here looking for ghosts?" he said with a sheepish grin.

I laughed and told him we were just here doing a project, trying to be as vague as possible.

"So you're not?" he asked and smiled. I knew he was reading my body language. And I could tell he didn't believe me. "So it's just a 'project,'" he added.

I had to smile. The officer obviously knew more than he was letting on.

"Yep."

"I was told y'all were here," he admitted with a chuckle.

I just smiled. We weren't supposed to talk about the project, and I'd already signed a non-disclosure agreement to that effect.

"I heard there were a lot of ghosts here," he said and raised his eyebrows.

I chuckled to myself, thinking, *You got that right, buddy*!

Word travels quickly in these parts. In a small town like this, where everybody knows everyone, people tend to take notice when out-of-towners show up with their Yankee accents. Apparently, the townsfolk had seen cameramen filming locations around town and exterior shots of Madison Dry Goods, which roused everyone's interest. Plus, one never knows when they might get discovered by Hollywood!

After some small talk about the weather, and once he realized that he wasn't going to get anything out of me, the officer bid me a good night and continued on his way, leaving me alone with my thoughts once again.

* * *

Today would've been my good friend Ed's funeral. I hate that I'm unable to make it. It's eating me up inside. But I know that Ed would understand. That's just the way he was.

I still can't believe he's no longer with us. He was the last person who deserved this. He was such a loving and caring person. Like how he always sent me songs he thought I might like. I miss his big bear hugs, calling him handsome and seeing how his face would light up, and just hearing him chuckle. God, I'm gonna miss that man. I started this journey with Ed, and now I'll carry him with me to the end.

I finally decided to go inside around 7 a.m. as downtown started to come alive. Seeing the sun come up always made me feel better, and safer, knowing I'd survived another night. Plus, the energy inside usually seemed to settle down after sunrise. Light truly does dispel the darkness. In more ways than one.

Just as I was getting up from the bench, Jereme rushed outside in a panic.

"The spirits are everywhere!"

"Wait, what are you talking about?" I asked.

"The spirits! They're everywhere!" Jereme said again.

Did he just wake up from some crazy nightmare? Were the spirits rallying for their final stand? Or was Jereme in the throes of a mental breakdown?

I tried to calm him down, but he was out of his mind with fear. I'd never seen him like this. Up until now, he'd always been the one trying to talk *me* down off the ledge and trying to convince *me* not to quit.

The dark forces were breaking him down, and now *he* seemed to be the one ready to tap out.

"Now you know how I feel!" I said.

I did my best to keep Jereme's agitated state of mind from affecting me. It wouldn't be good for us both to be freaking out. Up until now, Jereme had been my rock. I guess it was my turn to return the favor.

After we finished our cigarettes, I managed to help Jereme calm down. I'm sure the nicotine didn't hurt, either. I reminded him we were in this together, and I had his back, no matter what.

We still had, what, ten days left? It was so hard to keep track of the days now. It felt like this lockdown was never going to end. It was like the COVID lockdowns all over again! But we both made commitments to see this through to the end.

It looked like it was about to storm here. I could smell the ozone in the air. For us, that can be good *and* bad. On one hand, it tends to heighten all my abilities and strengthen my connection to the spirit world. On the other hand, it also empowers the spirit energies since they can feed off the electrical current from the lightning and the static electricity in the air. Plus, water is a natural conductor, making for a perfect confluence of energy. For good and bad.

I decided that I'd better try and get some sleep now. It looked like tonight was going to be a pretty active one.

DAY 13 - Tobacco Room Investigation

Thanks to the calming rhythm of the rain, I could finally get some sleep. I awoke around 3:00 p.m. and glanced over to find Jereme snoring away. I decided to get out of bed and clean up a bit. If I don't, who will? Even here, I'm the mom.

After washing the dishes, I kicked back and contemplated the day ahead. I hate just sitting and doing nothing. I'm usually always going between work, kids, readings, and investigations. But there isn't much to do here when we aren't investigating. What am I supposed to do, sleep all day? So far, I've been lucky to get three to four hours of sleep a day since I've been here.

Without kids to take care of (unless you count Jereme, who sleeps most of the time now) and no phone or internet for distraction, I'm beginning to get stir-crazy with boredom. I glanced at the games on the table, but they all required at least two players. Still exhausted and unable to think of anything better to do by myself, I decided to go back to bed and catch up on some of the sleep I'd missed.

I woke again around 6:00 p.m. and saw that Jereme was still asleep. After staring at the ceiling for a while, I dozed off again.

I finally woke up for good around 9:00 p.m. to the sound of Jereme talking upstairs. It sounded like the producers were interviewing him. I stayed downstairs so I didn't interrupt their recording. After several minutes, they ended the interview, and Jereme came back downstairs.

223

Jereme lamented how tired he was and how he didn't have any energy. It's like a repeat of this morning where he's threatening to tap out, and I'm the one striving to convince him to gut it out. It's strange seeing our roles reversed. But I guess it's better than us both wanting to tap out at the same time.

"We've only got about a week or so to go," I told him. "We got this!"

"I don't know, Brandy."

"You just think you're tired because you're bored," I said. "C'mon, let's plan our next investigation.

For some reason, I find myself drawn to the Tobacco Room on the second floor.

"Why don't we investigate up there tonight?"

Jereme sighed, "All right."

"It's settled then," I said, holding my hand out for Jereme to shake. "Tonight, we investigate the Tobacco Room."

* * *

We began the night's investigation around 11:30 p.m. I was still so drained. I can't wait to leave this place. I'm sure I'll be up until sunrise again. I really am turning into a vampire!

It's a lot like being a police officer—hours of boredom punctuated by moments of sheer terror. But we agreed to do this job, so I'm determined to do my best and push through until the end.

We wanted to pull out all the stops tonight and incorporate all the various equipment we might use during a typical paranormal investigation. We needed to capture everything possible if we hoped to solve this mystery.

Jereme set up a video camera aimed into the Tobacco Room to capture any visible manifestations that might arise. We both grabbed a digital recorder to capture EVPs. That way, if one of our recorders failed, we'd have a backup. It's common for spirits to drain a device's batteries to use that energy to communicate or even materialize. Hopefully, we'll capture something with two digital audio recorders and the audio from the video camera.

This time, we also introduced a new plasma spirit box device. Not all spirit boxes are the same. For example, some scan frequencies forward, some backward, and others contain a prepopulated database spirit energies can pull words from. A couple of the spirit boxes we used at Detroit Paranormal Expeditions, which have given us some of the best results, were custom-made out of wood from known haunted locations. The thinking was that haunted artifacts act like a magnet for spirit energies.

What's different about this spirit box is the addition of a plasma disk. The plasma disk reacts whenever energy touches it or draws near enough to its surface. When this happens, the plasma disk indicates the direction the spirit energy is coming from by displaying bolts of electricity across its surface. Plasma disks and spheres also produce energy that spirits can draw from to gather enough strength to communicate or even manifest themselves. These devices are based on technology originally invented by Nikola Tesla.

For tonight's investigation, I decided to make another attempt to communicate with the father who murdered his family. In our previous investigations, I connected with the oldest daughter and mother energies. Based on those encounters, I've concluded that the father murdered his wife and his children. But I also sensed that there was still more to the story. During tonight's investigation, I hoped to find out for sure whether there was a connection between his daughter's pregnancy and the murders.

I took a seat in the Tobacco Room - a small room decorated with dried tobacco leaves and what appeared to be tobacco farming paraphernalia. A single bare bulb hung from the ceiling, casting the room in a dim yellow glow. I nervously scanned the vintage artifacts decorating the Tobacco Room and was startled to find a pitchfork and a scythe. Having vinyl records hurled at me was one thing, but sharpened farm implements was quite another!

Jereme fired up the spirit box as I reached out to the father.

"I need to speak with the father energy," I announced.

I waited for a response, but all I heard was static.

"Are you with us right now?"

A man's voice came through the spirit box.

"Uh-huh."

I looked at Jereme to see if he heard it. He raised his eyebrows.

As the spirit box continued to fill the room with white noise, I glanced around me for any sign of his presence.

And to make sure the pitchfork hadn't moved.

Opening myself up more, I reached out to the father energy, hoping to connect. Suddenly, I heard the hollow sound of boots walking across the wood floor.

"Did you hear that?" I asked Jereme.

The footsteps continued.

I stood up, and Jereme cautioned, "Brandy, no... no." He worried I might try to take this entity on by myself.

"I'm not," I assured him.

"Are you walking around us?" Jereme asked. It was quiet for a moment. "Walk around some more if you're with us."

The footsteps returned.

"Who is that?" I shouted. "I need to know!"

At first, there was no response. 'Please, I need to know."

A voice pierced the static from the spirit box and said, "Charlie."

Jereme and I gawked at each other.

"Did you say your name was Charlie?" I asked.

A haunting, raspy voice answered through the spirit box, "Chaaarles."

The hair on my neck bristled, goosebumps rising on my arms.

Jereme gasped. "Holy shit!" he said. "Charlie? Charlie, listen to me."

BOOM! Something upstairs apparently didn't want Charlie talking to us.

"Charlie?" Jereme continued. "Did you just make a noise upstairs?"

I reached out to the father. "What would cause you to do something so horrible to your family?"

Jereme grabbed his head. "Oh my God!" he shouted. "I've got a freakin' headache all of a sudden." Jereme started rocking, obviously in great pain.

"Charlie? I need you to stand back." I said.

A voice from the spirit box said, "Out."

"You want us to get out?" Jereme asked, still grimacing from the pain.

Could this really be the father from the photograph? Or was something else trying to manipulate us? Whatever or whoever it was, I could tell it was powerful.

Why were we drawn to the Tobacco Room? The answer to this mystery came later when we discovered that the father had been a tobacco farmer. And his name was Charlie Lawson.

Jereme attempted to provoke this entity to reveal itself so we could see exactly what we were dealing with. It's hard to know for sure since demons often masquerade as the spirit of someone who died to trick us into lowering our guard so they can manipulate or even possess us. Jereme reminded me about the verse in 1 John 4:1, which tells us not to believe every spirit.

Losing sight of this is dangerous. The devil isn't called the "Father of Lies" for nothing.

I decided to try a different tact. "The faster we get answers," I offered, "the faster we can get out of here and leave you alone."

Something moved in the room. I jumped to my feet.

"Do you hear that?" I asked Jereme.

"Brandy, just wait right there. It'll be all right."

"That's easy for you to say!"

"Calm down," Jereme said. "This son of a bitch don't scare me."

"Well, it scares the shit out of me!"

And with that, I was finished investigating for the night. I'm not too proud to admit when I'm scared. And this place scared me shitless.

We turned off all the equipment, especially the plasma box since we didn't want to give the dark entities here enough energy to wield the pitchfork or scythe. Then, we retired to the workroom to review the evidence we'd captured. With the intelligent interaction we encountered through the spirit box, I couldn't wait to see what EVPs we might've captured.

When we went to play the recording from the first digital recorder, we discovered it was blank. I could've sworn we hit record on them both. Oh well, that's why we used two recorders. We turned to the second recorder and... it was blank, too! Was it possible that we both forgot to turn them on? It's not unusual for spirits to completely drain batteries and mess with electronic devices, so I guess we shouldn't be too surprised. But we'd had so much interaction tonight that I thought we must have captured something.

Fortunately, we still had the audio and video from the camera and wireless microphones they made us wear all the time. I wondered what kind of EVPs the microphones caught up till now.

* * *

By 1:00 a.m., Jereme was already asleep. I hated to say it, but it's all he seemed to do anymore. I was doing all the work here: cooking, cleaning, and even performing most of the investigation work by myself lately. It was getting to the point where I just wanted to tell him that I wasn't his momma or his wife and that he needed to start cleaning up after himself.

I was at a loss to know what to do. It was like something was wrong with him. I don't know if he was just sick of being here, if he had a medical condition, or if the dark entity here had gotten ahold of him and stolen all his energy. But something wasn't right.

I lay awake for a few more hours, mentally rehearsing what I wanted to say to Jereme. Maybe after a long night's sleep, he would be more energetic in the morning.

Left: Tobacco Room Right: Haunted Hallway

DAY 14 - Hallway Investigation

I tossed and turned most of the night, but at least Jereme seemed to get a solid night's sleep. We took it easy most of the day, just trying to re-energize for another late-night investigation.

Tired of being blocked by the dark energy haunting the upstairs, I decided tonight I would go for it to see if I could finally get the answers I needed directly from the father. I had to figure out what would drive him to murder his whole family.

Since I was able to get the spirit who identified himself as Charlie to communicate through the spirit box last night, I figured there was a chance tonight might finally produce the breakthrough we needed. But I must admit, I was terrified because I had no idea what this spirit was capable of.

Jereme and I set up REM pods in the second-floor hallway, along with the spirit box. The box we chose tonight was a customized radio designed to rapidly scan multiple frequencies, creating primarily white noise. Paranormal experts believe spirits can manipulate these devices to commune with the living. I don't totally understand the science behind it all. But my DPX team and I have had some spectacular success using our spirit boxes to prompt intelligent responses from spirits at many locations using them.

I was still exhausted from only a few hours of sleep last night, so this may not have been the best time to connect with the spirit of a potential homicidal maniac. I felt completely drained, spiritually, which makes me incredibly vulnerable. But I needed to keep going if we wanted any chance of uncovering the truth of what happened and why.

"Can you light up one of these lights," I asked, "or move something around for me to let me know you're here?"

After the words left my mouth, I nervously surveyed the hallway to ensure no pitchforks were around.

The room was silent except for the static emanating from the spirit box.

"Who is the head guy here who keeps standing in the middle of the doorway?"

I still wasn't getting anything.

"You made yourself known to me last night," I reminded.

Still nothing.

It was Jereme's turn now. He wanted to test the spirit of Charlie to see if it was evil or even demonic. He began reciting a prayer of protection over me from Isaiah 43. If we were dealing with a dark entity, this would likely provoke it to react.

"When you pass through the waters, I shall be with you," Jereme read. "And through the rivers, they shall not overflow you. When you walk through the fire, you shall not be burned, nor shall flames scorch you. For I, the Lord, am with you."

As Jereme read from scripture, I started to feel strange. The more scripture he read, the angrier the energy in the room became.

He then transitioned to reciting the Lord's Prayer.

The air around me grew heavier as if the room was filling up with water and I was sinking deeper and deeper.

Jereme began another prayer, determined to provoke the dark forces to reveal themselves.

My head now felt like it was being squeezed in a vice.

"Let not your heart be troubled," Jereme prayed over me. "He will not forsake you."

I interrupted him, unable to take the pressure building in my head as the REM pod screamed to life.

"Please, stop!" I cried.

Jereme leaned over and laid his hand on my forehead.

I finally broke down and began to sob. As Jereme comforted me, I suddenly realized who impregnated the oldest daughter and why they didn't want me to know the truth.

A historian later confirmed my reading that, before the father murdered his family, it was believed that a dark secret was about to be exposed—the father, Charlie Lawson, had impregnated his daughter, Marie.

Once the secret was finally revealed, a voice shouted through the spirit box.

"Get her!"

I knew it was only a matter of time before we broke through if we kept at it long enough. But I wasn't naïve. I knew the dark energies haunting this place would likely retaliate if we got too close to their deadly secrets. And that chilled me to the bone. The more Jereme provoked them, the stronger they pushed back... AT ME!

But what should I expect? I'm a psychic medium in a freaking funeral home filled with negative energy and the spirit of a murderer!

I finally reached the point where I had nothing left to give.

Jereme rose with an intense look in his eyes. He shouted at the entity that called for the other spirits to get me.

"I guarantee that is not going to happen," Jereme said. "If you want to get to her, you're going to have to go through me!"

I was a total mess, tears streaming down my face. Everything was just so overwhelming. The full weight of my situation hit me all at once. What if this evil energy followed me home? Who's going to help me then?

Nobody!

The people behind the show get to go home after it's all over. They get to go on with their lives as if nothing ever happened.

Not me.

I've had to endure uncomfortable living conditions, separation from family and friends, sleep deprivation, haunting visions of blood and death, strange voices tormenting me all night, an evil entity choking me, and now, something just ordered evil spirits to attack me!

My tears devolved into sobs. Dealing with evil energies like this was no joke. There was no way I was taking this shit home with me and risking something horrific happening to my children.

Screw that.

The REM pod continued to shriek, the red LED shining steadily.

"Back off!" Jereme yelled.

"I'm tapping out," I finally told Jereme. "I'm done."

My mental and physical well-being was worth far more than some TV series.

We shut off all the devices and returned to our work area to regroup. When I went to take a seat, my knees were shaking so badly they just gave out. I told Jereme I didn't think I could do this anymore. This grueling experience had taken too big of a toll. And I knew it would only get progressively worse from here on.

To his credit, Jereme was very understanding. "I can't ask you to stay and put yourself at risk," he said. "That would make me responsible for whatever happens to you."

That put a ton of pressure on me because I didn't want Jereme to feel he had to leave because of me. Or worse yet, stay here by himself and take on these dangerous forces alone. If some negative energy or demon were to take him over, who's going to have his back?

Jereme looked me straight in the eye and said, "Don't worry about me."

* * *

It was now 3:00 am. Jereme and I escaped outside to get a break from the heavy energy and escalating activity. As we often did, we smoked and talked about the day and the craziness of the previous night's investigation.

By 4:30 a.m., we were still outside, deciding what to do next. I did not want to go back into that building. Jereme was conflicted. He sought to banish the evil energies in this place once and for all and help the family move on. But he admitted that he couldn't do it without me.

I was torn. I didn't want to run away because that's what the dark forces want us to do. Besides, I'm not wired that way. I'm a rebel and a fighter.

And what if we did hightail it out of here? Then what? My heart told me to stick it out, but my intuition said, "Run like hell!"

I concluded that whatever was attacking me, whether it was the father's energy or, even worse, something demonic, was also tormenting the spirits of this family in the afterlife. And I feared that if I left, the family would never get the closure they were seeking or ever be able to heal. And that put a lot of pressure on me.

So what do I do? I want to complete the task I was hired to do and help the Lawson family tell their story. And I longed to solve the mystery of who haunted Madison Dry Goods and why. I wanted to do all of that. But how do I do that without jeopardizing myself, Jereme, or my family?

The clock turned 5:00 a.m. I was still pacing outside and pulling my hair out, striving to figure out what to do.

By 6:00 a.m., the sun was coming up. I came to realize we were fighting a spiritual battle here. A battle that's taken a terrible toll on me. My body could only take so much. I was becoming physically ill from all this.

Jereme realized that I was the primary target here now that the energies knew that I could communicate with them. But he also knew he was just as vulnerable to their attacks. He may be a demonologist, but he's still a human being.

DAY 18 — Confronting Demons

W e took a break to rest and work up the courage to seek out the spirit identifying as Charlie. I'd had some success in the second-floor hallway, so we figured it would be an excellent place to start. Plus, I didn't want to step foot in that attic again.

As we mounted the stairs, my psyche was already telling me not to go up there. Jereme thought my approach of calmly questioning the entity calling itself Charlie wasn't likely to work. Jereme's plan was to directly provoke the Charlie entity to find out if it was indeed the spirit of the father from the photo, who we believed murdered his family, or if it was something demonic. Since Jereme was a demonologist, I let him take charge as this was his specialty.

The thought of connecting with "Charlie" terrified me. I questioned whether provoking this energy was a good idea. I feared we were playing with fire.

Against my better judgment, I powered up the spirit box and let Jereme take control. Whenever you work with a spirit box, it's critical not to take what you hear at face value. It could be a trickster spirit or something worse.

"I've come here to address the spirit of Charlie," Jereme began. Then, he quickly ramped up the provocation. "I want to know what kind of sick man would kill his entire family, including his own kids!"

Shit, here we go.

The spirit box reacted, but I couldn't understand what it said.

"You killed your entire family in cold blood! And if anyone deserved to die that day, it was you, Charlie." Jereme shouted.

I attempted a less confrontational approach, hoping a good cop, bad cop technique might prove more successful.

"Why did you do it, Charlie?" I asked.

"You know what, Charlie?" Jereme said, "You deserve to rot in hell for what you did."

BAM!

A loud noise shook the hallway. I felt the atmosphere change as darkness descended over the hallway.

"Brandy, get out of here!" Jereme shouted. "Go, please."

He didn't have to tell me twice. I bolted for the stairs. I had a sick feeling confronting this dark entity was a bad idea.

Now, it was Jereme's turn to be the target of attack. He abruptly doubled over, holding his head. "Get off of me!" he shouted.

I tried to watch from the upstairs landing. Whatever was attacking Jereme wasn't Charlie. This was a full-blown demon.

Jereme held out a crucifix and shouted, "In the name of God and by the cross and resurrection of Jesus, I say get back!"

I ran the rest of the way downstairs, terrified and shaking, not wanting anything to do with the battle ensuing upstairs.

"Get back!" I heard him repeat.

His pacing stopped, and I heard him groan.

"Jereme!" I called. 'Come down here!"

"Get off of me!" he shouted again.

"This shit ain't worth it to me," I mumbled.

The intensity in the building continued to escalate. There was still over a week left to go, and it was only going to get more dangerous the longer we stayed.

Paranormal expert and head of the Warren family estate, Tony Spera, told us that Ed and Lorraine Warren's 28-Day Cycle theory suggested that the veil became thinnest during this stage of the investigation. And, most frightening, this was also the point where we were most susceptible to demon possession.

If I had known this upfront, I would've tapped out long ago. Which is probably why no one told us ahead of time.

The pressure and pain finally became too much for Jereme, and he was forced to retreat, ceding this battle to the dark forces. But the war was still far from over.

DAY 20 – Troubles Can Cause

Jereme hasn't been the same since he provoked that entity in the hallway the other night. It's like he's been completely drained of energy. All he wanted to do was sleep. He's had absolutely no motivation to do anything.

Once again, it was Jereme's turn to talk about tapping out, which was somewhat ironic since I made up my mind to see this experiment through to the end.

"Well then, you can be the hero," he said.

His comment stunned me. Where did that even come from? It didn't sound like Jereme at all. Ever since that last encounter, Jereme was constantly complaining about headaches and just acting strange.

Not sure how to respond, I just glared at him as he sat at the work table, absently writing something. My curiosity got the better of me, so I snuck behind him to look over his shoulder at what he had written. To my surprise, I discovered a cryptic message hastily scrawled over and over again in his notebook.

TROUBLES CAN CAUSE

What in the world did that mean? When I asked Jereme where that saying originated, he replied, "Voices in my head."

Was he joking, or was he serious? Although I was afraid to ask, I needed to know. What if it was a clue?

"What do you think it's related to?" I asked.

He just shrugged and shook his head. 'I don't know."

"So you got this message from a voice in your head?"

"I've been hearing it for well over a week now," he said sheepishly. "It's probably nothing."

But I knew it was much more serious. The typically light-hearted Jereme was now angry all the time. He began complaining that *he* had to suffer because *I* couldn't sleep.

"Seriously?" I shot back, frustrated. "You've been sleeping for three days straight! All you do anymore is sleep or bitch about having to get up and work!"

That's the problem with being an empath. I was mirroring his anger. At the peak of my frustration, I finally blew my top and told him what had been building up inside me for weeks.

"You need to either man up or go home!"

I'd reached the end of my rope. Despite having investigated some of the most actively haunted locations in the country, I realized that I was not prepared for this. And the way Jereme was acting, I worried he wasn't either.

DAY 21 – 1 on 1 with Charlie

By the end of the third week, we had reached our limits. Jereme and I stepped outside to have a smoke and talk it out. It pained me to see Jereme's temperament continually spiral into anger and depression. I needed to know if he thought we'd reached a dead end in this investigation and, more importantly, whether he thought he'd reached that dark place where he might potentially harm himself or others. And seeing that I was the only other person here... that person would be me.

So I asked him point blank whether he thought that might be possible. His answer floored me.

"You're only asking because you're scared that I'll snap and kill you," he said with an unsettling smile.

Wow. I couldn't believe what I just heard. Jereme's behavior since our encounter with the "Charlie" entity had convinced me something more dangerous was happening here. Had a demon attached itself to Jereme?

And what if the same thing that caused Charlie to snap and kill his whole family was what was manifesting in Jereme? It was like I was living in a Stephen King novel!

Here I was, alone with a man twice my size who might be under the influence of an evil spirit. There's no way the producers, who may or may not be watching at the time, could get here fast enough to save me if he actually snapped!

Could a demon have driven Charlie to kill his family? And what if that same demon now possessed Jereme?

* * *

With my partner's strange and unpredictable state of mind, I chose to contact Charlie while he was sleeping. I knew it was a risk going one-on-one with Charlie, but if Jereme was being controlled by the same demonic entity Charlie was, I could end up outnumbered two-to-one. I decided it was better to risk confronting Charlie alone than to take them both on simultaneously.

I've been temporarily taken over by spirits several times as a paranormal investigator. And it's terrifying. If it wasn't for others intervening, I don't know what would've happened. Please, do not be fooled into opening yourself up to channel a "friendly spirit." There are no such things. If something wants to possess you, it's a demon.

After years of communicating with those who have passed on to the other side and facing demons who masquerade as them, I've learned how to close myself off and resist being possessed. But even after decades of experience, if a demon catches you in a weakened state, you are in big trouble. Remember, even at our best, we are still only human. Demons are fallen angels, far more powerful beings than us mere humans.

DO NOT TRY THIS AT HOME!

As I nervously set up in the second-floor hallway, the REM pod and spirit box would have to act as my paranormal investigation partners. These tools assisted my psychic abilities by confirming the messages I received internally. REM pods were excellent for getting answers to yes or no questions, allowing the spirits to interact with them and trigger the appropriate response. The spirit box was a great tool to elicit words and phrases and confirm what I intuited. It might also help provide new clues for our investigation.

As I turned the REM pod and spirit box on, I thought of my investigation partners over at DPX. I so wished Todd and Jeff were here with me right now.

"Hello?" I called out tentatively. "Charlie?"

A raspy voice exhaled through the spirit box.

"Can you come toward my energy?"

Looking back now, I must've been crazy to try this.

"Charlie? I have a question for you."

Something unintelligible broke through the static.

"Charlie? Was there a negative energy force that made you kill your family?"

I waited but got no answer. I pressed forward.

"Or even to make you sexually abuse Marie? If that's correct, can you make that red light go on for me?"

The REM pod lit up.

If true, this would be an incredible breakthrough. I had to confirm the signal from the REM pod wasn't random and that Charlie was indeed confirming the question.

"If I hear correctly, Charlie, you are saying something made you do this?"

A male voice came through the spirit box loud and clear.

"Yes."

I was blown away. It sounded as if I'd finally gotten to the root of the mystery of why Charlie Lawson killed his family. The voice from the spirit box further confirmed my suspicions.

"Evil."

Negative energy suddenly surrounded me. To my left, I felt something dark crawling across the floor toward me. Oh shit, what did I stir up?

The responses from the REM pod and spirit box seemed to imply that Jereme might be in danger. Could the same evil entity

that drove Charlie to kill his family now be attached to my partner?

I quickly ended the session and hurried downstairs to tell
Jereme what happened. I felt it was vital that he knew what this
Charlie energy was alleging. Was it possible that an evil force
drove him to commit those heinous acts?

When I came downstairs, I was shocked to see Jereme sitting
there, waiting for me. He had a strange look in his eyes. When I
shared the results of my solo investigation, Jereme's response
startled me. Raising his hand, he extended two fingers like devil
horns.

"Sweet. Rock and roll!"

Then he gave me a sinister wink.

No, there was nothing sweet about any of this. I've never
seen Jereme act this bizarre before. I had to walk away from
him. There was no longer any doubt in my mind that Jereme
was under the influence of something evil.

I didn't know what to do. I was at my wit's end. Something
was definitely wrong with him. But how could I be sure what? If
it was what I suspected, what could I even do about it? He was
supposed to be the demonologist!

"Oh, Lord," I prayed silently. "Show me the way."

What if my intuition was correct and Jereme was under the
same evil influence as Charlie? My very life could be in danger!
I finally decided to sneak away and contact someone from the
production team using one of the emergency walkie-talkies.

A short while later, Tom, the head producer of the show, arrived outside of Madison Dry Goods. I slipped outside without
Jereme knowing and told Tom about my partner's strange behavior and how I was sure it would not stop on its own. It was
something weird every day now, and I began to fear for my life.
I was forced to spend the bulk of my time sitting outside

because, when Jereme wasn't sleeping (which was most of the time now), he was acting aggressively. Both of these behaviors were significant red flags for me. We were dealing with something much bigger than us.

Although I didn't know it at the time, Tony Spera and Aaron Sagers were behind the scenes, monitoring the footage at each location. When Tony reviewed the recording of the last couple of days, he too was convinced that Jereme was in the oppression stage and likely influenced by a demonic entity. And with the oppressive state Jereme was in, Spera felt it was very likely it could lead to a full-blown demonic possession.

Actual demonic possession takes control of the soul (the mind and emotions) and even the body. It can produce physical illness and, at times, even criminal behavior. Jereme was demonstrating all the signs of early-stage demonic attachment, if not possession. This was as serious as it got. There was a spiritual battle raging inside of Jereme, and it was clear that he was in for the fight of his life.

Confirming Our Findings

To get a deeper insight into how evil forces may have influenced Charlie and to confirm what may have been going on in the days leading up to this father of seven snapping and killing his family, the producers got me in touch with local historian Trudy Smith. Smith authored the book *White Christmas, Bloody Christmas*, which chronicled the infamous Lawson family murders. If anyone would know about the homicidal father's behavior before the murders and had insight into Jereme's behavior now, it would be her.

The hope was to determine if Jereme could snap out of this oppression on his own or if we needed to take more drastic measures.

The producers set up a Zoom call between Trudy and me to discuss our current findings and hopefully provide insight into what we might be dealing with. I told her what I had already intuited and what I'd gleaned from the female spirits in the photograph. And how I felt a distance between the father and the rest of his family. I also relayed the visions of the father with a shotgun, the blood-spattered wall, and the blood pooled on the floor. Finally, I recounted the mental images of kids running and hiding from their mysterious stalker.

When I finished telling her all that I'd uncovered, Trudy confirmed every single one of my suspicions. Amazed, she recounted the tragic events that transpired nearly 100 years ago.

Bloody Christmas

O n a cold Christmas morning in 1929, tobacco farmer Charlie Lawson murdered his wife and six of his seven children. Those who knew the man said that in the months leading up to the murders, Charlie had been acting erratically. Lawson's brother later divulged that Charlie complained about sleepless nights and how he'd been suffering from blinding headaches.

Sound familiar?

His wife, Fannie, told others how she awakened one night to discover Charlie's side of the bed empty. Worried, she trudged outside looking for him, only to find him out in the cornfield on his knees, crying.

When she asked him what was wrong, he said his headache was so bad he couldn't bear it anymore. Once she finally convinced him to come back inside, he wiped the tears from his eyes and slowly got to his feet. To Fannie's horror, she discovered her husband had brought a shotgun.

Charlie was known for his temper and had experienced a couple of violent run-ins with locals. Fannie confided in close friends that her husband had become increasingly abusive in the weeks leading up to the "Christmas Surprise" that he'd been promising the family. Others had also heard whispers of ongoing domestic abuse, but in those days, most thought it best not to meddle in another man's family affairs. Especially not one with Charlie's violent history.

One of the strangest examples of Charlie's uncharacteristic behavior occurred shortly before the murders. Charlie gathered up his family and drove them into the town of Winston-Salem to buy all new outfits and pose for a family portrait. Quite unusual for a struggling tobacco farmer in the 1920s. Little did the family realize they were picking out their burial clothes.

Top Row: Arthur (19), Marie (17), Charles (43), Fannie (37) with baby Mary Lou
Bottom Row: James (4), Maybell (7), Raymond (2), Carrie (12).

On that fateful Christmas morning, Charlie and his oldest son Arthur had planned to go out rabbit hunting. After spending an hour or so plinking tin cans in the snow-covered yard, Charlie handed Arthur some money and asked him to go into town to buy more ammo for the hunt. While his son was away, Charlie gathered up his guns and the remaining ammo, then circled behind the tobacco barn to lie in wait.

Before long, Lawson's youngest daughters, Carrie (12) and Maybell (7), trudged through the crisp snow on their way to their Uncle Elijah's house to visit their cousins and exchange Christmas gifts. Charlie watched as his daughters came within range. Stepping from behind the tobacco barn, Charlie raised his Winchester .25-20 rifle.

Carrie lifted her small hand in a vain attempt to protect herself as her father pulled the trigger. The bullet traveled through her hand and blew a hole through her face.

To Charlie's dismay, the rifle jammed, giving Maybell a chance to recover from her shock and make a run for it. Afraid Maybell might get away and spoil the rest of his "Christmas Surprise," Charlie swapped the rifle for one of his 12-gauge shotguns. Before Maybell could escape, he blasted her in the back, lead shot tearing through her lungs, dropping the seven-year-old in her tracks.

Already low on ammo, Charlie chose not to waste any more rounds on his young daughters and instead grabbed a two-by-four from the barn. As his daughters lay bleeding in the snow, Charlie finished them off by bludgeoning them to death with the two-by-four.

Once the heinous deed was done, Charlie dragged his daughters' lifeless bodies into the tobacco barn and hid them from sight. In a bizarre show of sentiment, Lawson placed rocks under his daughters ' heads like pillows, crossed their hands over their petite chests, and closed their eyes as if laying them to their final rest. Lawson reloaded his 12-gauge and headed for home.

As he reached the house, Charlie found his wife, Fannie, on the front porch gathering firewood. Seeing her husband level the shotgun at her, Fannie dropped the firewood and turned to flee into the house. Before she could reach the door, her husband shot her in the back, literally and figuratively piercing her heart.

Inside the Lawson home, oldest daughter Marie had just finished baking a special Christmas cake for dessert, carefully decorating it with raisins. She'd set hair rollers next to the fireplace to heat up since she planned to attend a Christmas function at church later in the day with a boy she liked. Ironically, her suit-or's name was also Charlie.

Hearing the commotion from the kitchen, Marie rushed into the living room to investigate, followed by a neighbor boy who had stopped by earlier in the day. She swung open the front door, only to find her father standing over her hemorrhaging mother and holding the murder weapon. Marie backpedaled as her father stepped over her mother's body and followed her into the house. The neighbor boy bolted through the kitchen and escaped out the back door, not waiting to see what Marie's dad planned to do with that shotgun.

Marie pleaded for her life as her father fed another shell into the 12-gauge. With her mother's life bleeding out on the porch and her father reloading, Marie lunged for the fireplace poker. But it was too little, too late. Charlie shot his eldest daughter point blank, blowing a hole in her back large enough to see through.

The autopsy later confirmed that Marie's front teeth had been knocked out, and her neck was snapped. It's unclear whether these injuries were caused by the force of the shotgun blast propelling Marie face-first into the fireplace or if her father had bludgeoned her just like he had her little sisters to ensure their silence.

The clock on the fireplace mantle stopped at 1:25 p.m. But Charlie Lawson did not.

The two youngest Lawson boys, James (4) and Raymond (2) fled and attempted to hide from their father, hoping to avoid the same fate as their mother and sisters. But Lawson wasn't fin-ished doling out his "Christmas Surprise." James tried to hide under his parents' bed next to the fireplace, but his father grabbed hold of the toddler's leg, dragged him out from his hiding place, and bludgeoned him to death with the barrel of his shotgun.

Two-year-old Raymond escaped into the kitchen and hid behind the stove. Unable to reach the little child, Charlie kept shoving the barrel of his gun behind the stove to root the boy out of his hiding place. Terrified, his youngest son eventually ran out the other side. But before Raymond could escape, Charlie swung the shotgun, bashing his son's head in and sending him sprawling across the floor, just like the lad's older brother.

At last, only one other family member remained alive in the house: Charlie's four-month-old baby daughter, Mary Lou.

Charlie strolled over to the baby's crib, raised the bloody shotgun toward the ceiling, and drove the butt end of the 12-gauge into his baby daughter's head, crushing Mary Lou's fragile skull and ending her life before it even had a chance to begin.

The heinous massacre left so much bloodshed that Charlie slipped and fell in the pool of blood coagulating on the floor. Despite the brutality of his acts, Charlie Lawson took the time to perform one last act of sentimentality and madness. Marking the wall with a bloody handprint as he climbed the stairs to the second floor, Charlie retrieved each of his children's pillows, leaving bloodstains on their sheets. Then, he tromped downstairs to finish his work.

Charlie dragged his wife's corpse from the porch and across the threshold, far enough to be able to close the front door. After retrieving her pillow from their bed by the fireplace, Charlie placed it under his wife's head, much like he'd done with the rocks for Carrie and Maybell in the tobacco barn. Next, he closed her eyelids and crossed her arms over her chest.

One by one, Charlie dragged the limp bodies of each of his children across the living room floor, lined them up next to their mother, and placed their pillows under their heads. For the final touch, Charlie closed each of their eyes and crossed their hands over their chests, completing the gruesome tableau.

James (4), Maybell (7), Raymond (2), Carrie (12).

Carrie and Maybell Lawson's death certificates

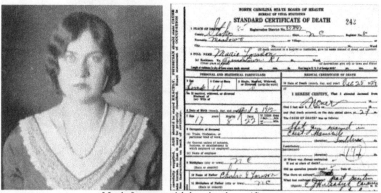
Marie Lawson with her death certificate

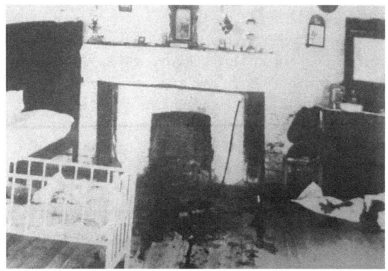

Marie's bloody murder scene

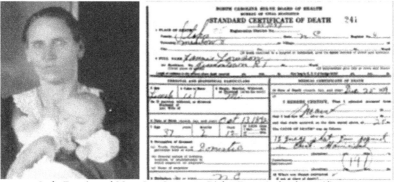

Left: Fannie and Mary Lou Lawson   Right: Fanny's death certificates

Once Charlie completed his "Christmas Surprise," he loaded his single-shot 12-gauge shotgun one last time and headed out the back door toward the woods, alone.

As Lawson fled the crime scene, his two beagles ran alongside him, man's best friends to the end. Reaching the cover of the nearby pines, Charlie slowed to a stop and leaned against a tree to catch his breath. He stared at the 12-gauge in his hands, contemplating the last round in the chamber.

Lawson paced around the tree, considering what he'd done, working up the nerve to finish what he started. Turns out, it's easier to shoot other people than yourself. As he continued to pace, it occurred to Charlie that maybe he should leave behind a note. An explanation. A confession. A swan song.

Digging through his pockets, he retrieved $60.00 – all that remained of the life savings he'd withdrawn from the bank days earlier, a pencil stub, and a pair of receipts.

Lawson scribbled a few words on the back of the receipts, but no one could decode their cryptic meaning because he never finished the thoughts. In the end, Charlie failed to articulate what was going through his head or why he murdered his entire family.

Hearing police and townsfolk closing in on him, Charlie sat on the ground and leaned back against a dogwood tree. He placed the lengthy barrel of the shotgun against his chest but quickly realized he couldn't reach the trigger. Hearing the approach of boots crunching through the snow, Charlie had to think fast before he was discovered. Lawson scavenged a branch with a forked end, hoping to extend his reach. Propping the butt-end of his loaded shotgun against the ground and the business end against his chest, Charlie used the forked branch to activate the trigger.

The final life 43-year-old Charlie Lawson took that snowy Christmas day was his own. I wonder about Charlie's final thoughts when the lead shot blasted that gaping hole through his cold, black heart. The only clue to this mystery is the unfinished thoughts he penned on the back of those two receipts found in his pockets.

Secrets Revealed

After hearing the details of the Lawson Family Massacre, everything seemed to come into focus. The visions of Marie with her younger siblings, the blood-spattered walls, the shotgun blasts, children running and hiding. But there were still a couple of details I needed final clarity on.

First, I had to know what Charlie had written on those receipts and if there could be any connection to the strange message I'd seen Jereme writing in his notebook. When I asked Trudy, this is what she said.

According to her research, when the police found Charlie's body in the woods, they discovered that he had two notes on him. On the back of one receipt, he'd scribbled, *"Nobody to blame."* It's unclear what this fragmented thought meant. Was he trying to explain that the horrific events of that fateful Christmas morning were nobody's fault but his own? Or was he trying to escape blame as well, chalking the incident to fate?

As I pondered the meaning of the first note, Smith revealed the message Charlie had written on the back of the other receipt. It hit me like a ton of bricks.

"Troubles can cause."

My jaw dropped, and my heart nearly skipped a beat. Was this confirmation that my partner was under the influence of Charlie himself? Or did the same evil entity that influenced Charlie now control Jereme?

Hoping to better understand what was happening to Jereme, I asked Trudy what she thought might have influenced Charlie before his killing spree and if others may have seen any signs or strange behavior I should be looking out for.

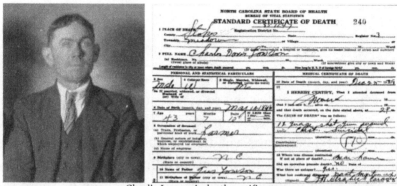

Charlie Lawson's death certificate

Trudy proposed some possible motivating factors that may have led to the heinous murders. Two months before the murders, Black Friday, the day the stock market crashed and sent the US economy into a depression, rocked the nation. This could be devastating news for a struggling tobacco farmer. But there was another factor that likely became the final catalyst, one that I had already suspected.

After interviewing surviving relatives and neighbors, Smith believed she had finally unlocked the Lawson family's dark secret: Marie was pregnant.

She also uncovered a far darker secret: Charlie Lawson was the baby's father.

After the murders, it came to light that Marie had shared her painful secret with her closest friend, Ella May. The daughter of a fellow member of the same Masonic Lodge as Charlie, Ella May confided in Marie that she was also molested by her father.

It's believed that Charlie found out about his daughter's loose lips and feared Marie might tell others. And if the news spread, like it always does in small towns, it would stain his reputation and the Masonic order he belonged to.

The picture became clearer as Trudy helped connect the dots between what Jereme and I uncovered during our investigations and her research of the Lawson family murders. But I still had a couple of questions that needed answers.

First, I wanted clarification about the location of the murders. In my visions, I kept seeing a tall, wooden cabin that didn't look anything like the Madison Dry Goods building. Was it possible that the murders occurred on the same property, but the house was later torn down and Madison Dry Goods built over top of it? Why else would the spirits of the Lawson family be haunting this place?

Lawson family home

As hoped, Smith confirmed that the cabin I described from my visions did match the Lawson family home. But the Lawsons' residence, which was no longer standing, was on Brook Cove Road, roughly 20 miles from Madison Dry Goods. So why would the Lawson family spirits be trapped here?

Once again, Trudy provided the answer. Due to the number of victims, their local funeral parlor was unable to accommodate that many cadavers. The funeral director recommended that the Lawson family's bodies be taken to a larger funeral home in downtown Madison. T.B. Knight-Sugg Funeral Home hosted Rockingham County's largest embalming room. And, as you've probably guessed by now, the Knight-Sugg Funeral Home that embalmed the Lawson family and hosted their funeral used to be located in what is now the Madison Dry Goods building.

It finally all made sense!

As if being secluded in the same funeral home where the Lawson family's funeral was held wasn't bad enough, I also discovered that our second-floor sleeping quarters were where their bodies were embalmed! That would certainly explain the heaviness and paranormal activity we were experiencing on the second floor.

And, due to the sheer number of bodies, the coffins were displayed not only in the viewing rooms on the second floor but also in front of the building where Jereme and I retreated to escape the negative energy inside. No wonder it felt like we had nowhere to run from the oppressive energy in this place!

Lawson family funeral outside Knight-Sugg Funeral Home

Graveside service for the Lawson Family

The Men in Black

S peaking of oppressive energies, I couldn't help but think of the dark spirits surrounding me as I lay in the coffin during our first investigation. The entities I call *The Men in Black*. Whenever I got close to uncovering the Lawson family secrets, these shadowy figures would appear in the room and surround me, driving the other spirits away.

But who were these entities manifesting as bearded men in black suits and Quaker-style hats? And how were they related to the Lawson family, if at all? Trudy thought she might have the answer to that, too.

It turns out that Charlie was a longtime Mason. After news broke about the Lawson Family Massacre, the Masonic Lodge where Charlie belonged reportedly called an emergency meeting. All lodge members who were 21 yrs. or older, were forced to swear an oath to keep Marie's pregnancy and the details of the murders a secret forever.

The roots of Freemasonry date back to the Middle Ages, although the earliest Masonic texts trace masonry back to ancient Egypt, where the Hebrews introduced the craft to them during their time there. Early Masonic writings place the first Masonic lodge in the porchway of King Solomon's Temple and credit the origins of the craft to Jabal, son of Lamech, as documented in Genesis chapter four.

Masonic orders and their rituals are steeped in ancient mysteries. Their secret practices have been closely guarded for centuries, so it wasn't surprising to hear them swear their local members to secrecy regarding the Lawson family murders.

Was it possible that, even in death, this mysterious brotherhood was still trying to guard these horrible secrets to protect their reputation? Neither one of us was prepared to rule that out.

Before ending our call, I needed to address the most pressing issue: Jereme's recent erratic behavior. I told Trudy about what my partner was going through and how he seemed depressed and slept all the time, had no motivation, experienced severe headaches, and lashed out with angry outbursts seemingly out of nowhere. I was hoping she might provide some insight on whether there was any correlation between Charlie's behavior before he snapped and Jereme's.

Trudy revealed that there was more than one thing affecting Charlie's similar behavior leading up to the murders, according to neighbors and relatives. Before shooting his family, Lawson had also been complaining of severe headaches and appeared depressed—the exact same behavior Jereme was manifesting.

Stepping Up

After ending the call with Trudy, I called Jereme to come to the second floor to discuss what was happening with him. He huffed and grunted, obviously unhappy that I'd summoned him up there, but he eventually joined me in our workroom. Jereme dropped into a chair across from me with a sigh and just glared at me.

"I need to know what's going on with you," I told him. "You've been doing nothing but laying around, not wanting to participate in anything, and I'm having to do investigations by myself. I feel like I'm on my own here."

I hated calling him out but didn't know what else to do. I felt like I was on overload, and something had to change.

"Brandy," he said. "Don't you think that if I knew, I would tell you? I don't know."

"Well, what is it you're feeling? What's going on?" I asked.

By now, I was so mentally, physically, and spiritually drained with all this negative energy surrounding me that I couldn't put myself at risk doing this alone anymore.

Jereme's excuse was that he couldn't help being tired all the time.

"What am I supposed to do?" he asked. "And haven't I told you about the massive freaking headaches I've been having? Have you ever had a headache before and tried to do an investigation?"

"Are you serious right now?" I asked him, incredulous. "Of course I have."

At this point, I was so frustrated with him that I just came out and told him what was on my mind.

"You may not want to hear this, but I believe you are on the verge of possession."

Jereme scowled, his eyes shooting daggers at me. It was so unlike him. Until that experience with the entity calling itself Charlie, he had been such a jovial guy.

I told him of my conversation with local historian Trudy Smith regarding Charlie's depression and angry outbursts in the days leading up to the murders. And how, two weeks before Charlie killed his family and himself, he also experienced extreme headaches. Then, I hit him with the final blow.

"And the expert told me that when Charlie's body was recovered, they found a note on him where he'd written the words, 'Troubles can cause.'"

Jereme's jaw dropped. He looked like he'd just seen a ghost.

"Everything that you are feeling, Jereme, Charlie was experiencing, to a tee."

Then, Jereme's scowl returned. "What are you saying, Brandy, that Charlie is affecting me?"

"I honestly believe that the negative energy that affected him is now doing the same thing to you!"

Jereme's face softened as the reality of the situation hit him.

And then he started to cry.

"I need you to step out of this," I said, "and be the Jereme you were when you first came here. Because this is not you."

Jereme's tears turned to sobs.

"Doesn't this all add up to you now?" I asked.

He nodded.

It was almost as if Charlie was forcing Jereme to feel what he'd been going through before he went berserk. I needed

Jereme to step up and be a part of the team again. Before it was too late. Before he followed in Charlie's footsteps.

Jereme hung his head and looked utterly defeated.

"Listen," I said. "I need you. We came here as a team, and we're going to end as a team. The only way we're going to get through this is as a team."

Jereme slowly looked up, his face streaked with tears.

"I can beat this," he said. "I know I can."

DAY 24 — Going Head-To-Head with Charlie

We took a break for a couple of days while Jereme pulled himself together. He was determined to step up and fight through it. We had reached an impasse since our last encounter with the Charlie Energy. Something seemed to be blocking us from effectively communicating with Charlie's spirit. Was it Charlie's reluctance? The Men in Black? Or was it our lack of faith?

After my heart-to-heart talk with Jereme, he resolved to fight this entity together. And since we were running out of time here, we needed to pull out all the stops. Jereme suggested we jumpstart our stalled investigation by incorporating an experimental new technology that its designer had dubbed *The God Helmet*.

The God Helmet was a tool Jereme tried out on the *Ghosts of Morgan City* series, which aired on the Travel Channel. After the positive results he obtained the first time, he asked the producers if he could use the device in case our investigation needed a boost. The concept behind the God Helmet was to leverage magnets embedded in the helmet to stimulate nerve cells in specific areas of the brain that psychic mediums like myself utilize naturally. This can help the wearer better open themselves up to commune with the spirit realm.

Jereme realized he needed to fight whatever was trying to possess him. But to do that, he would have to make a psychic

connection with the spirit of Charlie himself. The helmet's ability to use neuromagnetic pulses to amplify specific frequencies
while filtering out the noise from the rest was believed to help
the wearer better connect with a particular entity one-on-one.

With his weakened state, Jereme hoped this device would
give him the boost he needed to block the dark energy from The
Men in Black and channel a private connection with Charlie for
the first time. Only then could Jereme determine the demon's
influence on Charlie for what it was and how he might overcome it.

We decided to return to the attic, the source of the darkest
energies haunting this place. Despite the nagging voice warning
me not to, I knew we didn't have much time left, so it was either
now or never. I tried to convince myself that since Jereme
would be wearing the God Helmet, maybe there was a chance I
wouldn't be the target this time. God, I hoped I was right.

Jereme sat cross-legged on the floor while I tried to give him
space, being careful not to influence the experiment. As he prepared to don the God Helmet, he hesitated.

"I'm having trouble breathing," he said. "I need you to keep
a watch on me, Brandy."

"Remember," I told him. "Just calm your energy first."

Jereme took a deep breath, then strapped on the God Helmet,
repeating his caution.

"Brandy, you watch my ass, okay?"

"I got ya," I assured him.

Jereme powered on the helmet and took another deep
breath, attempting to calm his nerves. He remained still for a
time, not saying a word.

I opened myself up a little, just enough to sense what might
be happening around us but not enough to allow anything in. It's
always much easier to open that door than to close it.

"It's cold," he said.

I felt the energy in the attic grow heavier. Before long, I sensed a dark presence creeping up on Jereme.

"Damn, It's freezing in here," Jereme said.

The temperature felt like it dropped twenty degrees.

I'd never worked with anything like the God Helmet before. I was terrified of what doors it may open and what kind of things it might invite in.

"Back!" Jereme shouted, recoiling from some unseen energy. "You'd better stay back!"

Jereme shifted his position, turning his back on the encroaching apparition.

He slowly lowered his head as if descending into a trance. His lips moved soundlessly.

Suddenly, he sat bolt upright.

"Oh, shit... what did you do?" Jereme shouted. "What did you do!"

I glanced around the room, sensing the dark energies surrounding me again. What were we thinking coming up here again? Especially with Jereme wearing a veritable lightning rod on his head!

All of a sudden, he jerked as if struck by lightning.

"Oh my God, oh my God!"

Jereme tore the helmet off his head and threw it across the room. His whole body was shaking.

"Holy shit, holy shit!" Jereme shouted. He looked at me, eyes wide with fear. "We need to get out of here. Now!"

I didn't need any convincing. We bolted out of the attic and never looked back.

The First Casualty

As we returned to the first floor to catch our breath and gather our thoughts, I was struck by Jereme's appearance.

"Are you okay?" I asked.

"No," he said. "I am not okay. Something is trying to take me over."

Jereme paced like a caged animal, totally out of breath. "Feel my heart," he said.

I put my hand on his chest. He was ice-cold, and his skin felt clammy. His heart pounded like it was trying to smash through his chest.

"You need to go to the hospital," I told him.

I ran, grabbed the emergency walkie-talkie, and called for help.

We determined over the walkie-talkie that Jereme's symptoms required immediate medical attention. I just hoped that help would arrive in time.

Our head producer, Tom, showed up about 15 minutes later, concern clouding his expression. Seeing how pale my partner looked, he quickly rushed Jereme outside and loaded him into a van. Tires squealed as he sped off to take Jereme to the closest emergency room.

Fortunately for Jereme, the producers were quick to get him to the hospital before his health condition worsened. While there, the doctors ran a battery of tests on Jereme before deciding to keep him overnight for observation.

For the first time since all of this started, I was forced to spend the night alone in Madison Dry Goods. Of course, in this place, I was never really alone...

DAY 25 — Final Girl

The next morning, I paced around the first floor, waiting for word on Jereme. I was up all night worrying about my partner's condition. I'd been kept completely in the dark about what was happening with him, except that he'd been taken to the ER. I worried that something demonic had attached itself to him and possibly even caused permanent harm. What if Jereme had a heart attack or a stroke?

I assumed the hospital staff was skilled at dealing with people with heart conditions, but I seriously doubted they were equipped to perform an exorcism.

I stepped outside to grab a smoke, get some fresh air, and pray for Jereme.

Around 7:30 a.m., a van pulled up in front of Madison Dry Goods. To my amazement, out stepped Jereme. How could he be back so soon?

"Are you all right?" I asked. "What happened?"

"Don't ask me," he said. "Some things are better left unspoken."

After that cryptic message, he stopped and turned to me, sounding more like himself again.

"I reckon I'm okay," he said. "I think I was able to break free from whatever was trying to possess me."

He *thinks* he broke free of the demon?

I'm sure it had to help getting away from this place, even if it was just overnight. Putting some distance between himself and the demon's stranglehold could only help break its grip on Jereme. But I still wanted to keep a close eye on him.

Despite our bickering the last few days, I must admit it was good having the big lug back. I needed Jereme by my side if I was going to be able to finish this. I can't do it on my own. With the producers' hands-off approach, I needed at least one person I could count on in this place.

I told Jereme about my sleepless night and asked him how his night was.

"Brandy," he said. "It was horrible."

The hospital diagnosed Jereme with heart attack symptoms. But, after completing a battery of tests, they were unable to diagnose a physical cause for his symptoms. They told him what he had was virtually unheard of.

Since Jereme went to the hospital right after the God Helmet experiment, I didn't get to find out what progress, if any, he made when he contacted Charlie. Now that he was back, I needed to know if he had unlocked any more of the mystery. Or if he discovered anything new about Charlie that could help us obtain closure here.

Jereme confirmed that his experiment wearing the God Helmet did allow him to connect with the spirit of Charlie. And during this radical experiment, he'd vicariously experienced what Charlie had seen and felt that fateful day. The ordeal also allowed him to connect with the demonic entity that had assumed power over Charlie.

That was when Jereme admitted it became too much for him to withstand, and he was forced to bail on the experiment. He believed that close encounter with the demon was what put him in the hospital.

"I never thought I'd be so happy to see your face," Jereme said with a smirk.

"You and me both," I laughed.

* * *

After Jereme spent a restless night in the hospital being poked and prodded and me up all night pacing and worrying, we both just crashed. We were so exhausted we slept the rest of the day.

The next couple of days after that, whenever we weren't investigating, we were recuperating. I knew it would be challenging, but I never dreamed how much of a toll this would take on me.

After we awoke and got moving again, I noticed that Jereme was acting more like himself, which was refreshing. I needed the old Jereme back if I was to make it until the end with my sanity intact.

Armed with what I'd discovered through my mediumship abilities and Trudy Smith's research, plus Jereme's renewed understanding from his experiment with the God Helmet, we thought we might finally be ready to help the Lawson family move on from here and hopefully banish that demon in the attic back to the underworld where it belonged.

Fog Machine

There was still some uncertainty over whether we had been communicating with Charlie Lawson himself, and to be fair, the same could be said about Fannie and Marie. However, I felt pretty confident that I had been communicating with the Lawson women. But in a place as active as this, there was always the possibility we were being played by a trickster demon.

So far, I'd been given visions of Marie Lawson, her mother, Fannie, and Marie's younger siblings. I'd also received intelligent communication from "Charlie" through REM pods and multiple spirit boxes. The God Helmet had helped Jereme contact Charlie himself and possibly even the dark entity that likely influenced Charlie to kill his whole family, enabling Jereme to vicariously experience the Lawson family murders. But until now, we hadn't captured any visual evidence outside of what we'd seen in our mind's eye.

In talking with Jereme, we both felt we needed to try something different to validate whether these energies were indeed who we thought they were. If there was only something more we could do to get the spirits to reveal themselves.

Jereme and I discussed various options, including incorporating a Jacob's ladder to energize the spirits in the second-floor hallway to get them to manifest themselves. This could be our last chance to coax Charlie out of hiding. Until now, he had mostly kept his distance. Whether it was because of shame for what he had done or something else holding him back, there had to be some way to lure him out. Maybe a Jacob's ladder would do the trick.

For those unfamiliar with these devices, Jacob's ladders create a high-voltage arc that travels up a pair of wires or electrodes until the distance between them grows too far apart and the resistance too great to maintain conductivity. Then, a new spark is created at the base of the electrodes, and the electrical arc begins its ascent all over again.

The electrical discharge from a Jacob's ladder heats and ionizes the surrounding air, creating an energy field that many believe can be leveraged by spirits to better communicate with our dimension or even to manifest themselves. The EMFs produced also help amplify the psychic energy I send out into the atmosphere when I connect with spirit energies. We hoped to boost both the transmission and reception of energy in the second-floor hallway to provide us with the best chance of helping the spirits manifest themselves.

Jereme surprised me by suggesting we amplify the energy even further by adding one additional component to the mix: fog. Jereme said he'd tried this before and it had produced incredible results. I had never heard of this procedure before, let alone tried it, but I was game to give it a shot if there was a chance it could help our investigation.

The concept was to use a fog machine to fill the hallway with a dense vapor cloud and then power up the Jacob's ladder to ionize or charge the water particles, acting as conductors to magnify and extend the energy throughout the hallway.

Now that we had our plan, we were ready to put it into action. We set up the fog machine inside the hallway and waited in the adjacent workroom as the hall slowly filled with fog. Once the hallway was thick with vapor, we set the Jacob's ladder inside the mist and turned it on.

The device buzzed and zapped as the electric arc worked its way up the electrodes, energizing the water vapor and super-charging the hallway. The ozone in the air smelled like a mid-summer thunderstorm.

My heart pounded as we waited for something to materialize in the hallway. Could this crazy experiment actually work? Not seeing anything initially, I began sending out psychic energy to draw the spirits from the hallway toward us. I knew this was risky, but we'd already come too far to quit now.

Jereme called out to the oldest daughter, the mom, the kids, and to Charlie, asking them to show themselves to us. I started taking pictures with a Nikon digital camera at intervals, looking to capture an apparition. I couldn't see anything yet, but I hoped the camera would eventually capture an image visible on the bigger computer screen when we reviewed the pictures later.

"Is there anyone in here?" Jereme called out. "If you want to reveal yourselves, use this energy to make yourself known."

I snapped a few more pictures but couldn't make out anything in the fog through the lens finder. So, I stepped into the fog-filled hallway, opened myself up, and reached out to the spirits of the Lawson family.

"You don't have to be afraid," I encouraged. "Please show yourself if you want to be heard."

I felt the atmosphere in the hallway change. The Jacob's ladder appeared to be working. I snapped more pictures as I sensed the mother's energy come forward. Then I felt her joined by the spirit of her oldest daughter, Marie. I continued to snap pictures at regular intervals as I felt their presence draw nearer.

One of the tips I learned when investigating haunted loca-tions is to always take pictures in at least three or more consec-utive shots. Many times, it's not the first or second picture but the ones after that which capture an image. It's not easy for spirits to manifest, so even when they do, it may only be for an instant. The more snapshots you take, the better opportunity to capture a ghostly apparition.

It was time to see if I could finally get Charlie to appear.

"Charlie, are you here with us?"

The father had been the most reluctant family member to come through. I wasn't sure whether it was because he was ashamed of what he had done or if something else was holding him back from communicating with us. But if we were ever going to get a glimpse of Charlie, this was the perfect environment for it.

"Charlie? Can you come forward?"

The energy changed as I detected Charlie's presence. I quickly snapped more pictures as I encouraged him to reveal himself.

Jereme joined in. "Is there anything you want to tell us, Charlie?"

I took another series of pictures.

As Charlie's energy grew stronger, his wife and daughter's energies began to fade. Was he scaring them off? Since I'd already had great success communicating with Fannie and Marie, I decided to focus on Charlie's energy to draw him out.

A wave of sorrow suddenly enveloped me. Was I starting to empathize with Charlie?

The Jacob's ladder continued to buzz and snap as the energy in the hallway grew more and more negative. I sensed something else join Charlie. I snapped another series of pictures as I struggled to differentiate the energies converging in the hall.

"Charlie, is that you?" I asked. "At least show yourself so we know that it's really you that we are communicating with."

There was definitely something else here with us, a sinister energy that appeared to be gaining strength, eclipsing Charlie's energy.

I started backpedaling from the hallway as the dark force grew in strength. And it was coming closer. I snapped one last series of pictures before retreating into our work area.

"That's it. I'm done," I said, staring at the eerie fog rolling into the room from the hallway. Hopefully, the malevolent entity behind Charlie didn't use the energized fog to invade our "safe space."

I made Jereme unplug the Jacob's ladder and fog machine while I collapsed on the couch and tried to get my heart rate under control. With the Jacob's ladder off, the negative energy seemed to be diminishing, and my anxiety levels declined.

Anxious to find out if we'd captured any visual evidence, we downloaded the pictures from the digital camera to the computer to get a closer look. Did the camera record any apparitions of the spirits I sensed but couldn't see with the naked eye?

I started clicking through the photos one by one on the computer. At first, all I could see was a wall of fog illuminated by the electrical arc from the Jacob's ladder. My heart sank, fearing the experiment failed. But as I kept scrolling, something emerged from the electrically charged mist. Was that a face?

I couldn't believe my eyes. As I cycled through the photos, a woman's face slowly manifested out of the fog. I recognized that face from the family photo we'd found. It was the face of the mother, Fannie Lawson! And it was clear as day.

"Jereme, do you see what I'm seeing?"

He was as shocked as I was. I continued to arrow-key to the next picture, and the next, creating a disturbing strobe-like effect. Soon, another image emerged from the fog: the face of the oldest daughter, Marie. She seemingly materialized from the fog itself! Marie appeared beside her mother, corroborating what I'd sensed in the hallway.

Of all the energies in this place, I seemed to connect the strongest with Marie. She seemed the most intent on seeking my help to tell her story. The next strongest connection was with her mother, who also appeared to be reaching out for help.

When it came to the younger children, they tended to gather around Marie the most. When they did come forward, and one of the dark entities emerged from the shadows, they would usually hide behind Marie and disappear with her. As a mother of five, it made sense. Remembering the portrait with Fannie holding a baby made me think how common it was for an older sister to care for her younger siblings like a mother, with the baby requiring so much of their mother's attention.

Encouraged by what we'd captured so far, I continued to scroll through the photos.

Wait! Was that what I thought it was? Jereme and I leaned in. Another face faintly emerged in the background.

My heart raced as I scrolled to the following picture and the next. A familiar face appeared deep in the fog and slowly came into focus with each key press. I recognized that face from the family photo. It was the face of the murderer, Charlie Lawson.

I gasped as Charlie emerged through the fog, sneaking up behind his wife and daughter who he'd slain in cold blood. I was almost too afraid to continue, seeing Charlie drawing closer and closer.

But as he approached his victims, and his image became more and more distinct, their images began to fade. Was he usurping their energy to manifest himself, or were they still afraid of Charlie and fleeing from his presence?

As I continued to scroll, I noticed another presence materialize behind Charlie. At first, all I could make out was a black shadow. Then, as I advanced through the next series of shots, a dark phantom took shape. Charlie's advance appeared to slow, almost as if this dark entity was pulling him back to the in-between. I suddenly recognized the shadowy form. It was one of the Men in Black I'd seen before—the one with the top hat.

This finally confirmed my earlier suspicions that Charlie was willing to communicate, but something was restraining him. I assumed it was a sense of sorrow and remorse that held him back. But could it have been this Man in Black who was blocking him? Or was it both?

With the arrival of the top-hat-clad Man in Black, the mother and daughter faded completely. And just when it seemed that Charlie was reaching out to us, perhaps to confess or convey the remorse I empathically felt from him, he too faded away.

Jereme and I were stunned. We stared at the monitor for a while, mouths agape. I don't recall ever capturing any apparitions this clear before. It seriously was mind-blowing.

Right about now, if you've seen 28 Days Haunted on Netflix, you are probably saying to yourself, "Hey, I don't remember seeing those pictures when I streamed the show." And you'd be right.

I wish I could give you a good explanation as to why the fog machine and Jacob's ladder experiment weren't included in the show. And why the incredible photos we captured never saw the light of day. Jereme and I were just as shocked when we watched the show for the first time. The only reasons I can think of for omitting the photos would be if there was a technical problem on their end, perhaps due to the fog, or if they thought the pictures looked too good and that the audience would assume they were Photoshopped or something. Or was it just a matter of time restraints? I'm afraid we'll never know.

As great a job as they did culling through 28 days' worth of raw footage from three locations down to six 45-minute episodes, this is the evidence I most wished had been included. I even went so far as to inquire about these photos, but so far, I have been unable to get my hands on them. Sadly, once our investigation ended, we had to turn in all our evidence to Netflix. After that, the rest was out of our control.

Don't get me wrong, the team did an amazing job editing the mountain of footage into one of the top five most-watched Netflix shows in the entire world. But if there was one thing I could get my hands on from my time there, it would be those photos.

After reviewing the photos, Jereme and I took a break outside, like usual, to grab a smoke and discuss the recent investigation. It dawned on me that I hadn't had a cigarette in two days. I'd been doing so much nervous smoking here that I was actually sick of them. Which wasn't a bad thing.

I think I've lost about 10 lbs. since I arrived here. Part of the reason was likely the fact that I hadn't had any Mountain Dew in almost a month. All I drank here was coffee, water, and the occasional Sprite. And since we weren't allowed to leave the premises, I didn't have any fast food either. I felt like I was going through junk food withdrawals!

As Jereme and I smoked and talked, we kept coming back to how successful the experiment with the fog machine and Jacob's ladder turned out. We were both amazed at how clear those photographs turned out.

The more we talked, the more we agreed that we needed to finish strong and do our best to help free the spirits trapped in this place. We knew releasing the Lawson family from this purgatory wouldn't be easy. The powers of darkness were sure to mount a mighty counteroffensive. But what would be the extent of their opposition? Would we only have to confront Charlie?

Or would we also have to battle the Men in Black and potentially even a full-blown demon? The thought of encountering a demon sent a shudder through me.

We headed back inside, knowing we needed to be well-rested and adequately prepared for the final battle in this war between light and dark.

* * *

It was 4 a.m., and I was still tossing and turning. Jereme snored in the bed next to me. I couldn't seem to shut off my mind. Knowing we were only days from this all being over and finally going home made me think of all the things I missed. I missed my babies so much. I'd never gone this long without seeing or even talking to them. I never want to be away this long again. Hopefully, they realized why I did this and were proud of their mom. I couldn't wait to see all my friends again. But there were also all the little things I missed, like my smartphone and all the comforts of home.

How many other people could've made it this far? I wondered how all the other teams were faring. Did they have the same struggles? Were their locations as active as ours?

As proud as I was of myself for stepping out of my comfort zone and for not quitting, I never wanted to do this again. It was hard to believe I'd survived almost a month locked in this crazy, haunted location already. It wasn't just the daily investigations where we encountered so many spirits, both light and dark. It was everything. The isolation and even just the silence in a place like this could drive the average person crazy, let alone a psychic medium battling an extremely active location haunted by the spirit of a mass murderer.

I swear, I must've been crazy to do this. But maybe this was my destiny. I thought back to my years growing up in a haunted house and how it helped prepare me for this day. Despite all I'd been through here, I didn't let it break me. If anything, it made me stronger. I'm starting to feel unstoppable. I want to encourage my kids to reach the same heights and even greater.

I wrote all this in my journal so I wouldn't forget my time here. I had to journal at precisely the right angle to keep the cameras from seeing everything. Because the cameras were everywhere here. But this journal was for me and my kids. And maybe someday, for my book.

I suddenly realized I had to pee, but the thought of using the bathroom here creeped me out. Even in the most private of places, I felt I was being watched by something. Even though there weren't any cameras in the bathroom, I constantly felt like a goldfish in a fishbowl. I couldn't even fart without worrying about a microphone picking it up and some guy in a sound booth somewhere yelling, "Gross!" They wouldn't let us turn off our microphones unless we were going to sleep.

Wait, what was that?

I was starting to hear things again. It sounded like there was someone upstairs whistling. Was something up there trying to get our attention? Were they trying to trick us into going up there to check it out? Or worse, were they trying to lure me up there by myself?

The eerie whistling gave me the chills. Did Charlie whistle while he worked? Was he whistling while he murdered his family?

I finally got up and went outside because I couldn't take the whistling anymore. It was making my skin crawl! I envisioned Charlie with a five o'clock shadow, smiling and whistling as he delivered his Christmas surprise.

I knew Jereme needed rest, so I didn't want to wake him. But I also couldn't stay inside another minute with that damn whistling! I tiptoed past my slumbering partner and snuck outside.

Sitting on the bench outside, I stared at the stars, alone with my thoughts. It was much cooler out in the night air, even if it was a bit humid. It felt good to get away from that creepy whistling and finally clear my head. It's so quiet out here. Gazing into the night sky, I thought maybe it wouldn't be so bad to be a vampire.

I ended up staying outside until 7 a.m. when the sun began to rise over the Main Street shops. Unable to keep my eyes open any longer, I quietly slipped back inside and crawled into bed.

DAY 26 – Preparing for Battle

I had the weirdest dreams last night. For some bizarre reason, I dreamed I was dating Lionel Ritchie, and this blonde girl gave me this beautiful Coach purse! Where the hell did that come from? I really must be losing it!

Then, something startled me out of my dream. I glanced around and listened for a few minutes, wondering what had awakened me. But everything was quiet. The sun shone brightly through the storefront window. I rolled away from the glare and put the pillow over my head.

After several minutes, I dozed off again and dreamed I was in a building where they were cloning humans. I've never had such weird and vivid dreams like this before. What was this place doing to me? I was starting to feel like a psychiatric patient at Eloise!

I awoke around 1 p.m. and lay there for a while, just zoning in and out. I felt totally spent, spiritually and investigation-wise. I promised myself that when I got home, I would take it easy with investigations and psychic readings for a while. I felt like I had PTSD from all the crazy supernatural encounters between mass murderer Charlie Lawson, the Men in Black, and whatever that evil thing up in the attic was.

But I'm not the type to sit around and do nothing all day. I enjoy being out of the house. And, knowing my paranormal investigation friends, I'm sure it won't be long before they pull me into another one of their intriguing investigations.

We only had a couple more days left, and let me tell you, the end couldn't come soon enough. Anyone who knows me would know how hard it was to be isolated here for 28 days straight. These last few days, we worked from 5 p.m. to 3 a.m., full throttle, to make sure we ended strong. I was so worn out that I wasn't sure how much more I could take. You'd think I'd be used to it by now, but this wasn't something you could ever really get used to.

* * *

The producers got ahold of us on the walkie-talkies and asked us to recap some missing fill spots. That was TV jargon for talking to the camera about some of our experiences and discoveries that may not be evident from the raw footage. It could be difficult for some of our paranormal experiences to translate to the audience, especially when it was things I felt or visions I saw inside my head. A great example was when that dark energy rushed me and practically bowled me over. The camera only captured my reaction, not what I sensed or saw charging toward me.

The producers also suggested that we try some solo investigations. Sometimes, an energy may want to connect to one person but not another. For example, the female spirits may be scared off by a strong male energy like Jereme's and prefer to communicate with me. Or an old-school male energy might feel more comfortable communicating with another man.

Paranormal investigating isn't an exact science or some cookie-cutter formula. Every location, every spirit or energy, is different. What might work in one situation may not work in another. What one spirit might respond to may not get you anywhere with another entity.

Coming into an investigation cold, like we did for this show, had its challenges. Since I didn't know the history of the place beyond what the spirits chose to share with me, I didn't know what triggers, like objects or topics of conversation, might spark a response from the energies haunting this place. Fortunately, I was able to confirm some things with historian Trudy Smith that we could now use to better connect with the family haunting this place and hopefully help them move on.

At one point today, I nearly ran out of the building and never looked back. Out of the blue, we heard a woman scream bloody murder upstairs! Her scream was so loud it reverberated throughout the whole building. It made the hair on my neck stand up! Were the screams coming from Marie, reliving the moment she saw her father drag her mother's shotgun-riddled body into the house, or when Charlie pointed the 12-gauge at her before pulling the trigger?

With only a few days left, we needed to wrap up some things, like reviewing the audio recordings we'd made to see if we'd captured any EVPs. We were shocked, not just by the number of EVPs, but by their tone. The messages were all so negative. Some were even downright violent.

Listening to hours and hours of audio can be tedious. After not finding anything for long stretches, it can lure you into the false assumption that you didn't catch anything at all. And most of the time, you don't. But when you finally hear that disembodied voice or scream, the rush is incredible... and often downright blood-chilling.

The most terrifying EVP I've ever heard was still the one we captured when our DPX team visited the Beaver Island lighthouse off the coast of northern Michigan. The second? The one we caught while investigating Madison Dry Goods. Jereme and

I had been listening to recordings for quite a while, and I was beginning to zone out when suddenly, a raspy voice hissed.

"I will kill you!"

It chilled me to the bone. I don't like being threatened. Especially by an enemy I couldn't even see! Was this an idle threat or a promise? We still had a couple more days here—plenty of time to make good on that threat.

As we continued to review the audio files, the lights suddenly flickered! Did listening to the EVPs trigger something? If the lights had gone out just then, I probably would've had a heart attack! It wasn't the first time the lights had flickered on us here. Was it just old, sketchy wiring? Or something supernatural?

The fact it happened right after hearing the death threat freaked me out. We tried to finish playing the rest of the recordings, but the EVPs we captured were all so dark and menacing that I couldn't take it anymore. I had to get out of this place. I needed some fresh air and sunlight to cleanse all the negativity off me.

We tried to take it easy the rest of the afternoon. Jereme felt much better after his overnight hospital stay, and my mind felt much clearer after some time outdoors. But we still needed to recharge our batteries as much as possible. It was critical to clear our minds before confronting the evil entity tormenting the Lawson family in the afterlife.

Now that we had a better idea of what we were facing, we knew we had to prepare for a spiritual battle. It wasn't just an angry spirit we were dealing with here. We were now convinced that a powerful demon dwelled here as well.

It's been difficult dealing with the constant negative energies surrounding us and the persistent attacks. The challenges ahead were sure to push us to our limits.

✳ ✳ ✳

From Jereme's experience and information gleaned from Ed and Lorraine Warren, there was usually one final battle before a demon could be banished once and for all. Demons do not like to give up their domain easily. That's why I do my best to avoid them altogether. Unfortunately, locked in the Madison Dry Goods building, we had no choice.

I spent the evening preparing myself spiritually while Jereme studied and prayed. It was comforting seeing him with his head buried in his Bible and reviewing exorcism resources. We're going to need the full armor of God for this fight. This final battle would be the most demanding and dangerous of our lives.

I'm not sure if it was just nerves, the fact that we'd rested most of the day, or a combination of both, but I was still lying awake in bed at 6:30 a.m., and so was Jereme. Our days and nights were still switched, which didn't help our circadian rhythms. The weather down here didn't help either.

Jereme decided to get up and take a shower. It's so hot and sweaty in this place. It helps to take a cool shower right before bed to cool off. I can't stand sleeping when it's sweltering like this. I turned the fans on us, but it didn't help much.

Unable to keep our eyes open any longer, we both finally passed out.

DAY 27 – Arming for Battle

It was our second to last day at Madison Dry Goods, and I was so ready to be done. Oddly, things around here were especially quiet today. I was worried that this might be the calm before the storm. Jereme and I spent the day resting and preparing for our upcoming battle with the dark forces here. Were they quiet because they were also gathering up the strength to fight one last battle? The thought made me shudder.

"You know how drained I am?" I asked Jereme. "Physically, mentally, spiritually, everything. And it isn't just us. We are all being affected by this negative force here, and it needs to stop so this poor family can cross over and find the light. This is what we spent 28 days here to do."

"You know, Brandy," Jereme said. "I think you're right."

"Good, because I think it's time that you did your job as a demonologist and banished this demonic entity from the property once and for all."

If Jereme could do that, I felt confident we could cleanse this place and guide the Lawson family to the other side. This was our last chance to finally free this family after 100 years of bondage. If we didn't do that, then we failed our mission.

Jereme locked eyes with me and said, "Let's do it."

Jereme prepared for tomorrow's final battle by visualizing the confrontation and asking God to give him *His* power to fight the demon. As a demonologist, he knew there was no way he could defeat a fallen angel on his own. He was merely the vessel for the Holy Spirit to do His job. Jereme's job was to allow God to manifest His power through him, here in the physical realm, a realm the demon had invaded.

Not long after God created the universe and its heavenly hosts, evil was introduced into the world when Lucifer and his angels rebelled, leaving the heavenly realm to come to Earth and begin wreaking havoc, tempting and tormenting God's beloved creation.

Our biggest challenge in the fight ahead was that the real battle took place in the unseen realm, but we lived in the physical realm. That's why we had to prepare ourselves spiritually to engage these forces head-on.

I thought about how much I'd been through here and all the negative energy that had collected around me, and I knew that I needed to release that negative energy. I went outside barefoot, and although we weren't supposed to leave the property, I stepped off the sidewalk to ground myself to a more earthy, positive energy. I had to get my body, soul, and spirit back in tune. I gazed up toward heaven, took a deep breath, and visualized fresh energy coming down from heaven, flowing through my body and grounding to the earth beneath my feet.

With our time here running out, I figured we'd only get one shot at this. And to be honest, I didn't know if I could handle more than one battle with the dark forces here, especially if they all decided to gang up on us at once. Any one of these entities would be a challenge to face, but if we had to battle the spirit of a homicidal maniac, the Men in Black, and possibly even a demon, we would need all the help we could get to engage in the battle of our lives.

DAY 28 – The Final Battle

W e spent our last day readying ourselves for the final battle. Jereme prepared himself by reading his Bible all day. I showered and cleansed myself physically and spiritually. Through prayer, meditation, and visualization, we emptied ourselves and asked the spirit of God to empower us for the battle ahead.

At 11 p.m., Madison Dry Goods was unnervingly quiet. Gathering our courage, we marched up to the second-floor waiting area just outside the main funeral parlor viewing rooms. Since we had gotten most of our interaction on this floor, we felt it would be the ideal place to make our final stand.

We strategically placed the spirit box and REM pods around us. I gazed at the Lawson family photograph I'd brought to use as a trigger.

"You ready?" Jereme asked.

"Let's do this."

I reached out to the Lawson family. By now, I felt like I knew the Lawson women and kids. I even reached a point with Charlie where he had opened up a little, maybe even expressing a modicum of sadness or even remorse for what he'd done.

They must have known we were coming because the energy in the room ramped up quickly, almost as if they'd been lying in wait for us.

I let Jereme take the lead in confronting the demon.

"Did you drive Charlie to kill his family?" Jereme called out accusingly.

An angry, inhuman voice erupted from the spirit box. Something did not like Jereme calling it out.

"By the grace of my God," Jereme said, pacing the floor like a prowling tiger, "through the power of Christ, I weaken the forces of evil set against me and banish them so they can no longer speak or do harm to me or anyone else in this place. In Jesus' name, I pray, amen."

The energy in the room spiked.

BAM!

A noise startled us from somewhere in the room. We both rubbed our arms, feeling the goosebumps rise. I stood and began pacing, unable to sit still. I also didn't want to be a sitting duck.

Suddenly, a loud voice cried out from the spirit box, scaring the crap out of me. While I was temporarily off-balance, an invisible force rushed me, driving me backward and right into Jereme's lap! Had that noise been meant to distract me so something else could mount a sneak attack on me?

I jumped to my feet, somewhat disoriented, and glanced around, bracing myself for what might come next.

I heard my mom's voice yell, "Brandy, get out!"

I ignored her at first, thinking this was our last chance to free the spirits of the family trapped here. I couldn't abandon them now.

It gave me confidence knowing that my mom still had my back. She was like my guardian angel. I'm sure she observes things from the other side that I can't see, so it was wise not to ignore her warning for too long.

Another squawk from the spirit box made me jump again.

Jereme echoed my mom's message, "Brandy, Get Out!"

With both Jereme and my mom warning me to get out of there, I knew I'd better listen. I bolted down the stairs, shouting, "Fuck this!"

On a humorous note, some of my friends placed bets on how long it would take before I used the F-word on the show. Anyone who knows me knows I cuss like a sailor when I'm scared. I'm sure people will give me shit about being a chicken, but there's a big difference between watching something on TV and experiencing it firsthand.

This shit gets real, very fast. Plus, I have kids to think about. I need to be there for my children after all this is over. I didn't want to bring any of this crazy shit home. Besides, it was Jereme's turn to step up. He was hired as the big, bad demonologist. That's his specialty. It was now time to see what he was made of.

To his credit, Jereme stood his ground. He was convinced that after all we'd learned over the last 28 days, the only way to defeat this evil energy was to confront it head-on. He knew it was finally do-or-die time.

By 2:30 a.m., Jereme had been fighting a spiritual battle for almost three hours. His weapons? The power of God's word and prayer. Whatever this enemy was, it was not going to surrender easily. This had been its domain for far too long, and it wasn't about to relinquish it now.

A loud KNOCK shook the ceiling above me, where Jereme was still fighting the dark powers.

"You better stay back," Jereme shouted. "I am not running from you no more, and there ain't a damn thing you can do about it!"

The strategy was to convince the evil entity that we were not leaving until it did. Hopefully, it worked. I stayed downstairs, monitoring the situation with my psychic abilities, not wanting to get between Jereme and the demon, but ready to intervene if forced to.

"Jereme, watch your back!" I called upstairs.

I could hear Jereme pacing above me, shouting, "I have run long enough. You have put fear into me, and you tried to distract me from what I came here to do. But I am not going to let it happen anymore!"

I stood at the bottom of the steps, joining my energy with Jereme's.

"Lord, banish all the powers of evil and darkness in this place for all eternity!" Jereme cried out.

Loud knocking and crashing sounded above me in response to Jereme's prayer.

"What was that?" I yelled.

"I don't know," he replied. "You can make all the noise you want up here," he continued, "but it's not going to deter me!"

A door slammed somewhere on the second floor.

"Get away from that door!" Jereme shouted. He marched toward the noise when, all of a sudden, something shattered upstairs.

"No, you will not! You will not—you stay back! You stay back!" he repeated. "You cannot make me flee!"

"What was that crashing sound?" I yelled, fearing for Jereme's safety.

After reviewing the footage from the second floor, we discovered that a vase had flown off the shelf and shattered, seemingly by itself!

"Listen to me!" Jereme commanded, "By the name of my father in heaven, and my savior and God Jesus Christ, I will not give in to fear!"

I sensed a dark presence heading for Jereme.

"Jereme, watch out!" I yelled. "There's a shadow figure!"

SLAM!

The sound of the door slamming sent Jereme reeling, his feet shuffling for balance.

"Get back! You get back!" he shouted again. "I'm going to make this known right now, right here. You are banished! This will end now!"

"Jereme, be careful!" I yelled up to him. "This is not a fucking joke!"

"I am not backing down!" Jereme shouted. "You have no right to hold this family hostage in death like you did in life. No right! And I am determined to bring them home. You are set free!"

With that, the commotion and chaos upstairs ceased. Finally, all was quiet.

A feeling of peace washed over me.

Jereme told me later that when the demonic make their final push and think they are cornered, that's when they physically attack. So when that dark entity lashed out by throwing the vase, Jereme knew we were winning.

Positive and negative energy cannot occupy the same space simultaneously. By following the Warren's 28-day method, we showed the negative energies here that *they* were not welcome. And by letting our lights shine and calling upon the light of the world, the dark forces had no choice but to vacate.

We know from the laws of physics that energy never dies; it can only transform itself from one state to another or from one location to another. Jereme's plan was to corner the evil energy so it had nowhere else to go. One of his strategies was to visualize the darkness completely surrounded by light. Light dispels darkness, not the other way around. Darkness can't exist where the light is. Instead of fighting the darkness under his own power, Jereme called upon a higher power, the one who created light and all the angels, even those who later rebelled.

But there was no guarantee that Jereme's efforts sent the demon to hell, where it belonged. Humans aren't powerful enough to destroy demons. But we do know that someday, they will be cast into the lake of fire for all eternity. For now, I hoped Jereme's work was sufficient to dispel the fallen one long enough for us to free the Lawson family.

Once things calmed down after the flying vase incident, I went back upstairs and examined the shelf where the vase launched itself from, to make sure it wasn't some gag that the show's producers had rigged up for dramatic effect. I carefully examined every square inch of that shelf and the wall behind it but found nothing that could have sent it flying like that. I also checked the vase for a fishing line that could've been used to pull it off the shelf, but again, I could not debunk the phenomenon.

There was no doubt left in my mind that the origin of this incident was paranormal.

At this point, we both needed a break. The spiritual battle we'd just experienced, plus all the things we'd endured the whole time we were here, had taken a major toll. Jereme and I went outside to get some fresh air and looked up into the clear night sky to thank God for getting us through this.

Crossing Over

Before leaving this place, I needed to connect with Fannie and Marie to thank them. They'd guided me through this whole investigation and have suffered so much, not just in life but also in the afterlife. And, more importantly, I needed to know they had moved on.

Jereme and I decided to perform a cleansing ritual in Madison Dry Goods before we left to help the spirits of the Lawson family cross over. And to hopefully drive away any negative energies that might still linger here.

We planned to start up in the attic and work our way downstairs to the second floor, then finally, the first-floor general store. Jereme prepared a holy water sprinkler, or aspergillum, which was basically a metal, mace-like wand filled with holy water. The ball at the top included holes to allow the holy water to sprinkle out when the holder flicks their wrist. In his other hand, he carried his well-worn, leather Bible.

Jereme carried his crucifix, and I walked alongside him with an incense holder filled with smoldering frankincense and sage, hoping to smudge the area and drive away any remaining negative energies.

After cleansing the attic, we descended to the second floor and cleared every room there. Jereme read from his Bible and sprinkled holy water as I did my best to push out any negative energies.

As we traversed the former funeral home floor, I reached out to the Lawson family spirits, attempting to tune into the mother and all of her kids. Fannie came forward first, her smile filled with hope, yet her eyes were questioning.

I told her it was okay to go into the light and that she didn't have to be trapped here. I sensed Fannie telling me she hadn't moved on because she refused to leave her family behind. Even in death, she only wanted to keep her family together. But she felt she didn't have the energy to take everyone with her, so she'd rather stay behind than cross over without all of her children.

Next, I sensed Marie come toward me and join her mother. She smiled the kind of smile that lit up a room. It was downright angelic. Of all the spirits here, I've had the closest connection with Marie, even since the beginning. Like her mother, Marie also resisted crossing over without the children.

Soon, the kids gathered one by one around Fannie and Marie. They each looked at me expectantly, as if standing on a train platform waiting for the conductor to cry, "All aboard!".

"Everything will be okay," I assured them. "There is nothing to fear. Enter into your rest."

Jereme continued to pray and read from his Bible.

I did my best to mentally guide them toward the light, encouraging them to cross over. Then, as one, I sensed them all slowly fade away into the light. I was suddenly overwhelmed with emotion, tears streaming down my face. But they were tears of joy.

Jereme came over and put his arm around me.

After a moment of silence, I took a deep breath and tried to pull myself together. But then, it struck me. I hadn't seen Charlie.

The last time I'd communicated with him, I'd felt a sense of remorse and guilt, sadness even. Despite our best efforts, I believe that Charlie chose to stay. Whether it was the brotherhood of the Men in Black and the other dark entity we encountered holding him back, or if Charlie was just afraid to cross over and face judgment day for taking the lives of his family, I guess I'll never know. But as best as I can tell, Charlie remains at Madison Dry Goods to this day.

Once Jereme and I finished smudging and cleansing the first floor, we went outside to let it all out. We had both emptied our tanks and left everything inside this place. As we stood outside enjoying the cool, fresh night air, we looked at each other and smiled. It felt like we'd just completed a marathon. I was proud of the work we accomplished during our harrowing mission.

The two of us chilled outside for a while, smoking and talking like we did most every night, but this time it was different. Jereme and I were completely exhausted, but we felt good. That feeling you get when you've given it your all without regret.

We spent the rest of the night sitting on the bench in front of the general store, recouping our energy and allowing things to settle down inside. The process cannot be rushed. It takes time for the atmosphere inside to clear and everything to take its course.

As the sun came up, I wandered back inside and looked around, taking everything in, wanting to record this moment in memory. As difficult as this experience was, it had become my home for the last month. The general store really did have a sweet, nostalgic charm about it, especially in the golden morning light.

I reached out, sampling the energy. And, for the first time, the atmosphere in Madison Dry Goods felt... light. It was as though the spirits of Fannie, Marie, and the children were now free from the evil forces trapping them here, and they had finally crossed over. I honestly felt that what we'd done had worked!

Jereme and I decided to tour Madison Dry Goods one last time. The atmosphere in there felt so much brighter than when we'd first arrived. I could finally breathe freely again. I believe our work here broke the hold that the demon, and possibly Charlie, held on the Lawson family's souls. And now, after a century of imprisonment, they were finally free.

This is why I do what I do.

Saying Goodbye

I t was 6:30 a.m., and Jereme and I debated what our last requests should be before leaving Madison Dry Goods. Soon, the conversation turned to food and how far it might be to the closest Waffle House. Jereme suggested we give the crew our last meal request since we felt like prisoners here. Just for grins, we wrote out our demands on sheets of paper and held them up to the cameras.

On Jereme's sign, he'd written,

All-Star Demands
-eggs - scrambled
-steak - medium well
-2 hash browns w/cheese and ham chunks
-white toast
-O.J.

On my sign, I'd written,

-Sausage, egg, and cheese hot sandwich
-hash browns
-sweet tea
-scrambled eggs.

Our mouths were watering just thinking about it. Unfortunately, we never got any of it. But if we were blessed to get renewed for a second season, I would have to talk to the producers about the food. Would it really be so bad for us to get to eat out once in a while? I'm sure the Warrens ate out once in a while!

I'd been looking forward to our last day here and finally meeting all the people working behind the scenes who made this show happen. I'm excited to get to know the owners of this place and to be able to swap stories with them.

I'm also hoping to visit the gravesite of this tragic family before I leave, although it makes me sad to think about all the lives that were taken so early.

I hope to meet Trudy Smith, the historian, in person someday. She was so helpful with verifying all the impressions, visions, and communications I gathered from the spirits here. It helped give me the confidence to persevere and hopefully bring closure to the Lawson family.

After Jereme and I finished packing all our stuff, the van came around to pick us up. It felt so good to escape this place after being locked down for 28 days straight. The crew turned out to be super nice. We all wanted to get a picture together to commemorate our experience on the show and for Jereme and I to put a face to the names of all the vampires working behind the scenes.

28 Days Haunted crew

This month-long investigation was a massive learning experience to see how far I could go with my abilities and how much I could physically and mentally endure. I'm not ashamed to admit that I was terrified much of the time. I nearly bailed more than once. But deep down, I knew I had to keep pushing. If I had quit and walked away without helping the Lawson family, I knew I would've regretted it for the rest of my life.

I prayed that I was able to help the Lawson family cross over. It's such a tragedy to think they'd been imprisoned here for almost a hundred years.

Before taking us to the airport, I asked if the driver could take us to the cemetery where the family was buried.

Lawson family tombstone

As the van approached the cemetery, my stomach was full of butterflies. Why was I so nervous? It was like the anticipation you felt when you were about to reunite with someone you hadn't seen in years and weren't quite sure how you would be received.

Jereme and I meandered through the old cemetery, searching for the Lawson family plot. Finally, we spotted the massive headstone. And they were all there, buried in one mass gravesite. Looking at all the names, I felt like I knew these people.

I was suddenly overcome with emotion. As a mom myself, it broke my heart to see the babies' names inscribed on the tombstone, knowing they never got a chance to grow up, especially after the connection I made with Fannie. With all the horrors this family experienced, I knew there was no way their mom would stop until all her babies were set free.

As the gravity of it all hit me, I broke down and wept over their graves. For me, liberating Mrs. Lawson and her children was the most important achievement of our investigation. It felt so good knowing that they were no longer stuck in that murder house. After all this time, they were finally free. And after 28 days of hell, so were we.

Brandy's sad farewell to the Lawsons

Post-Production

B y the time production wrapped, more than 2,000 hours of raw footage had been recorded. Now, it was time for the editors to begin wading through all that material to pare it down and structure it into a compelling narrative. When all was said and done, the production team was able to edit all that content into just six episodes, comprising only three and a half hours of total runtime.

I don't envy the production team, who had to pore over 28 days' worth of raw footage for each of the three locations. Not only did they have to watch all that footage, but they also had to clip all the highlights and then weave them together into one cohesive storyline for the series.

You're probably wondering if what you saw on 28 Days Haunted and on other reality shows is real. I can only vouch for my experience on the shows I've been on, where I'm upfront with the production companies that I will not fake anything. For one, it's unethical. For another, I have a reputation to uphold. If I ever faked anything relating to the paranormal, I would likely lose the trust of my peers and my clients. And rightfully so!

That doesn't mean other "Reality" series don't manipulate reality. I've heard plenty of stories to that effect. But I hope you believe me when I tell you that everything you saw me do on 28 Days Haunted and other TV series, at my various paranormal events, and the readings I give to clients is all legit.

Unscripted/Reality shows are different from regular scripted TV shows. Scripted/Fiction TV series start with a script where everything that's going to happen is predetermined by the showrunner and writers ahead of time. Then, the script is acted out and filmed based on that structure, with some minor changes based on the director's vision and sometimes input from the actors and crew.

Unscripted/Reality series are mostly "scripted" during the editing process since you don't know everything that will happen ahead of time. The only predetermined elements are the setting, the cast, and specific situations the cast will be put in. If you place the right people in certain environments and situations, you can expect a particular outcome, but you still never know exactly what you'll get until you see how it all plays out.

For example, by putting a psychic medium and a demonologist in a highly active haunted location, you could probably expect some crazy paranormal shit to go down, but it's not guaranteed. Spirits don't act according to a script or perform on cue.

Once all the recorded footage was reviewed and the production team saw what actually happened, they could edit the show together and structure what the audience ultimately sees around the most exciting events. They can also look for any themes or overarching storylines that developed to help them decide what to keep and what ends up on the cutting room floor.

After all of the footage has been edited down, there are always things that need to be added in post-production to help clarify certain things, to provide additional context, or to insert segues from one scene to another to make sure the story flows. A big part of that process includes having the talent record voiceovers, commentary, or re-record any audio that the microphones may not have picked up clearly. For that, they needed to fly us out to California.

California, Here I Come!

It was so exciting flying to California, staying in a hotel in downtown Los Angeles, and going into a professional studio to record the interview and voiceover segments. I was actually way more nervous being in front of a camera under the studio lights with a film crew watching us than I was doing the show in a haunted building. At Madison Dry Goods, the cameras were hidden everywhere, and after a while, we forgot they were there.

During our time in California, we recorded six hours of interviews where we discussed what we experienced, both personally and investigation-wise, during our 28 days at Madison Dry Goods. Those interviews were later edited into the series. Some of the things we recorded were just do-overs of things we said during our video journals, where maybe we misspoke, the audio wasn't clear, or we left some things out. They also asked us to describe what we felt during some of the more nerve-racking moments so the audience could better understand what we were going through internally.

Our time in California turned into a whirlwind trip. We were only there for two days (not counting travel), so we didn't get to do much outside of our interviews and voiceovers. We did get out of the hotel one evening to walk around downtown LA for a bit and check out some stores. Unfortunately, we weren't near any interesting landmarks and didn't have time to venture very far. I wish we had more time to take a day and see some sights like the Hollywood sign, the Hollywood Forever

Cemetery, go to Venice Beach to see all the freaky people, dip my toes in the Pacific Ocean, and walk along the beach.

But it was amazing to finally meet all the people who investigated at the other locations. Since everything was done so secretively, Jereme and I had no idea who any of the other investigators were. This was by design, as producers like to keep as much under wraps as possible so nothing leaks out ahead of time. The entertainment world is a very competitive business, after all.

But, with all of the talent staying at the same hotel, it was inevitable that we would run into each other in the elevators or lobby. It was fun to hang out with fellow paranormal investigators, have some drinks at the hotel bar, and talk shop. I had never met any of them before, but I knew a couple from other series. Because we were locked down at different locations, none of us knew where the other teams were investigating or what kind of paranormal run-ins they may have experienced.

Since the producers didn't want us spoiling anything before the show aired, we were all a bit nervous to share too much about our experiences during our 28-day lockdowns. We mainly just introduced ourselves and talked about the paranormal in general. After going into this adventure blind, we were still in the dark about what the others encountered at their haunted locations until the day the series aired.

We did compare which team had it the roughest, and Jereme and I won that trophy easily. If you've seen the show, you've seen the beautiful Victorian mansions that the other teams got to stay in, which are now lovely bed and breakfasts complete with full kitchens and four-poster beds. Jereme and I slept on mattresses on the floor and had to cook on a hot plate. But I'm not bitter. Much.

There was definitely a buzz in the air when we all got together. Everyone wondered how the series would turn out and hoped they wouldn't look bad. Overall, I was pleased with how the series turned out. I just wish we could've had more episodes to show everything that happened. Hopefully, this book helps make up for that.

THE AFTERMATH

My top priority after I got home was to spend time with my kids and attempt to regain some sense of "normal" again. Everything about my experience being locked down at Madison Dry Goods was traumatic. I seriously don't feel like the same person anymore. This wild ride left me in serious need of some self-care. Maybe a little time off would help me renew my energy.

Trying to adapt to life again on the outside took longer than I expected. This must be what people recently released from prison must feel like.

I knew I would miss my kids, but it was great to see how much they missed me, too. The first thing I did was hug them all and catch up with what was going on in their lives. They obviously had lots of questions about my time away on the show.

One thing I didn't expect when I got home was struggling with social anxiety. Everyone who knows me knows how social I am. But after being isolated for a month, it seemed strange to interact with other people (especially the living variety). It was almost like I was released from solitary confinement. Even getting used to having my phone again and engaging on social media took time to adjust.

The 28 Days Haunted experience took such a toll on me mentally, physically, and spiritually that I didn't do any investigations or psychic work for the next three months. My biggest concern after leaving was that nothing followed me home. Once I returned to my home in Michigan, I felt I needed to close myself off completely for a while to ensure that none of the dark entities I connected with there could find me here.

While locked down at Madison Dry Goods, I didn't get to do much in the way of grounding or cleansing. It was like I kept collecting more and more negative energy without being able to shed any of it or hit the reset button. I had nowhere to escape there. No matter where I was, I knew I was being watched by people in the control room or the spirits haunting the place.

Every single room was fitted with hidden cameras except one—the bathroom. Every mother will tell you (and as a mother of five, trust me, I know!) locking yourself in the bathroom can be your only escape. It's like Superman's fortress of solitude. But at Madison Dry Goods, even the bathroom possessed a dark presence! The only relief from the negative energy was when Jereme and I would slip outside for a smoke. But even there, the three-story haunted building loomed over us, almost taunting us as if it knew we would eventually have to return.

After the show, I closed myself off completely. I tried not to think about the Lawson family and the shocking murders. I was afraid even to say the name Charlie! I hoped that if I took enough time off, the visions and memories would eventually fade.

I was determined not to let Charlie find me.

As a psychic medium who often embarks on paranormal investigations and regularly performs psychic readings and mediumship for clients, it felt strange and even frightening to open myself up to the unseen realm and exercise my gifts again. The first time I tried to intentionally connect with the other side, since leaving Madison, I feared it might not work. After not using my psychic gifts for months, was it possible to lose the capability altogether? My psychic abilities have become such a part of my identity that I was afraid of what it would be like not to have those gifts anymore.

I tried my hardest to put the negative energy from Madison Dry Goods out of my mind and leave it in North Carolina. But the thought of those dark entities following me home kept me closed off for months. I'm not sure what I was more afraid of now, testing my mediumship abilities and them no longer working, or having them work too well and have Charlie or the Men in Black come through and not be able to close that door again.

First Investigation After – Middle Point High School

After a few months of my paranormal investigator friends encouraging me to get back out there and investigate with them, I finally gave in. I accepted an invitation from my Ohio friends to drive down for a public investigation they were hosting at Middle Point High School. The building was constructed back in 1885 as a college for teachers before it was shuttered in 1903. It was later reopened and expanded, becoming a high school before it eventually closed in the 1950s.

I don't know this with absolute certainty, but I have a strong feeling this property used to be home to a Native American tribe. I feel a strong Indigenous presence here, which I will elaborate on in a moment.

I have been to Middle Point High School probably fifty times, since I have good friends who live nearby, and it's only about two hours from my home. The school's been closed for so long it's become dilapidated, creating the kind of spooky atmosphere that comes with abandoned buildings.

It's also extremely haunted.

I hadn't seen my Ohio friends since I embarked on my 28 Days Haunted adventure, so I couldn't say no when Austin Maynard invited me down for a public paranormal investigation he was hosting. Austin is like a brother to me, always challenging and encouraging me to expand my capabilities. He likes to talk me into testing the new paranormal gadgets he's always tinkering with. It's like I'm his favorite Guinea pig.

When my fiancé Shane Vernaroli and I got to Middle Point, we met up with Austin and his wife Calleen, Becky and Eric Mohr, Courtney Casares, Derrick Coil, and Michael Ring. It was so good to see them again and give them all big hugs.

Austin and the gang greeted the attendees and reviewed the logistics and rules. Once the open investigation began, Austin's team broke into three groups, each leading a third of the participants on one of the floors. One group went down to the basement, another to the gymnasium, and the last group went upstairs.

When I attend events like this, I usually just float between groups. But once I start sensing things, I can't help but join in the fun. Sometimes, lost loved ones of those attending the events come through wanting to send them a message. This time, I was mainly here just to hang out with friends, not to conduct any tours or mediate with the spirit world.

Shane and I started with the group investigating the old gymnasium on the first floor, led by Derrick. The gym was a large multi-purpose space with a basketball court and vintage hardwood floors. But water had gotten in over the years, and the boards were now worn and buckling up in places. It was like we had unearthed a time capsule from the 1950s.

On one side of the gymnasium, there was a stage once used for student assemblies, theatrical plays, and other events for the student body. There were also rows of theater-style wooden seats for spectators and a small ticket booth. Looming over it all, the ceiling was cracked with peeling paint and chunks of plaster missing, revealing gaping black holes. The floor was covered in dust and broken plaster chunks that had fallen from the ceiling, creating a virtual minefield. It looked like a remnant from a war-torn country.

When our group first entered the gymnasium, everyone gawked at everything as if we'd just stepped out of a time machine and discovered that the world had ended. Soon, people began wandering around to get a closer look at the warped floor boards, abandoned stadium seats, and the arched windows and doorways around the ticket booth. Some people had their K-2 meters out searching for paranormal hotspots.

I overheard Derrick ask Shane how I was doing, knowing this was my first investigation since I'd been locked down for 28 Days Haunted. I was touched by his concern, but it also made me pause and take stock of myself. Was I okay? Could I really do this again so soon? It had already been a couple of months since leaving Madison, but how soon is too soon?

I'll admit I was nervous stepping out on my first investigation after the 28 Days Haunted experience. But I knew I had to get on with my life. I enjoy exploring old historical locations and seeing what spirits still lurk in their halls, basements, and attics. Having my good friends accompany me definitely made it a lot easier.

I promised myself I would take it easy and hang back, observe the others, and enjoy the company of my friends. But old habits die hard, and once the spirits still roaming a place realize I can see them, I become like a magnet and draw them to me whether I want to or not.

Knowing how low my energy was after my 28 Days Haunted experience, I worried my resistance might be weakened. I was determined not to open up my energy at first but to just get a feel for everything. I could always open up more as the investigation went on. I'll admit that I was super nervous to start the investigation part. My palms began to sweat when the spirit box came out.

Derrick announced that he was ready to fire up the spirit box to see if any spirits wanted to communicate with us. My anxiety skyrocketed when the LEDs lit up. Static hissed from the spirit box's speakers as the modified radio inside rapidly scanned the frequencies.

The former funeral home from Madison Dry Goods flashed in my mind. I quickly shook the image out of my head. This was going to be even more challenging than I thought.

I did my best to keep myself closed off, not letting anything in, afraid to draw any lingering spirits to me. I strained to shut out the white noise from the spirit box and ignore the pops and random indistinguishable voices that broke through. I reminded myself that I was just here to hang out. This wasn't my investigation.

My anxiety levels maxing out, I decided to leave the gymnasium and wander over to one of the other groups. Since I'd investigated this place many times, I knew exactly which hot spots to avoid. I planned to stay clear of the top floor and the basement since they were the most active areas, each filled with tons of negative energy. I knew I wasn't ready for that yet.

Stopping in the hallway to catch my breath and regroup, I waited for my anxiety levels to go down. After a deep cleansing breath, I wandered upstairs to the second floor. The crew was up there investigating two more notoriously active rooms on this floor, the "Dark Room" and the "Mirror Room." I realized then this wouldn't get any easier, so I might as well ease my way back in, one step at a time. I slowly opened myself up again, hoping I wouldn't live to regret it.

The Dark Room

I strolled down the narrow hallway to the Dark Room as Shane caught up to me. Peeking inside, Austin and Calleen smiled and waved me in. Having them here and Shane by my side made it possible for me to step foot into one of the more active rooms in the building. An old 70s-style couch, covered in a loud floral pattern, was pushed against the wall. I took a seat with my back against the wall to prevent anything from sneaking up behind me.

A metal folding chair was placed in the middle of the room where we often set a spirit box or REM pod. I usually sat in that chair when I led investigations here, especially if we planned to stay for a while. But, since the chair was in the center of the room, I knew I'd feel too vulnerable. Plus, the couch was more comfortable. I still wanted to hang back and not open myself up too much yet.

Brandy, Austin, and Calleen investigating the "Dark Room."

317

The scariest thing about the room was the dark male presence lurking in the left-hand corner. This shadow figure possessed such a powerful negative energy! Although he didn't speak, I felt he controlled a lot of the other energies in this place. I also detected a female presence here at times, but she primarily haunted the upstairs. Frequently, when I tried to connect with this female spirit, I felt as if the male energy prevented her from speaking to me. It's like he had some sort of control over her and wanted to silence her. It reminded me of how Charlie and The Men in Black controlled the Lawson family's spirits.

I had to be careful not to push either of those energies too hard because when the shadowy figure in the corner got mad, his energy ramped up to dangerous levels. Strong enough to act out physically against the living.

My anxiety rose along with the shift in negative energy. I think the man in the corner remembered me or at least detected my abilities. I could sense him warning me not to push it, *or else*. I didn't want to find out what the *or else* was, so I didn't stay in the Dark Room very long. I was still trying to ease my way back into investigating again.

After opening myself up a little, I quickly shut it down again. I was still gun-shy after the traumatic experience at Madison Dry Goods. I didn't feel comfortable opening myself up completely. I needed to take baby steps, only opening up a little at a time for fear my psychic resistance was still too weak. I couldn't risk something bursting through that door if I opened it too far.

An image flashed in my head of Charlie standing in the doorway of his cabin with the shotgun in one hand and a fistful of his dying wife's hair in the other, eyeballing me as if I were Marie.

A chill ran up my spine, and I knew I had to get the hell out of there. I fled into the hallway, where the energy was lighter. Steadying my breathing, I waited until my heart rate slowed before moving on. Surviving my first encounter with a dark entity since Madison felt good. So far, so good. But this was definitely going to take time.

Shane and I decided to head down the hall to the room where another group was investigating. A room known as the "Mirror Room."

As soon as I stepped into the Mirror Room, I was immediately hit with the same eerie feeling I encountered in the basement. I won't even go down there anymore; it creeps me out too bad. There are some places I avoid because of things I've felt there. Others because of what I've seen. In the basement of Middle Point School, it's both. But mostly, it's to avoid running into the dead guy who lurks down there.

Man in the Basement

Not all spirits of the dead present themselves as they truly are... or were. Some spirits present themselves how they want to be perceived. Some want to represent themselves in the best light so they don't scare you away. Whether that's because they want you to listen to them or because they want to trick you into lowering your guard so they can jump you, like the dangerous ones who present themselves as children. That kind really scare me because I know they are likely demons.

Other spirits intentionally misrepresent themselves to scare you off because they don't want you disturbing them. They may do this by presenting themselves as much bigger than they are or by taking on the image of something they think will terrify you. Some appear just like they were when they died—like the man in the basement of Middle Point High School. And believe me, it wasn't pretty.

When descending into the basement, the stairway dumps you into a big, open room with a concrete floor and cinderblock walls. The atmosphere is cold and suffocating. If you walk deeper into this room, you'll find the old janitor's area to the right. It's so dark and oppressive down there, and the sense of dread only grows stronger the closer you get to the janitor's room.

The first time I saw the man in the basement, I was terrified and ran out of there as fast as my feet would take me. The mysterious figure stood in the doorway, glaring at me. He was clothed in dingy gray-blue coveralls stained with soot, his collar singed. The coveralls had patches that were burnt through, revealing charred flesh. His entire face was burnt, his features melted almost smooth except where his cheekbones and nasal bone jutted out from his skull. He reminded me of Freddy Krueger but without the charm.

Whenever the charred figure appeared in the basement, I sensed a powerful, dark energy emanating from him. Even before my time at 28 Days Haunted, my guard immediately went up when I felt his presence, wary of what evils this entity was capable of.

Every time the smoldering janitor manifested, he would be followed by a powerful, protective Native American spirit. This spirit, who I dubbed *The Chief*, interceded and warned me to stay away from the dangerous entity, often shielding me so I could escape.

The Mirror Room

Mike Ring led the investigation in the Mirror Room. I must confess that I didn't spend more than a few minutes there because of its heavy energy. The source of that dark energy appeared to come from the giant mirror on the wall. It was as if it was a portal to the underworld.

After only a few minutes in the Mirror Room, I sensed spirits flowing through the mirror toward me, bringing back frightening memories from the Old South Pittsburgh Hospital and the creepers flying out of that portal.

Did these spirits remember me from my previous visits here, or did they just sense my weakness and want to exploit it?

I hate mirrors. If I ever enter a strange room with a large mirror hanging on the wall, I'll usually just turn around and head right back out. My aversion to mirrors started with the mirror portal in the Old South Pittsburgh Hospital, but believe it or not, there's another mirror that haunts me even more... the mirror in the Old Licking County Jail in Ohio that nearly stole my soul.

Old Licking County Jail

Back in 2018, my partners at DPX, Todd Bonner and Jeff Adkins, traveled with me down to investigate the old Licking County Jail with some of my other paranormal investigator friends—Jeff Fent, Teri Long, and Teena Pare-Duchesne. It brought back great memories of when I met Teena while investigating another jailhouse—the 6th Precinct.

Built in 1889, the old Licking County Jail was praised as the best and most secure jail the state had ever seen. It was designed to house up to 68 prisoners, as well as the local sheriff and his family. The building shares the same Richardsonian Romanesque style of architecture found in one of my favorite places, the Ohio State Reformatory, like the stonework arches and turrets.

It's no wonder I immediately fell in love with the place as we drove up to it for the first time. The old Licking County Jail has a number of unusual architectural features, including gargoyles sculpted into the window sills and a water spout that looks like a frog.

The property was surrounded by an ornate wrought iron fence, giving it a gothic look perfect for ghost hunting. The jail also possessed a dark history. Over time, the prison conditions became so awful that many inmates opted for suicide over living in one of its cells. Their method of death varied from poison to hanging to slitting their own throats. After only 45 minutes of being locked in her cell, one woman burned herself alive! Were all of these horrific incidents mere acts of desperation? Or were they driven by something much darker?

One of the more notorious inmates of the jail was 72-year-old Laura Belle Devlin, who was incarcerated for having bludgeoned her husband to death and sawing off his arms and head before burning his extremities in their oven. Unfortunately for Mrs. Devlin, her husband's torso was too large to fit in their stove. Police later discovered the rest of his remains in a backyard fire pit.

Needless to say, the facility housed its share of unsavory prisoners during its lifetime, and who knows how many, even after their deaths. Since its closing, the old Licking County Jail has been notorious for paranormal activity, including shadow figures, disembodied screams, banging cell doors, footsteps, and haunting moans.

The sun was beginning to set when our DPX team arrived. Jeff Fent met us in the parking lot along with Teena and Teri. I'd been chatting with Jeff through Facebook, but it was our first meeting in person. He came up to me all excited and said he had a surprise for me. Jeff showed me a special spirit box he had made based on the Geobox technology initially created by George Brown.

The GeoBox device rapidly scans radio frequencies and converts them, along with fluctuating electromagnetic fields (EMFs) and ambient vibrations, to audio.

I climbed into Jeff's car, and he fired up the spirit box. Since my friend Teena had experienced success connecting with my mom before, he wanted to see if he could communicate with her spirit while Teena and I were together, thinking it could improve our chances.

At first, nothing came through but the typical white noise. Concerned that the problem might be the reception in the area,

Jeff drove us around the block to see if that helped. We kept trying until we returned to the parking lot but still couldn't get any intelligent communication. Jeff then suggested we take the spirit box inside the building to see if that helped. Maybe the problem was more spiritual than technical. He wasn't sure about the reception, but he knew the spirits were strong in this place.

While Todd and Jeff Adkins explored the other parts of the building with Teri, Jeff Trent led Teena and me up to the second floor, where the warden and his family used to reside. Their living quarters were in the tower section, so the room we entered was round on one side. Teena and I sat on the floor with the spirit box while Jeff paced around us. We began asking questions to see if we could get any spirits to talk with us.

"Is there anyone here who would like to communicate with us?" I asked.

We took turns asking questions and listening for responses from the spirit box.

"Are you stuck here?" I asked.

The white noise was interrupted by radio snippets and other muddled sounds, but no intelligent responses yet. I decided to talk directly to my mom instead of waiting for her to come through on her own.

"Mom? It's Brandy. Are you here?"

Jeff knelt next to the spirit box. "Renee, Brandy needs you to come through for her. She needs to hear from you," he said. "This is very important to Brandy."

Teena took a turn at reestablishing the connection she'd made before with my mom.

"Renee, you can talk to Brandy right now," Teena said. "Can you give her a message?"

"You need to come closer." Jeff encouraged.

I closed my eyes and reached out to my mom. I missed her so much and wanted to hear her voice again so badly. To know that she was okay on the other side.

"Mom, this is Brandy. I need to hear from you. I love you."

Finally, a familiar voice pierced the static. "I love you, too."

My heart leaped in my chest, and I started crying. I knew it was her voice. Her presence in the room was so strong!

"I miss you more than you know."

My mom's voice replied, "Miss you too."

Teena looked at me, shocked and amazed.

"The kids really miss you, too," I said, smiling.

I didn't know how long I'd be able to keep the communication going, so I asked the one question that weighed on my heart most.

"I have an important question I need you to answer for me," I said. "Was your death accidental, Mom?"

I listened intently, not sure I wanted to know the answer. Then, as clear as a bell, I heard my mom say, "Naturally."

"Did you hear that?" Teena said with a giant smile. "She said Naturally. Like in natural causes."

"Thank you!"

I pressed on, not wanting my mom to go.

"Did you move on to heaven, or am I keeping you here?"

No answer at first.

"Mom, am I holding you here?" I said. "I'm afraid I'm keeping you here, being in so much pain from missing you."

I waited nervously for an answer, trying to hold back the tears.

"Mom?"

My mom's voice came through the spirit box again.

"Don't be frightened."

I choked up, hearing my mom trying to comfort me and telling me not to be afraid. It was the kind of thing she used to say when I got scared as a little girl.

Teena hugged me, and Jeff smiled. The whole room was filled with her angelic presence—a beam of light inside the dark jailhouse.

"Mom," I asked. "Who is with you?

A familiar name came through the spirit box.

Jeff asked me, "Did she say Frankie?"

I was stunned to hear that name but also grateful. My mom had a brother named Frank. Uncle Frankie died two years prior to my mom's passing.

"Thank you, I needed that." The thought of my mom reuniting with her brother warmed my heart.

"I'm going to let you go now," I said. I wanted to keep talking with my mom for as long as possible, but I didn't want her getting stuck here in this jail.

Now that I think back on it, I'm so glad I did. The thought of my mom imprisoned at the haunted Licking County Jail like the Lawson family at Madison Dry Goods would torment me for the rest of my life.

"Thank you for coming through," I said, wiping my eyes. "I need you to go back where you were now."

Teena and I did our best to release my mom back to the other side. And just as quickly as she arrived, I felt my mom's presence disappear, and the darkness returned.

I hugged Teena and thanked her for helping me contact my mom. Then, I embraced Jeff and thanked him for letting me use his custom spirit box. They knew how important this was for me and how much I missed my mom. And Jeff was thrilled at the success of his new creation.

Ever since we contacted my mom, I've had a special connection with that Geobox. I even gave it the nickname "Baby Geo." From that time on, Jeff and I shared custody of the box. We each took the spirit box for six months at a time before trading it back.

Eventually, Jeff made me my own spirit box with wood from Eloise Psychiatric Hospital. He even engraved "Eloise Hospital" on top, Mom's face on one side, and "Angel Box" on the other. The spirit box even lights up in my mom's favorite color—turquoise. The Angel Box is definitely one of a kind!

After that highly emotional experience, it took me half an hour to regroup before I was ready to investigate the rest of the Licking County Jail building. We caught up with Todd, Jeff Adkins, and Teri and told them about our breakthrough in the warden's family quarters. They said there was something down in the basement that I had to see. Something that would change how I looked at mirrors for the rest of my life.

The most frightening part of the old Licking County Jail was the haunted mirror in the basement that stretched from floor to ceiling and ran nearly the entire length of one wall. It was incredible. I'd never seen a mirror that large before.

While investigating the basement, a voice came through the spirit box telling us to look in the mirror. I walked over and gazed into the looking glass. Old mirrors weren't made like they are now; the glassmaking process back then created imperfections during the shaping and cooling process that created wavy patterns that can be quite disorienting.

The longer I gazed at its reflective surface, the more I felt it drawing me in. The powerful energy emanating from the mirror created a hypnotic effect as my reflection stared back at me. But there was something *off* about it. Although I knew I was looking at my own reflection, it was like staring at someone else! It was my face but someone else's eyes! No matter how hard I tried, I couldn't break the mirror's spell over me. I was frozen.

A numbness spread over my body until it no longer felt like mine. My lifeless body stared at its doppelganger in the mirror. It felt as though its energy was trading places with mine! I gradually lost control of my body as the doppelganger took over. Like a fool, I let my guard down temporarily, and something sinister took advantage. It was like the doppelganger evicted my spirit, creating an empty vessel for its dark energy to move into.

Unable to move, I could only stare helplessly at the Doppelganger-Brandy smiling back at my defenseless form. I didn't know what to do. I felt so helpless! Finally, I attempted to communicate with one of my partners to see if they could do something to bring me back.

"Jeff," my voice whispered from somewhere far away. "Come here. What do you see?"

I didn't feel my lips move. It was as if I was communicating telepathically. But would anyone else receive my message?

Jeff Fent came over and looked in the mirror. Thank God he heard me!

His head cocked to one side as he stared at my reflection. He could tell something wasn't right.

"Your eyes... they—they're not blue. They're green!" He frowned. "And your face... It's like it's changing into someone else's!"

Now, I was terrified. What if this entity permanently took over my body and replaced me? Is that even possible? Then what would happen to me? Would I become trapped in the mirror, waiting for someone else to someday swap places with?

My friend Teena, who's also a psychic medium, came over to see what Jeff was talking about.

"Brandy, that's not you!"

I could hear the horror in her voice. Teena grabbed me and physically spun me away from the mirror. When I finally broke eye contact with the Brandy in the mirror, the spell was broken. I felt my spirit rush back into my body, retaking control.

I blinked a couple of times, gradually regaining my senses. I tried to move, unsure if I could still control my appendages, like a puppet whose strings had been cut. Lifting my hands in front of me, I stared at them, wondering if they were mine. I pinched myself to make sure. The feeling in my body slowly returned.

I couldn't get away from that mirror soon enough. I bolted out of the jailhouse in a panic. Teena shadowed me out of the building to make sure I was okay. As I ran outside, I inhaled the cool night air and slowly let my breath escape, trying to calm down. I took a quick inventory of myself and the energy around me to ensure nothing from the other side of the mirror followed me outside.

Teena lit some sage and joined her energy with mine in an impromptu cleansing ritual to help me get grounded again. That was one of the craziest things I ever experienced. And now you know why I get nervous around mirrors.

The Missing Boy

S taring at my reflection in the mirror room at Middle Point High School, I questioned whether I was really ready for this. But deep down, I knew the only way to get back to my former self was to face my fears and put the spirit world on notice that they were no longer in control.

I quickly put up my defenses, avoiding eye contact with the mirror or the spirits around me as I backed slowly toward the exit and excused myself into the hall.

Shane and I wandered around the school building awhile, investigating some more, testing myself little by little. My anxiety was high the whole night, but over time, I began to relax and just enjoy my time with all the other investigators.

As the evening progressed, I opened myself up more, reaching out to the benevolent spirits that might be there. Whenever I'm in a group setting like this with the public, I like to open myself up to see if any spirits want to communicate with those around me. Many times, lost loved ones will come through with messages for someone on the tour. It always brings me great joy to provide closure and healing for others.

After spending the first half of the evening closed off, I resolved to open up more during the second half. But I shut the door again whenever the energy ramped up too high. I didn't want to take any unnecessary risks until I felt more confident that I was back to my old self and had regained my previous strength.

As we continued to walk the halls, I reached out to see if one of the spirits haunting the school might want to communicate with me. I thought of the spirit I often saw near the Middle Point School entrance, which I referred to as "The Missing Boy."

I first encountered The Missing Boy when he came through the spirit box during one of my early investigations at Middle Point High School. Over time, he revealed that he was lost and couldn't find his way home. He kept showing me woods with a narrow stream flowing through it. Over and over, he pointed and told me that he was under the water.

The boy's spirit was so insistent that I asked around if anyone from the area might know anything about the missing boy. I found out that there had been a young boy who'd gone missing many years ago but was never found. I also discovered there was a creek next to a wooded area about a mile from Middle Point School. Other mediums have also reported picking up similar messages from a young male spirit that pointed them to where they believed was his watery grave.

I eventually worked with law enforcement when they reopened the decades-old case. We searched the area from my visions, and authorities even dug up one section near the creek but ultimately came up empty. I reached out to the boy to tell me where we were going wrong, and he kept repeating the word "deeper."

But after failing to find any remains at the first dig site, the search was called off, and the case went cold again. The boy's case still remains open.

Although The Missing Boy didn't come through this time, I wasn't too surprised since he usually revealed himself when I first arrived. But I'd kept myself closed off most of the night, so I may have missed my window.

Shane and I switched groups again and returned to the gymnasium/auditorium where we started.

Gymnasium

By this time, it was getting pretty late, and I was beginning to wind down. The stress of being in such an active location after so much time off had really taken its toll. The more tired I get, the more vulnerable I become, which is dangerous for a psychic medium.

Shane, Derrick, and I conducted one more investigation with one of the groups in the gymnasium. Since this was going to be our last investigation of the night, I decided to go ahead and open myself up more to see what would happen. I was still nervous, but I reminded myself that I could always close myself off again if things got too stressful.

I wanted to push myself a little more this time. I couldn't spend the rest of my life afraid of opening myself up to the paranormal. It was part of my identity now. Plus I really enjoy it.

As I opened the door of my psychic abilities, I felt a loved one trying to come through. They wanted to speak to one of the ladies in the public group. I opened the door a little further, and her late husband came through.

Whenever I do mediumship for someone, I like to ask the spirit a few questions to verify that they are who they say they are. Most of the time, I can corroborate the spirit's message with their loved ones. But sometimes, the energy coming through is something dark with malicious intent. That's why it is always essential to test the spirits.

The first thing that came through from the lady's husband was the words "red car." For some reason, he kept mentioning it over and over. So, I asked the lady if "red car" meant anything to her. Her jaw dropped, and she began to tear up.

"He's talking about my red Mustang at home," she said. "He knows that's my baby."

Encouraged by her response, I asked the spirit one more question. How did he die? He told me that it was a heart attack. When I relayed this to his wife, she covered her mouth in shock. She was convinced that I was communicating with her late husband.

The spirit then started asking me about the car shows. A tear ran down her cheek.

"I still go to the car shows," she said and smiled.

At this point, Derrick turned on the spirit box to see if her late husband or anyone else might want to communicate. I passed along a few more messages from the lady's husband while the spirit box rapidly scanned the radio frequencies. I thanked the spirit I'd been communicating with and closed the connection.

The woman thanked me with tears in her eyes and a smile on her face. I guess I didn't lose my touch after all!

We now turned all our attention to the spirit box. A couple of indistinguishable sounds filtered through the static. I opened myself again to any spirits who may want to communicate.

"Is there anybody here?" Derrick asked. "We would like to talk to the spirits who are still here."

The rhythmic static continued with a few interjections, but nothing clear enough to make out.

"Are there any spirits here that want to talk to us?" I asked.

Suddenly, a man's voice cut through the white noise, clear as day.

"Charlie!"

I nearly screamed as my knees gave out. I grabbed onto Shane to keep from collapsing on the floor.

"Did you say, Charlie?" Derrick repeated.

Once again, that familiar voice pierced the veil of static. "Charlie!"

My heart was practically beating out of my chest. This couldn't be happening. I thought I had closed that connection when I left Madison Dry Goods! I quickly blocked Charlie's energy and any other dark energies that might try to piggyback on his. I was especially terrified of that demonic energy that followed Charlie.

I was shaking so badly that I could hardly stand up. The flurry of emotions bombarding me made my head spin. I told Shane I needed to leave.

My thoughts returned to Madison. Even though I was confident that I had helped the Lawson family move on, I could tell that Charlie remained.

"I knew it!" I told Shane on our drive back to Michigan. "Charlie and I still have a connection!"

The whole way home, I kept wondering how Charlie could still come through. What did I do wrong? Why was the connection still there? But as the miles ticked by and I thought more about it, I realized I knew the answer the whole time. I just didn't want to admit it.

No matter how much time passes, once you establish a connection with someone on the other side, that connection remains. It's like you have each other's address. If I ever want to reestablish one of those connections, it becomes easier each time. The downside is that it's also easier for them to connect to you. Despite my best efforts, I wasn't able to cut the cord with Charlie. And I probably never would.

Middle Point High School Gymnasium

Lingering Effects

Since the investigation at Madison Dry Goods, I've been on a number of paranormal investigations. The name Charlie continues to come through the spirit box over and over. And every time I hear Charlie's name, I cringe and tense up, instantly putting my block up in case he tries to connect.

To this day, I don't feel comfortable opening myself up 100% for fear that Charlie, the Men In Black, or that non-human entity from the attic will come through. Even now, I'm much more guarded during investigations and in my psychic work. Even though there are things people can do to cleanse themselves, it's almost impossible to sever those supernatural connections once they're established. Even if you slam the door and lock it, they remember your address, and when you least expect it, they will jiggle the door handle.

Watch Party

The day finally arrived for our 28 Days Haunted watch party. My good friends Austin Maynard and his wife Calleen booked an incredible venue for us to watch the show - Father John's Microbrewery in Ohio. They have a bar, restaurant, and even a bed and breakfast housed inside what used to be an old Methodist church and parsonage built back in 1895. The restaurant and bar, located in the basement, make you feel like you are stepping back in time with the vintage stone-and-mortar walls and period artifacts.

I was joined for the dinner and watch party by a few of my closest friends, including my fiancé Shane, Austin and his wife Calleen, Bryan Prince (who helped me write this book), and his wife, Deanne.

I originally booked a venue near my house and invited a bunch of Michigan family and friends and some more from Ohio. But at the last minute, I discovered that the bar and grille couldn't stream Netflix to any of their TVs. Fortunately, Austin saved the day and found us a room at Father John's. But with the short notice and long distance, most of my Michigan friends didn't make it.

I couldn't have asked for a better venue for our watch party than the gothic-style room they gave us. By the time we all got together, ate, and talked, it was already getting pretty late, so we ended up just watching the first and last episodes of 28 Days Haunted.

Waiting for the show to start, I was excited but also scared. I think most people are self-conscious of how they'll look before they get their picture taken, or when they know they're being recorded, how they'll sound. But imagine being filmed almost 24/7 for a month! I'm sure I wasn't at my best the whole time. Did I pick my nose? Did they get my good side? Do I have a good side? Did I say anything stupid? Knowing I don't have much of a filter, I'm sure I did. I wanted to think that they edited out anything too embarrassing, but the problem was that I didn't have any say in what the final cut looked like. It was entirely out of my control.

I was most nervous about reliving all those terrifying moments I've tried so hard to forget. Just the mere mention of the name Charlie made me shiver. Would watching Jereme and I investigate the spirits there reopen those connections? Could it act like a magnet for Charlie and the Men In Black to reconnect?

I think I have some level of PTSD from my time filming 28 Days Haunted. I still experience things that take me back to Madison Dry Goods and my battle with the dark forces there. It can be a sight, a sound, a smell, any of which triggers that sick feeling of oppression and paranoia. I fought off spiritual attacks day and night, surrounded by negative energies and disembodied voices, and I still bear the scars of those 28 Days.

I hoped that watching the series might help put some of those demons to rest. To face my fears, knowing that I've already survived my real-life encounter with those same spirits, should help me move on, right? Whatever doesn't kill you makes you stronger, as they say.

As we launched Netflix on the big screen, I began to fidget, nervous I might come out looking like a fool. I was curious to see what they included and what got edited out. We captured so much extraordinary evidence. Hopefully, they included the best stuff. The most important thing to me was that it came across as authentic because I knew it was. My professional reputation rides on how they presented my work.

I leaned forward as the opening teaser began to play. I can't explain how surreal it was to see my face and name on the screen, especially knowing that this was Netflix. It was so satisfying to finally see the fruits of all the hard work and sacrifice we endured during those 28 days. It was also exciting to see the people I met at the hotel in LA investigating their locations.

I was on the edge of my seat the whole time, although I admit watching some of it through my fingers. It was fun filling my friends in on some of the behind-the-scenes details that weren't shown and just laughing at myself and Jereme's antics. The experience was equal parts joy and embarrassment.

But there were times when I felt goosebumps spread up my arms and the hairs on the back of my neck bristling as I relived confronting Charlie and the other dark forces in the haunted halls of Madison Dry Goods.

Despite the subtle tug I felt to open myself up again, I quickly locked that door. Whether it was Charlie trying to come through or something from this former 19th-century parsonage trying to get my attention, there was no way I was going to let them crash my party.

As harrowing as the entire experience on 28 Days Haunted was, I would definitely do it again. Opportunities like that don't come along every day, and there are no guarantees in life, so it's important to seize them when they present themselves. Each opportunity is a chance to grow, to prove yourself, and to make critical connections, which can lead to even bigger and better things. I am grateful for the opportunities provided by 28 Days Haunted, and I look forward to what comes next. Hopefully, you'll come along for the ride...

28 Days Haunted watch party at Father John's Microbrewery in Ohio
From Left: Shane Vernaroli, Brandy, Calleen & Austin Maynard, Deanne and Bryan Prince

Right: Brandy watches herself on the big screen.

What's Next?

So, what's next for me? Mostly, I just want to enjoy more time with family and friends. Being cut off from everyone for 28 days straight made me appreciate those I love even more. And it reminded me of what's most important—to take each day as a new opportunity to enjoy life and continue to grow. I've gained a stronger drive to focus on my goals and to expand my career as a psychic medium and paranormal investigator.

I just moved into a new place that's a better fit for me and my kids, somewhere away from the hustle and bustle of the city but still close enough to visit my father and for the kids to still spend time with their dad.

I've begun doing psychic readings for clients again. I forgot how much I enjoyed interacting with people, helping them in their spiritual journeys, and providing comfort to those who have lost loved ones.

I wouldn't be where I am now without all of my wonderful clients over the years and all the new clients I've gotten since the 28 Days Haunted show aired. It's exciting to expand my reach to help more and more people, which, in turn, also helps me. By providing spiritual guidance, I learn more about the spiritual realm. The Lord teaches me new things all the time. The lessons God provides for my clients through me also teach me. Sometimes, I ask myself, why don't I apply this advice to my own life?

The most rewarding part of doing readings for people is when I help them connect with lost loved ones and bring a sense of closure. To help them on their healing journey. Sometimes, it's helping their loved ones move on. Many times, it's helping my clients tell their loved ones the things they always wanted to say but never got the chance because they died suddenly.

We always think we have more time with the people we love, but we never truly know how much time anyone has on this earth. That's why it's so important to let those special people in your life know how much you love them. I'm so glad my mom and I always ended every call saying, "I love you."

Sometimes, when the client's loved one passed away, they were on bad terms. Haunted with regret, they long to tell their loved ones the things they wished they would've said when they were alive. When I make these connections for people, I get this bright, angelic feeling, like I'm doing God's work. I believe He put me here on earth and gave me these gifts for a reason, and it's my mission to carry out His will in helping others, to continue to grow spiritually, and, most importantly, to share God's love with others.

After all, isn't that the greatest thing any of us can do?

 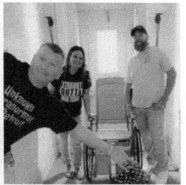

Left: My fiancé, Shane, who protects me and keeps me grounded.
Right: From Left: Joe Posey, Brandy, and Shane at Madison Seminary

Parting Thoughts

Sometimes, we lose ourselves in all of the chaos around us and in the world at large, which makes us anxious and depressed. We wonder why things in life don't change. In times like these, it's critical to take a minute and pause everything going on around you. It's okay to be selfish occasionally and take time to yourself to replenish and rejuvenate. It's okay not to fit into what society or family thinks you should be or do.

Always stay true to yourself. And, as long as you're happy, and the people who are meant to be on the journey with you are happy, that's what matters most. Take that minute to escape reality once in a while. Appreciate all that God has blessed you with. Love life and live it to the fullest.

Don't pay attention to all the hysteria on social media or the melodrama going on around you. Life goes by too fast, and those meaningless things can steal your joy and keep you from achieving your true potential. You can't turn back time. You only get one shot at life. So stop living in fear and appreciate your time here on earth so you can make the most of it. There is only one you in the whole universe. Don't worry what others think because only you can live the life you were meant to live. And maybe someday, people will tell stories about you.

Brandy Marie Miller

Brandy Marie is a 5th generation psychic medium who discovered her gifts at the age of five when she began seeing spirits in her childhood home. By the time she was 23, Miller was honing her abilities with help from various mentors, further expanding her supernatural talents. Since joining the paranormal field in 2014, Brandy has become a World-Renowned Psychic Medium, Paranormal Investigator, and Reiki Healer, traveling the nation investigating the paranormal and using her abilities to help bring healing to others.

Miller recently starred in the hit Netflix series *28 Days Haunted* and has been featured on such popular television series as *Fright Club* with Jack Osborne, *Destination Fear, Paranormal Caught on Camera,* and many more. She has also used her abilities to aid law enforcement on missing-person cases remotely and in person.

To follow Brandy or to book her for a reading, speaking event, podcast, or television appearance she can be reached at:

Facebook: facebook.com/brandy.miller.7370
Instagram: @la_vida_e_bella82
Bmiller031982@gmail.com.

B.D. Prince

B.D. Prince was born in Michigan—a dark fiction and comedy writer who credits these proclivities to growing up near a cemetery and being endowed with a freakishly long funny bone. The author moved to California to pursue screenwriting and get a tan. Prince got his start writing humorous greeting cards and penning one-liners for Joan Rivers. Now an award-winning screenwriter, Prince has published numerous short stories and novellas and is currently writing a new horror novel and developing projects for film and television.

You can follow B.D. Prince at...

BDPrince.com
Instagram: @clownprinceb
Facebook: facebook.com/bryan.prince.52
Twitter: @clownprinceb

Printed in the USA
CPSIA information can be obtained
at www.ICGtesting.com
JSHW022240171123
52029JS00003B/14